THE BRITISH ARMY OF AUGUST 1914

THE BRITISH ARMY OF AUGUST 1914

AN ILLUSTRATED DIRECTORY

RAY WESTLAKE

SPELLMOUNT
Staplehurst

For my
Uncle Ernest, Aunt Elsie and Cousin Pamela Child (age 8)
who were killed in an air raid on 11 October, 1940

British Library Cataloguing in Publication Data:
A catalogue record for this book is available
from the British Library

Copyright © Ray Westlake 2005

ISBN 1-86227-207-7

This edition first published in the UK in 2005 by
Spellmount Limited
The Village Centre
Staplehurst
Kent TN12 0BJ
Tel: 01580 893730
Fax: 01580 893731
E-mail: enquiries@spellmount.com
Website: www.spellmount.com

Design: Ian Hughes
www.mousematdesign.com

1 3 5 7 9 8 6 4 2

The right of Ray Westlake to be identified
as the author of this work has been asserted by him
in accordance with the Copyright, Designs
and Patents Act 1988

All rights reserved. No part of this publication may be
reproduced, stored in a retrieval system or transmitted in
any form or by any means, electronic, mechanical,
photocopying, recording or otherwise,
without prior permission in writing from
Spellmount Limited, Publishers.

Printed and bound in Singapore

CONTENTS

INTRODUCTION

In this book I have provided an alphabetical listing of the regiments and corps of the British Army that were in existence when war was declared on 4 August, 1914. Its scope is the Regular Army, Special Reserve and Territorial Force. Educational and training establishments (based on those appearing in the *Monthly Army List*) have also been included, along with contingents of the Officers Training Corps, recognised cadet units and Colonial (those appearing in the British *Army List*, but excluding the Indian Army) formations. Several groups of formations (listing the units that make up each), viz. Cadets, Cavalry, Cyclists, Infantry, Officers Training Corps, Special Reserve, Territorial Force and Yeomanry (under these headings) also appear.

The structure of the list is based on titles and designations that may be termed as "official", and therefore "correct". These are essential to know as researchers will certainly come across a problem if attempting to look up a record under some unofficial, but often more frequently used or shortened regimental name. To help with this, however, I have included in the listing references to the alternatives most likely to be used (the omission of "Royal" for example). The reader is then directed to the official version. I have not included nicknames. A complete study in their own right, these can often lead to confusion. Many, as they were, were made up on the spot, and were often known only to small groups within a regiment. There are, however, references to names that, although not strictly nicknames, have become more frequently used than the full and recognised designation, e.g. "Leeds Rifles", "Robin Hoods", "Liverpool" and "London Scottish". The essential qualification for these is that they appear as part of an official regimental name in publications such as the *Army List*.

The book is intended to help researchers – into military, local and family history – firstly to establish what constituted the British Army on the eve of war, and secondly to find easily the location of each unit. Certainly on a family-history front, knowing where relatives in the Regular Army were serving prior to their moving to the battlefields is essential to the construction of any family record. Local historians, likewise, will find the location references to the several Territorial Force detachments in their area an important contribution to their work. I have made no attempt to explain the function of each arm of service.

Hopefully my selection of illustrations represents a good example of what the British soldier looked like in the years preceding the Great War, on formal full-dress occasions, in training, and during the more relaxed atmosphere of camps. Uniform description has been kept to a minimum. Comments on colour usually apply to full-dress uniforms (khaki service dress being familiar to all), and where scarlet jackets/tunics are referred to it can be assumed that the trousers are dark blue. The term "facings" refers to collars and cuffs. All photographs and illustrations (unless otherwise stated) are from the Ray Westlake Unit Archives.

Ray Westlake
Malpas
August 2004

THE DIRECTORY

A

Aberdeen Batteries, 1st, 2nd, 3rd City of. See 1st Highland Brigade, Royal Field Artillery.

Aberdeen Fortress Engineers, City of. See City of Aberdeen Fortress Engineers.

Aberdeen University Officers Training Corps. One section field ambulance, Senior Division.

Aberystwyth University College Officers Training Corps. See University of Wales Officers Training Corps.

Ackmar School (LCC) Cadet Corps. Headquarters at the Guildhall, London. Two companies.

Aldenham School Officers Training Corps. Elstree, Hertfordshire. Two infantry companies, Junior Division.

Alderney Militia. See Royal Alderney Militia.

Aldershot Church Cadet Corps. See Wessex Divisional Transport and Supply Column.

Alexandra, Princess of Wales's Own Yorkshire Hussars Yeomanry. See Yorkshire Hussars Yeomanry (Alexandra, Princess of Wales's Own).

Alexandra, Princess of Wales's Own (Yorkshire Regiment). Two Regular (1st and 2nd), one Special Reserve (3rd) and two Territorial Force (4th and 5th) battalions. Depot, Richmond.

1st Battalion: Barian, India.

2nd Battalion: Guernsey.

3rd Battalion: Richmond.

4th Battalion: Northallerton with "A" and "B" Companies, Middlesbrough; "C" Company, Yarm-on-Tees (detachments at Great Ayton, Stokesley and Hutton Rudby); "D" Company, Guisborough (detachments at Eston, South Bank and Grangetown); "E" Company, Richmond (detachments at Catterick, Eppleby and Reeth); "F" Company, Redcar (detachment at Marske-by-the-Sea); "G" Company, Skelton (detachments at Carlin How, Lingdale and Loftus); "H" Company, Northallerton (detachments at Bedale, Thirsk, Easingwold, Brompton and Helperby).

5th Battalion: Scarborough with "A" Company, Market Weighton (detachments at Pocklington, Newbald and Stamford Bridge); "B" Company, Bridlington (detachments at Filey, Hunmanby and Flamborough); "C" Company, Beverley (detachment at Cottingham); "D" Company, Driffield (detachment at Sledmere); "E" and "F" Companies, Scarborough; "G" Company, Pickering (detachments at Helmsley, Kirby Moorside, Grosmont, Ebberston and Thornton Dale); "H" Company, Malton (detachments at Sand Hutton, Sheriff Hutton and Hovingham).

All Hallows School Officers Training Corps. Honiton, Devon. One infantry company, Junior Division.

Allan's School Cadet Unit. See 6th Battalion, Northumberland Fusiliers.

Ampleforth College Officers Training Corps. Oswaldkirk, near Gilling, Yorkshire. One infantry company, Junior Division.

Anglesey Royal Engineers Militia. See Royal Anglesey Royal Engineers Militia.

Angus and Dundee Battalion. See 5th (Angus & Dundee) Battalion, Black Watch (Royal Highlanders).

Antrim Royal Garrison Artillery. Special Reserve. Carrickfergus.

Ardeer Company. See Royal Scots Fusiliers.

Ardingly College Officers Training Corps. Hayward's Heath. Two infantry companies, Junior Division.

Ardwick Battalion. See 8th (Ardwick) Battalion, Manchester Regiment.

Argyll and Sutherland Highlanders. See Princess Louise's (Argyll and Sutherland Highlanders).

Argyll and Sutherland Infantry Brigade. See Highland Division.

Argyllshire Battalion. See 8th (The Argyllshire) Battalion, Princess Louise's (Argyll and Sutherland Highlanders).

Army Ordnance Corps. *Staff-Sergeant. Crossed hammer and pincers between crown and chevrons indicate the trade of Armourer. The cap badge shows a shield bearing three guns below three cannon balls – the ancient arms of the Board of Ordnance.*

Army Chaplains' Department. *The crowned Maltese Cross collar insignia are smaller versions of the cap badge.*

Argyllshire (Mountain) Battery. See 4th Highland Brigade, Royal Garrison Artillery (Mountain).

Army Chaplains' Department. Chaplains to the Forces were attached to stations throughout the world. The *Army List* records these under "1st Class" (Ranking as Colonels); "2nd Class" (Lieutenant-Colonels), "3rd Class" (Majors) and "4th Class" (Captains). Under "Acting Army Chaplains" five groups are listed – "Church of England", "Presbyterian", "Roman Catholic", "Wesleyan", "Baptist and Congregational" – and for the Territorial Force, those listed are recorded as "Honorary Chaplains".

Army Gymnastic Staff. Headquarters, and location of the Inspector of Gymnasia were at The Gymnasium, Queen's Avenue, Aldershot.

Army Ordnance Corps. AOC units (numbered companies) were grouped within Command areas: No.1 Company (Aldershot Command), Aldershot; No.2 Company (Southern Command), sections at Portsmouth, Tidworth and Devonport; No.3 Company (Irish Command), sections in Dublin, Curragh and Haulbowline; No.4 Company (Aldershot Command), Aldershot; No.5 Company (Western, Northern and Scottish Commands), sections at Burscough, Pembroke Dock, York and Stirling; No.6 Company (Eastern Command), sections at Chatham, Colchester and Dover; Nos.7 and 8 Companies (Eastern), Woolwich; No.9 Company (Mediterranean and South Africa Commands), sections in Egypt, Malta, Gibraltar, Pretoria and Capetown.

There were also (listed under "Independent Detachments") units located in Hong Kong, North

Alexandra Princess of Wales's Own (Yorkshire Regiment). *Known within the Regiment (due to its tall and slender appearance) as the "Eiffel Tower", the cap badge featured the cypher of the Danish Princess Alexandra entwined with the Dannebrog (or Danes') Cross. The date "1875" refers to the year in which the title "Princess of Wales's Own" was granted to the Regiment (formerly the 19th) – the Princess having married the Prince of Wales (later King Edward VII) in 1863. Based on the regimental cap badge (in 1914 this had a coronet in lieu of a crown), this postcard illustration shows the regimental crest.*

China, Singapore, Ceylon, Sierra Leone, Mauritius, Jamaica, Bermuda, Jersey and Guernsey.

Until 1918, and amalgamation as Royal Army Ordnance Corps, officers were grouped as the Army Ordnance Department, other ranks as Army Ordnance Corps.

Army Ordnance Department. See Army Ordnance Corps

Army Pay Corps. Until 1920, and amalgamation as Royal Army Pay Corps, officers were grouped as Army Pay Department, other ranks as Army Pay Corps.

Army Pay Department. See Army Pay Corps.

Army Remount Service. See Remount Service.

Army School of Cookery. See Army Service Corps Training Establishment.

Army Service Corps. Regular Army Service Corps units (companies) appear in four groups: Horse Transport Companies (these numbered from 1 to 43); Mechanical Transport Companies (numbered 45 to 65); Supply Companies (lettered "A" to "E") and Remount Companies (lettered "AA" to "DD"). The Territorial Force element of the ASC (all units recorded under their own titles) was created in 1908 and organised into two sections: Mounted Brigade Transport and Supply Columns (each of one company) – Eastern, Highland, London, Lowland, North Midland, 1st South Midland, 2nd South Midland, Notts & Derby, South Eastern, South Wales, 1st South Western, 2nd South Western, Welsh Border and Yorkshire (the brigades were allotted one to each Territorial Force division) and Divisional Transport and Supply Columns. These comprised four companies ("Headquarters" and three others allotted one to each of the three infantry brigades within the division) each and were designated according to division – East Anglian, Highland, Home Counties, East Lancashire, West Lancashire, 1st London, 2nd London, Lowland, North Midland, South Midland, Northumbrian, West Riding, Welsh and Wessex.

Horse Transport Companies: No.1 at Aldershot; No.2, Woolwich; No.3, Bradford; No.4, Dublin; No.5, Woolwich; No.6, Curragh; No.7, Aldershot; No.8, Edinburgh; No.9, Aldershot; No.10, Aldershot; No.11, Kensington Barracks, London; No.12, Portsmouth; No.13, Bordon; No.14, Woolwich; No.15, Bulford; No.16, Aldershot; No.17, Cork; No.18, Kensington Barracks, London; No.19, Dublin; No.20, Aldershot; No.21, Devonport; No.22, Bulford; No.23, Curragh; No.24, York; No.25,

Army Veterinary Corps.

Woolwich; No.26, Aldershot; No.27, Aldershot; No.28, Aldershot; No.29, Portsmouth; No.30, Devonport; No.31, Aldershot; No.32, Shorncliffe; No.33, Belfast; No.34, Devonport; No.35, Aldershot; No.36, Aldershot; No.37, Curragh; No.38, Dover; No.39, Gibraltar; No.40, Malta; No.41, Cairo; No.42, Pretoria; No.43, Potchefstroom, South Africa.

Mechanical Transport Companies: No.45 at Devonport; No.46, Woolwich; No.47, Woolwich; No.48, Dublin; No.49, Curragh; No.50, Fermoy; No.51, Curragh; No.52, Aldershot; No.53, Aldershot; No.54, Aldershot; No.55, Bulford; No.56, Bulford; No.57, Aldershot; No.58, Aldershot; No.59, Aldershot; No.60, Aldershot; No.61, Aldershot, No.62, Portsmouth; No.63, Bulford; No.64, Bulford; No.65, Chatham.

Supply Companies: "A" at Aldershot; "B", Gosport; "C", Aldershot; "D", Curragh; "E", Woolwich.

Remount Companies: "AA" at Woolwich; "BB", Dublin; "CC", Lusk; "DD", Dublin.

Army Service Corps. *19th Company, Middelburg, Cape Colony, 1908, in full-dress uniforms and foreign service helmets. Re-numbered as 50th (Horse Transport) Company in 1912, the Company in that year moved to Ireland. Note both Queen's and King's South Africa Medals. Their numerous bars (eight in one case) indicate wide service throughout the Second Anglo-Boer War of 1899–1902.*

Army Service Corps Training Establishment. Aldershot. Included the Army School of Cookery.

Army Signal Schools. Aldershot and Bulford.

Army Veterinary Corps. Veterinary officers and personnel were attached to Regular and Territorial Force units at various stations.

Army Veterinary School. Aldershot.

Arnold House School Cadet Corps. See 4th Battalion, Loyal North Lancashire Regiment.

Artists Rifles. See 28th Battalion, London Regiment.

Ashford Grammar School Cadet Corps. One company.

Aylesbury Grammar School Cadet Corps. See Buckinghamshire Battalion, Oxfordshire and Buckinghamshire Light Infantry.

Ayrshire Batteries, 1st, 2nd. See 2nd Lowland Brigade, Royal Field Artillery.

Ayrshire Royal Horse Artillery. Territorial Force. Ayr. Included the Lowland Mounted Brigade Ammunition Column.

Ayrshire Yeomanry (Earl of Carrick's Own). Territorial Force. Ayr with "A" Squadron, also at Ayr; "B" Squadron, Cumnock; "C" Squadron, Kilmarnock; "D" Squadron, Beith.

Army Service Corps. *52nd (MT) Company with Fowler Lion traction engine. "To Berlin" chalked on the side of the machine indicates that the photograph – although the 52nd Company did not go overseas – was taken after war was declared.*

Army Service Corps. *After war was declared some 100 civilian bus drivers of the London General Omnibus Company (centre) were employed by the ASC as instructors in the Hounslow/Osterley Park area of London. Most instructors wore the ASC cap badge to identify with their students.*

Army Service Corps. *Mobile workshop. Among the equipment carried was a lathe, drilling machine, tool grinder, hydraulic jack and power hack saw.*

Ayrshire Yeomanry (Earl of Carrick's Own). *A lion's head and neck winged, the cap badge shown is that approved in October, 1902 and worn until replaced in 1915 by a version incorporating the name of the Regiment on a scroll.*

B

Bablake School Cadet Company. See 7th Battalion, Royal Warwickshire Regiment.

Banff and Donside Battalion. See 6th (Banff and Donside) Battalion, Gordon Highlanders.

Bangor University College Officers Training Corps. See University of Wales Officers Training Corps.

Basingstoke and Eastrop Cadet Corps. See 4th Battalion, Hampshire Regiment.

Bays. See 2nd Dragoon Guards (Queen's Bays).

Beaumont College Officers Training Corps. Old Windsor. One infantry company, Junior Division.

Beccles Cadet Corps. See 3rd East Anglian (Howitzer) Brigade, Royal Field Artillery.

Bedford Grammar School Officers Training Corps. Three engineer companies, Junior Division.

Bedford Modern School Officers Training Corps. One engineer company, Junior Division.

Bedford Park Cadet Company. See 10th Battalion, Duke of Cambridge's Own (Middlesex Regiment).

Bedfordshire Regiment. Two Regular (1st and 2nd), two Special Reserve (3rd and 4th) and one Territorial Force (5th) battalions. Depot, Bedford.
1st Battalion: Mullingar, Ireland.
2nd Battalion: Roberts' Heights, South Africa.
3rd Battalion: Bedford.
4th Battalion: Hertford.
5th Battalion: Gwyn Street, Bedford with "A" Company, also at Gwyn Street; "B" and "C" Companies, Luton; "D" Company, Biggleswade (detachments at Sandy, Arlesey and St Neots); "E" Company, Ampthill (detachment at Olney); "F" Company, Luton (detachments at Dunstable and Leighton Buzzard); "G" Company, Fletton (detachment at Yaxley); "H" Company, Huntingdon (detachments at St Ives and Ramsey).

Bedfordshire Yeomanry. Territorial Force. Ashburnham Road, Bedford with "A" Squadron, also at Ashburnham Road; "B" Squadron, Biggleswade (detachment at Shefford); "C" Squadron, Dunstable (detachments at Leighton Buzzard, Woburn and Ampthill); "D" Squadron, Godmanchester (detachments at St Neots, Kimbolton, Ramsey, Somersham, Sutton and Chatteris).

Beefeaters. See King's Body Guard of the Yeoman of the Guard.

Belfast University Officers Training Corps. Two infantry companies and a section of field ambulance, Senior Division.

Bedfordshire Regiment. *1st Battalion, Aldershot, 1913, shortly before moving to Ireland.*

Bedfordshire Regiment. *Cap badge. The Bedfordshire Regiment, long associated with the military forces of the neighbouring county of Hertfordshire, featured in its cap badge the hart lodged in water from the arms of Hertford.*

Berkshire Yeomanry (Hungerford). *The cap badge (left) is based on the skeletal White Horse chalk figure cut into the Downs above Uffington, while the crescent and star collar badge (right) comes from the seal of Hungerford.*

Berkshire Yeomanry (Hungerford). *This trooper wears the standard 1903-pattern ammunition bandolier.*

Berkhamstead School Officers Training Corps. Three infantry companies, Junior Division.

Berkshire Regiment. See Princess Charlotte of Wales's (Royal Berkshire Regiment).

Berkshire Royal Horse Artillery. Territorial Force. Yeomanry House, Castle Hill, Reading. Included the 2nd South Midland Mounted Brigade Ammunition Column. The Battery also had a detachment at Ascot.

Berkshire Yeomanry (Hungerford). Territorial Force. Yeomanry House, Castle Hill, Reading with "A" Squadron, Windsor (detachments at Maidenhead and Wokingham); "B" Squadron, Reading (detachment at Wallingford); "C" Squadron, Newbury (detachments at Hungerford and Lambourn); "D" Squadron, Wantage (detachments at Abingdon, Faringdon and Didcot).

Buckinghamshire Yeomanry. *The hussar-style uniforms are green with scarlet collars and cuffs.*

Bermuda Cadet Corps. See Bermuda Volunteer Rifle Corps.

Bermuda Militia Artillery. Two batteries.

Bermuda Volunteer Rifle Corps. Four companies. The Bermuda Cadet Corps was attached.

Birkenhead Cadet Corps, 1st. See 4th Battalion, Cheshire Regiment.

Birmingham University Officers Training Corps. Two infantry companies, Senior Division.

Black Watch Infantry Brigade. Territorial Force. Bell Street, Dundee. Battalions – 4th, 5th, 6th, 7th Black Watch with 5th Argyll and Sutherland Highlanders attached.

Black Watch (Royal Highlanders). Two Regular (1st and 2nd), one Special Reserve (3rd) and four Territorial Force (4th to 7th) battalions. Depot, Perth.

1st Battalion: Aldershot.

2nd Battalion: Bareilly, India.

3rd Battalion: Perth.

4th (City of Dundee) Battalion: Dundee.

5th (Angus & Dundee) Battalion: Arbroath with "A" Company, Kirriemuir (detachments at Glamis and Newtyle); "B" Company, Forfar; "C" Company, Montrose (detachment at Craigo); "D" Company, Brechin (detachment at Edzell); "E" Company, Arbroath (detachment at Friockheim); "F" Company, Arbroath (detachments at Carnoustie and Monifieth); "G" and "H" Companies, Dundee.

6th (Perthshire) Battalion: Tay Street, Perth with "A" and "B" Companies, also at Tay Street; "C" Company, Dunblane (detachments at Bridge of Allan, Doune and Callander); "D" Company, Crieff (detachment at Comrie); "E" Company, Blairgowrie (detachments at Coupar Angus and Alyth); "F" Company, Auchterarder (detachments at Blackford and Dunning); "G" Company, Birnam (detachments at Pitlochry, Ballinluig, Stanley, Luncarty and Blair Atholl); "H" Company, Aberfeldy (detachments at Kenmore, Fortingall, Grandtully and Killin.

7th (Fife) Battalion: St Andrews with "A" Company, Dunfermline; "B" Company, Lochgelly; "C" Company, Kirkcaldy; "D" Company, Cowdenbeath; "E" Company, Cupar (detachments at Newburgh, Auchtermuchty and Abernethy); "F" Company, Leven (detachments at Colinsburgh and Largoward); "G" Company, St Andrews (detachments at Guardbridge, Anstruther and Crail); "H" Company, Leslie (detachments at Markinch and Thornton).

Blackheath and Woolwich Battalion. See 20th Battalion, London Regiment.

Bloxham School Officers Training Corps. Banbury, Oxfordshire. One infantry company, Junior Division.

Blundell's School Officers Training Corps. Tiverton, Devon. Two infantry companies, Junior Division.

Blythswood Battalion. See 7th (Blythswood) Battalion, Highland Light Infantry.

Bolton Artillery. See 3rd East Lancashire Brigade, Royal Field Artillery (The Bolton Artillery).

Black Watch (Royal Highlanders). *The Pipers seen here at White City, Manchester in 1910 wear green doublets with Dress Stuart tartan.*

Black Watch (Royal Highlanders). *6th Battalion. These Territorials are seen wearing a mixture of dress – scarlet full-dress doublets with their blue collars and cuffs, red and black hose tops, Black Watch pattern tartan kilts and trews, together with khaki service dress. (David Barnes Collection).*

Border Battalion. See 4th (The Border) Battalion, King's Own Scottish Borderers.

Border Regiment. Two Regular (1st and 2nd), one Special Reserve (3rd) and two Territorial Force (4th and 5th) battalions. Depot, Carlisle.
1st Battalion: Maymyo, Burma.
2nd Battalion: Pembroke Dock.
3rd Battalion: Carlisle.
4th (Cumberland and Westmorland) Battalion: Strand Road, Carlisle with "A" and "B" Companies, also at Strand Road; "C" Company, Keswick (detachment at Brampton); "D" Company, Penrith; "E" Company, Kirkby Lonsdale (detachments at Sedbergh, Endmoor and Appleby); "F" Company, Kendal; "G" Company, Kendal (detachments at Burneside and Staveley); "H" Company, Windermere (detachments at Ambleside and Elterwater). The Kirkby Lonsdale Cadet Company was affiliated.
5th (Cumberland) Battalion: Workington with "A" Company, Whitehaven; "B" and "C" Companies, Workington; "D" Company, Cockermouth; "E" Company, Egremont (detachments at St Bees and Cleator); "F" Company, Wigton; "G" Company, Frizington; "H" Company, Aspatria (detachments at Dearham and Bullgill).

Bournemouth School Officers Training Corps. One infantry company, Junior Division.

Bradfield College Officers Training Corps. Reading, Berkshire. Three infantry companies, Junior Division.

Bradford Postal Telegraph Messengers' Cadet Corps. See 6th Battalion, Prince of Wales's Own (West Yorkshire Regiment).

Brecknockshire Battalion. See South Wales Borderers.

Bridgnorth Cadet Company. See 4th Battalion, King's (Shropshire Light Infantry).

Bridlington Grammar School Officers Training Corps. One infantry company, Junior Division.

Brierley Hill Cadet Corps. See 6th Battalion, South Staffordshire Regiment.

Brigade, 1st Cavalry. Aldershot. Comprised 2nd Dragoon Guards; 5th Dragoon Guards; 11th Hussars; 1st Signal Troop, Royal Engineers with IV, VII Brigades, Royal Horse Artillery; 1st Field Squadron, Royal Engineers attached.

Brigade, 2nd Cavalry. Tidworth. Comprised 4th Dragoon Guards; 9th Lancers; 18th Hussars; 2nd Signal Troop, Royal Engineers with VI Brigade, Royal Horse Artillery attached.

Brigade, 3rd Cavalry. Curragh. Comprised 4th Hussars; 5th Lancers; 16th Lancers; 3rd Signal Troop, Royal Engineers with III Brigade, Royal Horse Artillery and 4th Field Troop, Royal Engineers attached.

Brigade, 4th Cavalry. Canterbury. Comprised 6th Dragoon Guards, 3rd Hussars; 4th Signal Troop, Royal Engineers with 19th Hussars; II and X Brigades, Royal Horse Artillery attached. Also forming part of this division was the Composite Regiment of Household Cavalry. To be formed upon mobilization from personnel supplied by 1st, 2nd Life Guards and Royal Horse Guards.

Brigade, 5th Cavalry. York. Comprised 2nd Dragoons, 12th Lancers, 20th Hussars; 5th Signal Troop, Royal Engineers with V Brigade, Royal Horse Artillery attached.

Brigade, 1st Infantry. See 1st Division.

Brigade, 2nd Infantry. See 1st Division.

Brigade, 3rd Infantry. See 1st Division.

Brigade, 4th Infantry. See 2nd Division.

Brigade, 5th Infantry. See 2nd Division.

Brigade, 6th Infantry. See 2nd Division.

Brigade, 7th Infantry. See 3rd Division.

Brigade, 8th Infantry. See 3rd Division.

Brigade, 9th Infantry. See 3rd Division.

Brigade, 10th Infantry. See 4th Division.

Brigade, 11th Infantry. See 4th Division.

Brigade, 12th Infantry. See 4th Division.

Brigade, 13th Infantry. See 5th Division.

Brigade, 14th Infantry. See 5th Division.

Brigade, 15th Infantry. See 5th Division.

Brigade, 16th Infantry. See 6th Division.

Brigade, 17th Infantry. See 6th Division.

Brigade, 18th Infantry. See 6th Division.

Brighton Brigade Sussex Cadets. See 1st Home Counties Brigade, Royal Field Artillery.

Brighton College Officers Training Corps. Two infantry companies, Junior Division.

Brighton Preparatory Schools Cadet Corps. See 4th Battalion, Royal Sussex Regiment.

Bristol Grammar School Officers Training Corps. One infantry company, Junior Division.

Bristol University Officers Training Corps. One infantry company, Senior Division.

Broadwater Cadet Corps. Broadwater Hall, Broadwater Road, Tooting, London. One company.

Bromsgrove School Officers Training Corps. One infantry company, Junior Division.

Broughton Lads' Brigade. See 8th Battalion, Lancashire Fusiliers.

Buchan and Formartin Battalion. See 5th (Buchan

Buffs (East Kent Regiment). *5th Battalion. The gentleman seated wears the crossed axes of a Pioneer and on his lower arm two efficiency stars. These were awarded (to Territorials only) one for every four years returned as efficient. The jackets are scarlet with buff (the title of the Regiment comes from this) collar and cuffs.*

Buffs (East Kent Regiment). *Cap badge. The origin of the Dragon badge is uncertain. One early reference (a Royal Warrant of 1751) refers to it as being the "ancient badge" of the Regiment.*

and Formartin) Battalion, Gordon Highlanders.

Buckinghamshire Battalion. See Oxfordshire and Buckinghamshire Light Infantry.

Buckinghamshire Yeomanry (Royal Bucks Hussars). Territorial Force. Buckingham with "A" Squadron, Buckingham (detachments at Stony Stratford, Bletchley, Newport Pagnell and Akeley); "B" Squadron, Aylesbury (detachments at Kimble, Quainton and Wing); "C" Squadron, High Wycombe (detachments at Stokenchurch, Taplow and Beaconsfield); "D" Squadron, Chesham (detachments at Cholesbury, Chalfont St Peter and Great Missenden).

Buffs (East Kent Regiment). Two Regular (1st and 2nd), one Special Reserve (3rd) and two Territorial Force (4th and 5th) battalions. Depot, Canterbury.

1st Battalion: Fermoy, Ireland.

2nd Battalion: Wellington, India.

3rd Battalion: Canterbury.

4th Battalion: Canterbury with "A" Company at Ramsgate (detachments at Birchington and Broadstairs); "B" Company, Canterbury (detachments at Chartham and Ash); "C" Company, Canterbury (detachments at Littlebourne, Wingham and Nonington); "D" Company, Folkestone (detachment at Hythe); "E" Company, Sittingbourne (detachment at Sheerness); "F" Company, Herne Bay (detachment at Whitstable); "G" Company, Margate (detachments at St Nicholas at Wade and Westgate); "H" Company, Dover. There were four cadet units affiliated – the Chatham House (Ramsgate) Cadet Corps; Depot Royal Marine Cadet Corps, with headquarters at the RM Depot, Deal; Herne Bay College Cadet Corps and New College (Herne Bay) Cadet Corps.

5th (The Weald of Kent) Battalion: Ashford with "A" Company at Cranbrook (detachment at Benenden); "B" Company, Hawkhurst (detachment at Sandhurst); "C" Company, Headcorn (detachments at Staplehurst, Marden and Sutton Valence); "D" Company, Horsmonden (detachments at Goudhurst, Lamberhurst, Brenchley, Yalding and

Paddock Wood); "E" Company, Ashford (detachments at Pluckley, Bethersden, Aldington and Ham Street); "F" Company, Ashford; "G" Company, Tenterden (detachments at Lydd, Woodchurch, New Romney, Appledore, Wittersham and Rolvenden); "H" Company, Ashford.

Burford Grammar School Cadet Corps. See 4th Battalion, Oxfordshire and Buckinghamshire Light Infantry.

Bury Grammar School Officers Training Corps. One infantry company, Junior Division.

Buteshire (Mountain) Battery. See 4th Highland Brigade, Royal Garrison Artillery (Mountain).

Border Regiment. *The five-pointed star seen on the right lower arm indicates that the wearer is a regular soldier qualified in distance judging. Regulations issued in 1914 direct that such badges were issued forty-eight per infantry battalion. As best shot in his company he also wears (lower left arm) crossed rifles with star above.*

C

Cadet Battalion of Cornwall, 1st. See 4th Battalion, Duke of Cornwall's Light Infantry.

Cadet Norfolk Artillery. See 1st East Anglian Brigade, Royal Field Artillery.

Cadets. Administered by their local Territorial Force Associations, cadet units were formed with establishments ranging from company to battalion strength. Each was required to gain recognition (from its local TFA) and having done so would normally be affiliated to a unit of the TF. Battalions/companies having gained recognition, as of Aug/September, 1914, were as follows: Ackmar School, Aldershot Church, Allan's School, Arnold House School, Ashford Grammar School, Aylesbury Grammar School, Bablake School, Basingstoke and Eastrop, Beccles, Bedford Park, Bermuda, 1st Birkenhead, Bradford Postal Telegraph Messengers', Bridgnorth, Brierley Hill, Brighton Brigade Sussex, Brighton Preparatory Schools, Broadwater, Broughton Lads' Brigade, Burford Grammar School, Cadet Norfolk Artillery, 1st Chatham, Chatham House Ramsgate, 1st Cheshire Regiment, Christ's College, Church of the Ascension, 1st Cinque Ports, City of Aberdeen, 1st City of Dublin, City of Liverpool, City of London, 2nd Civil Service, Colchester Royal Grammar School, Coopers' Company School, 1st Cornwall, Cowley, Cranbrook College, Dartmouth, Depot Royal Marine, Devonshire Fortress Engineers, Drax Grammar School, Dublin Schools, Dunoon Grammar School, Ealing, 1st Essex Regiment, Exeter Cathedral School, Frimley and Camberley, 1st Glasgow Highland, Gloucestershire Regiment, Gordon Boys' Home, Greenwich Naval, Haddington, Haltwistle, 1st Hampshire Regiment, 2nd Hampshire Regiment, Harrow, Haytor (Newton Abbot), Herne Bay College, 2nd Hertfordshire, 3rd Hertfordshire, 4th Hertfordshire, Hugh Myddelton School, Hull (St Mark's), Hutcheson's Grammar School, Ilford Church, Imperial Cadet Yeomanry (City of London), Imperial Cadet Yeomanry (Yorkshire), Imperial Service (Brighton), Imperial Service (Eastbourne), Kensington and Hammersmith Navy League Boys' Brigade, Kent Fortress Royal Engineers, Kilburn Grammar School, King Edward VI School (Chelmsford), King Edward's School (Witley), 1st King's Royal Rifle Corps, King's School Peterborough, Kirkby Lonsdale, Leeds Postal Telegraph Messengers', Lewisham, 1st London Regiment, 6th London Regiment, 19th London Regiment, Lymington, Macclesfield Grammar School, Macclesfield Industrial School, Magdalene (Camberwell), 1st Manchester Regiment, 2nd Manchester Regiment, Manor Park, Marner School, 1st Monmouthshire Regiment, Morpeth Grammar School, 1st New Brighton, 2nd New Brighton, New College (Herne Bay), Newport, Newport Market School, North Berwick, 1st North Paddington, Northampton School, Nottingham (Church), Ongar Grammar School, Oratory (London), Paddington Boys' Club and Naval Brigade, Palmer's School, Peter Symonds School, Plymouth Lads' Brigade, 1st Poulton, Prestonpans, 1st Queen's Own

Cambridgeshire Regiment. *The cap badge seen being worn here is the pattern that included an additional scroll (lower) bearing the battle honour "South Africa 1900–01". This was awarded in recognition of the volunteer contingents provided by the old Cambridgeshire Rifle Volunteers for service in the Second Anglo-Boer War. The jacket is scarlet (white piping, blue collars and cuffs) and includes the white metal shoulder designation of "T" over CAMBRIDGESHIRE.*

Cambridgeshire Regiment. *Cap badge. The more common single-scroll pattern. The crest is from the armorial bearings of Cambridge – a bridge (the bridge on the Cam from which the city takes its name) – this had superimposed the arms (three open crowns) of Ely.*

Cambridgeshire Regiment. *Drum-head service at camp, Ipswich, 1910.*

Royal West Kent Regiment, Queen's Westminster, Richmond County School, Royal Berkshire Regiment, Royal Engineers (2nd London), 1st Royal Fusiliers, 1st Royal Marine Light Infantry (Chatham), 1st Royal Scots, 1st Royal Scots Fusiliers, 1st Royal Warwickshire Regiment, 2nd Royal Warwickshire Regiment, Ruthin School, Rutland Street School, St Ann's School (London), St Gabriel's (Canning Town), St Leonard's Collegiate School, St Mark's (Peckham), St Matthew's (Custom House), St Peter's (Holland Park), St Phillip's (Arundel), St Thomas's (Wandsworth), Sandroyd School, Seaford College, Settle, Sir Walter St James School, Somerset Naval, Sunbury House School, South London, Southend High School, Southport, Steyne School, Sunbury House School, Surrey Yeomanry, Tollington School, Tranent Industrial School, University School (Hastings), Upper Tooting High School, Ventnor, Wandsworth Boys' Naval, Waring, Warley Garrison, Welbeck (Mansfield), West Croydon, West Ham, Westerham and Chipstead, Westminster, Weymouth Secondary School, Wimbledon Boys' Naval, 1st Woolwich, Woolwich Scout, Yorkshire Squadron Imperial Cadet Yeomanry. For details see under title of each.

Cambridge and County School Officers Training Corps. One infantry company, Junior Division.

Cambridge University Officers Training Corps. One squadron of cavalry, a section of field artillery, one company of fortress engineers, a section of signals, an infantry battalion and one section field ambulance, Senior Division.

Cambridgeshire Regiment. Territorial Force. 14 Corn Exchange Street, Cambridge. *1st Battalion:* "A" Company, Cambridge (detachments at Great Shelford and Burwell); "B" Company, Cambridge (detachment at Sawston); "C" Company, Cambridge (detachment at Madingley); "D" Company, Cambridge; "E" Company, Wisbech; "F" Company, Whittlesea (detachments at Coates and Thorney); "G" Company, March (detachments at Benwick and Doddington); "H" Company, Ely (detachment at Sutton).

Cameron Highlanders. See Queen's Own Cameron Highlanders.

Cambridgeshire University Officers Training Corps. *The colour-sergeant (second row from front, third man from right) wears full-dress uniform – grey with light blue collar and cuffs, together with the light brown leather pouch-belt and its silver badge, whistle and chain.*

Cameronians (Scottish Rifles). *1st Battalion officers, Glasgow, 1914. Full- dress uniforms are worn – green doublets, Douglas pattern tartan trews, black shakos, silver badges and ornaments. The Battalion landed in France on 15 August, 1914.*

Cameronians (Scottish Rifles). *8th Battalion Machine Gun Section, December, 1914. The Battalion embarked for Gallipoli in the following May.*

Cameronians (Scottish Rifles). Two Regular (1st and 2nd), two Special Reserve (3rd and 4th) and four Territorials Force (5th–8th) battalions. Depot, Hamilton.

1st Battalion: Glasgow.

2nd Battalion: Malta.

3rd Battalion: Hamilton.

4th Battalion: Hamilton.

5th Battalion: 261 West Princes Street, Glasgow.

6th Battalion: Muirhall, Hamilton with "A" and "B" Companies, also at Muirhall; "C" Company, Uddingston; "D" Company, Larkhall (detachment at Strathaven); "E" Company, Bothwell (detachment at Palace Colliery); "F" Company, Blantyre; "G" and "H" Companies, Motherwell.

7th Battalion: Victoria Road, Glasgow. The Hutcheson's Grammar School Cadet Corps in Crown Street, Glasgow was affiliated.

8th Battalion: 149 Cathedral Street, Glasgow.

Campbell College Officers Training Corps. Belfast. One infantry company, Junior Division.

***Cameronians (Scottish Rifles).** Cap badge. The Mullet star – taken from the arms of James Earl of Angus, the founder of the Regiment in 1689 – surmounts a bugle horn. This device is from the 2nd Battalion (formerly 90th Regiment) who were styled as "Light Infantry" in 1815.*

Carabiniers. See 6th Dragoon Guards (Carabiniers) and Hampshire Yeomanry (Carabiniers).

Cardiganshire Battery. See 2nd Welsh Brigade, Royal Field Artillery.

Carnarvonshire and Anglesey Battalion. See 6th (Carnarvonshire & Anglesey) Battalion, Royal Welsh Fusiliers.

Carnarvonshire Royal Garrison Artillery. See Welsh Royal Garrison Artillery (Carnarvonshire).

Castlemartin Yeomanry. See Pembroke Yeomanry (Castlemartin).

Cavalry. The cavalry, as far as the Regular army was concerned, was made up of two main sections – the Household Cavalry and Cavalry of the Line. Providing the Sovereign's Escort, the Household Cavalry comprised 1st Life Guards, 2nd Life Guards and Royal Horse Guards. Line regiments, which were styled as Dragoon Guards, Dragoons, Hussars and Lancers, were organised into two groups. The first comprised seven regiments of Dragoon Guards (numbered 1st to 7th in their own sequence), the second being twenty-one Dragoon, Hussar and Lancer regiments. The numbering of these was mixed: 1st Dragoons, 2nd Dragoons, 3rd Hussars, 4th Hussars, 5th Lancers, 6th Dragoons, 7th Hussars, 8th Hussars, 9th Lancers, 10th Hussars, 11th Hussars, 12th Lancers, 13th Hussars, 14th Hussars, 15th Hussars, 16th Lancers, 17th Lancers, 18th Hussars, 19th Hussars, 20th Hussars, 21st Lancers. Unlike the infantry, which included both Regular and Auxiliary elements, cavalry regiments had no Special Reserve, Territorial Force or affiliated cadet units within their regimental framework.

Cavalry School. Netheravon.

Central Flying School. See Royal Flying Corps.

Charterhouse School Officers Training Corps. Godalming, Surrey. Three infantry companies, Junior Division.

Chatham Cadet Company, 1st. See 5th Battalion, Queen's Own Royal West Kent Regiment.

Chatham House (Ramsgate) Cadet Corps. See 4th Battalion, Buffs (East Kent Regiment).

Cheltenham College Officers Training Corps. Four infantry companies, Junior Division.

Cheshire Batteries, 1st, 2nd, 3rd. See Cheshire Brigade, Royal Field Artillery.

Cheshire Brigade Company, Army Service Corps. See Welsh Divisional Transport and Supply Column.

Cheshire Brigade, Royal Field Artillery. Territorial Force. Old Prison Yard, Shipgate Street, Chester with 1st and 2nd Cheshire Batteries, also at Old Prison Yard; 3rd Cheshire Battery, Crewe and Ammunition Column, Shipgate Street, Chester. Redesignated in 1913, the Cheshire Brigade was until then known as 3rd Welsh Brigade.

Cheshire Field Company. See Welsh Divisional Engineers.

Cheshire Infantry Brigade. See Welsh Division.

Cheshire Regiment. Two Regular (1st and 2nd), one Special Reserve (3rd) and four Territorial Force (4th–7th) battalions. Depot, Chester.

1st Battalion: Londonderry.

2nd Battalion: Jubbulpore, India.

3rd Battalion: Chester.

4th Battalion: Grange Road, Birkenhead with "A", "B", "C" and "D" Companies, also at Grange Road; "E" Company, Tranmere; "F" and "G" Companies,

***Cheshire Regiment.** Cap badge. In the centre, the ancient regimental device of an acorn.*

Cheshire Regiment. *1st Cadet Battalion. This young bugler wears the regimental scarlet jacket with buff collar and cuffs. Note the acorn collar badge and embroidered shoulder designation.*

Liscard; "H" Company, Heswall (detachments at Parkgate and Hoylake). There were four cadet units affiliated – the 1st Birkenhead Cadet Corps at St Catherine's Institute, Tranmere; 1st New Brighton Cadet Corps, Mona House, New Brighton; 2nd New Brighton Cadet Corps, 65 and 67 Rowson Street, New Brighton and 1st Poulton Cadet Company, St Luke's Parish Hall, Poulton.

5th (Earl of Chester's) Battalion: Volunteer Street, Chester with "A" Company, Altrincham (detachment at Knutsford); "B" Company, Chester (detachment at Kelsall); "C" Company, Sale (detachment at Cheadle); "D" Company, Hartford; "E" Company, Chester; "F" Company, Frodsham (detachment at Lymm); "G" Company, Runcorn; "H" Company, Hartford.

6th Battalion: Stockport with "A" and "B" Companies, Stalybridge; "C" Company, Hyde; "D" Company, Glossop (detachment at Hadfield); "E", "F", "G" and "H" Companies, Stockport.

7th Battalion: Macclesfield with "A" Company, Congleton; "B" Company, Congleton (detachment at Bollington); "C" and "D" Companies, Macclesfield; "E" Company, Winsford; "F" Company, Nantwich (detachment at Crewe); "G" Company, Sandbach; "H" Company, Wilmslow. The Macclesfield Grammar School Cadet Corps and Macclesfield Industrial School Cadet Corps were affiliated.

1st Cadet Battalion: 12 St Peter's Square, Stockport and affiliated to the 6th Battalion.

Cheshire Regiment. *4th Battalion. This battalion was distinct from others within the Regiment with its grey uniforms (scarlet collars, cuffs and piping). One man illustrates this, complete with grey cap and white gloves. The remainder enjoy the relaxed atmosphere of camp and wear a mixture of khaki service dress jackets with full-dress grey trousers. (David Barnes Collection).*

Cheshire Yeomanry (Earl of Chester's).

Cheshire Brigade, Royal Field Artillery. This photograph was taken at the August, 1914 annual camp. Orders to mobilize were received by many Territorial Force units about this time.

Cheshire Yeomanry (Earl of Chester's). Territorial Force. Old Bank Buildings, Chester with "A" Squadron, Knutsford (detachments at Alderley Edge, Hale and Sale); "B" Squadron, Eaton (detachments at Chester, Farndon, Aldford, Pulford, Tattenhall and Kelsall); "C" Squadron, Northwich (detachments at Great Budworth, Appleton, Warburton, Nantwich, Winsford, Middlewich, Tarporley and Crewe); "D" Squadron, Macclesfield (detachments at Congleton, Stockport and Adlington).

Chestnut Troop. See I Brigade, Royal Horse Artillery.

Chigwell School Officers Training Corps. One infantry company, Junior Division.

Christ's College Cadet Company. See 7th Battalion, Duke of Cambridge's Own (Middlesex Regiment).

Christ's Hospital Officers Training Corps. West Horsham. Four infantry companies, Junior Division.

Church of the Ascension Cadet Corps. See 1st Cadet Battalion, Essex Regiment.

Churcher's College Officers Training Corps. Petersfield, Hampshire. One infantry company, Junior Division.

Cheshire Yeomanry (Earl of Chester's). The cap badge features the Prince of Wales's plumes, coronet and motto. Regimental blue full-dress uniforms (scarlet collars and cuffs, white piping) are worn with the addition of white shoulder cords.

Cinque Ports Brigade, Royal Field Artillery. See 3rd Home Counties Brigade, Royal Field Artillery (Cinque Ports).

Cinque Ports Cadet Corps, 1st. See 5th (Cinque Ports) Battalion, Royal Sussex Regiment.

Cinque Ports Fortress Engineers. Territorial Force. 16 Bench Street, Dover with No.1 Electric Lights Company.

City of London Yeomanry (Rough Riders). *The trumpeter (centre) wears the regiment's lancer-style full dress – bluish-grey with purple cuffs, collars and plastron (the breast covering). Note also (far left) the fleur-de-lys Army Scout arm badge.*

City of London Yeomanry (Rough Riders). *Collar badge.*

Coldstream Guards. *Cap badges - the Star of the Order of the Garter – officers (left), other ranks (right).*

City of Aberdeen Batteries, 1st, 2nd, 3rd. See 1st Highland Brigade, Royal Field Artillery.

City of Aberdeen Cadet Battalion. 31 Adelphi, Aberdeen. Four companies.

City of Aberdeen Fortress Engineers. Territorial Force. 80 Hardgate, Aberdeen with No.1 Works Company.

City of Bristol Battalion. See 4th (City of Bristol) Battalion, Gloucestershire Regiment.

City of Dublin Cadets, 1st. Ship Street Barracks, Dublin. Four companies.

City of Dundee Battalion. See 4th (City of Dundee) Battalion, Black Watch (Royal Highlanders).

City of Dundee Battery. See 2nd Highland Brigade, Royal Field Artillery.

City of Dundee Fortress Engineers. Territorial Force. 52 Taylor's Lane, Dundee with No.1 Works Company.

City of Edinburgh Batteries, 1st, 2nd. See 1st Lowland Brigade, Royal Field Artillery.

Cornwall Fortress Engineers. *Post-marked "Lostwithiel 22 July, 1910" this postcard includes the message "Just a few of our Lerryn chaps [a detachment of No.2 Works Company] who attended the King's Memorial Service [King Edward VII had died on 6 May, 1910] at Fowey. After the service we all formed up in the square and had our promotions read."*

1st City of Dublin Cadets. *Cadet Edward F. Pearson, age fourteen.*

City of Edinburgh Fortress Engineers. Territorial Force. 28 York Place, Edinburgh with No.1 Works Company and No.2 Electric Lights Company.

City of Edinburgh Royal Garrison Artillery. See Lowland Royal Garrison Artillery (City of Edinburgh).

City of Glasgow Battalion. See 5th and 6th (City of Glasgow) Battalions, Highland Light Infantry.

City of Glasgow Batteries, 1st, 2nd, 3rd. See 3rd Lowland Brigade, Royal Field Artillery.

City of Glasgow Batteries, 4th (Howitzer), 5th (Howitzer). See 4th Lowland Brigade, Royal Field Artillery (Howitzer).

City of Liverpool Cadet Battalion. Seaton Buildings, 17 Water Street, Liverpool. Eight companies affiliated to the Liverpool Infantry Brigade.

City of London Battalions, London Regiment. See 1st to 8th Battalions, London Regiment.

City of London Batteries, 1st, 2nd, 3rd. See 1st London Brigade, Royal Field Artillery (City of London).

City of London Brigade, Royal Field Artillery. See 1st London Brigade, Royal Field Artillery (City of London).

City of London Cadet Battalion (Lord Robert's Boys), 1st. Headquarters at the Guildhall. Seven companies.

City of London Horse Artillery, 1st, 2nd. See Honourable Artillery Company.

City of London Regiment. See Royal Fusiliers (City of London Regiment).

City of London School Officers Training Corps. Victoria Embankment. Two infantry companies, Junior Division.

City of London Yeomanry (Rough Riders). Territorial Force. 39 Finsbury Square.

Civil Service Cadet Battalion, 2nd See 15th London Regiment.

Civil Service Rifles. See 15th Battalion, London Regiment.

Clifton College Officers Training Corps. Four engineer companies, Junior Division.

Clyde Royal Garrison Artillery. Territorial Force. 2 King Street, Port Glasgow with No.1 Company, also at King Street; No.2 Company, Helensburgh (detachment at Dumbarton) and No.3 Company, Dumbarton.

Colchester Royal Grammar School Cadets. See 5th Battalion, Essex Regiment.

Coldstream Guards. Three Regular battalions.

1st Battalion: Aldershot.

2nd Battalion: Windsor.

3rd Battalion: Chelsea Barracks, London.

Composite Regiment of Household Cavalry. See 4th Cavalry Brigade.

Connaught Rangers. Two Regular (1st and 2nd) and two Special Reserve (3rd and 4th) battalions. Depot, Galway.

1st Battalion: Ferozepore, India.

2nd Battalion: Barrosa Barracks, Aldershot.

3rd Battalion: Galway.

4th Battalion: Boyle.

Coopers' Company School Cadet Corps. See 5th Battalion, London Regiment.

Cork Grammar School Officers Training Corps. One infantry company, Junior Division.

Cork Royal Garrison Artillery. Special Reserve. Fort Westmoreland, Spike Island, Queenstown Harbour.

Cornwall Fortress Engineers. Territorial Force. Falmouth with No.1 Electric Lights Company, also in Falmouth; No.2 Works Company at Fowey (detachments at Lerryn and Lanreath); No.3 Works Company, Penryn (detachments at Ponsanooth).

2nd County of London (Westminster Dragoons). *Cap badge – the armorial bearings of the City of Westminster.*

Cornwall Royal Garrison Artillery (Duke of Cornwall's). Territorial Force. Falmouth with No.1 Heavy Battery, Padstow (detachments at St Merryn, Charlestown, Bugle and Par); No.2 Heavy Battery, Penzance (detachments at St Just and St Buryan); No.3 Company, Looe; No.4 Company, Marazion; No.5 Company, St Ives; No.6 Company, Falmouth; No.7 Company, Truro.

Corps of Army Schoolmasters. Located at various stations worldwide.

County of Durham Brigade, Royal Field Artillery. See 3rd Northumbrian Brigade, Royal Field Artillery (County of Durham).

County of London Battalions, London Regiment. See 9th to 28th Battalions, London Regiment.

County of London Batteries, 4th, 5th, 6th. See 2nd London Brigade, Royal Field Artillery.

County of London Batteries, 7th, 8th, 9th. See 3rd London Brigade, Royal Field Artillery.

County of London Batteries, 10th (Howitzer), 11th (Howitzer). See 4th London Brigade, Royal Field Artillery (Howitzer).

County of London Batteries, 12th, 13th, 14th. See 5th London Brigade, Royal Field Artillery.

County of London Batteries, 15th, 16th, 17th. See 6th London Brigade, Royal Field Artillery.

County of London Batteries, 18th, 19th, 20th. See 7th London Brigade, Royal Field Artillery.

County of London Batteries, 21st (Howitzer), 22nd (Howitzer) See 8th London Brigade, Royal Field Artillery (Howitzer).

County of London Yeomanry (Middlesex, Duke of Cambridge's Hussars), 1st. Territorial Force. Duke of York's Headquarters, Chelsea, London.

County of London Yeomanry (Westminster Dragoons), 2nd. Territorial Force. Elverton Street, Westminster.

County of London Yeomanry (Sharpshooters), 3rd. Territorial Force. Henry Street, St John's Wood.

Cowley Cadet Corps. See 4th Battalion, Oxfordshire and Buckinghamshire Light Infantry.

Cranbrook College (Ilford) Cadets. See 4th Battalion, Essex Regiment.

Cranbrook School Officers Training Corps. One infantry company, Junior Division.

Cranleigh School Officers Training Corps. Two infantry companies, Junior Division.

Cumberland Artillery. See 4th East Lancashire Brigade, Royal Field Artillery (Howitzer) (The Cumberland Artillery).

Cumberland Battalion. See 5th (Cumberland) Battalion, Border Regiment.

Cumberland Batteries, 1st (Howitzer), 2nd (Howitzer). See 4th East Lancashire Brigade, Royal Field Artillery (Howitzer) (The Cumberland Artillery).

Cumberland and Westmorland Battalion. See 4th (Cumberland and Westmorland) Battalion, Border Regiment.

Cyclists. Although cyclist sections were included in most, if not all regiments, it was only within the Territorial Force that whole battalions dedicated to this role existed. These were generally numbered and placed within regiments viz. 7th Devonshire, 5th East Yorkshire, 8th Essex, 9th Hampshire, 25th London, 6th Norfolk, 10th Royal Scots, 6th Royal Sussex, 6th Suffolk and 7th Welsh. There were also four independent battalions designated Highland, Huntingdonshire, Kent and Northern.

Coldstream Guards. *Drummers. The scarlet tunics are adorned by rows of white lace bearing scarlet fleur-de-lys. Note the arrangement (in twos) of the buttons. On both tunic fronts and cuffs, this indicates the seniority of each of the four Foot Guards regiments – Grenadier Guards (1st), Coldstream Guards (2nd), Scots Guards (3rd), Irish Guards (4th). When the Welsh Guards were formed in 1915, uniforms carried the buttons in groups of five.*

D

Dartford Grammar School Officers Training Corps. One infantry company, Junior Division.

Dartmouth Cadet Company. See 7th Battalion, Devonshire Regiment.

Dean Close School Officers Training Corps. Cheltenham. One infantry company, Junior Division.

Deeside Highland Battalion. See 7th (Deeside Highland) Battalion, Gordon Highlanders.

Denbighshire Battalion. See 4th (Denbighshire) Batalion, Royal Welsh Fusiliers.

Denbighshire Hussars Yeomanry. Territorial Force. 1 Erdigg Road, Wrexham with "A" Squadron, Wrexham (detachments at Llangollen, Mold and Ruabon); "B" Squadron, Denbigh (detachments at Prestatyn, Rhyl and Ruthin); "C" Squadron, Bangor (detachments at Carnarvon, Llandudno and Beaumaris); "D" Squadron, Birkenhead.

Denbighshire Hussars Yeomanry. *Annual camp at Rhyl, May, 1914. The blue uniforms have scarlet collars and cuffs. Note also the white cord cap-lines and shoulder chains.*

Derbyshire Yeomanry. *Cap badge. Serving in the Second Boer War as 8th and 104th Companies, Imperial Yeomanry, the Regiment gained the battle honour "South Africa 1900–1901".*

Denstone College Officers Training Corps. Rocester, Staffordshire. Two infantry companies, Junior Division.

Depot Royal Marine Cadet Corps. See 4th Battalion, Buffs (East Kent Regiment).

Derby School Officers Training Corps. One infantry company, Junior Division.

Derbyshire Batteries, 1st (Howitzer), 2nd (Howitzer). See 4th North Midland Brigade, Royal Field Artillery (Howitzer).

Derbyshire Yeomanry. Territorial Force. 91 Siddall's Road, Derby with "A" Squadron, Chesterfield (detachments at Ripley, Belper, Beauchief and Eckington); "B" Squadron, Bakewell (detachments at Buxton, Tideswell, Matlock, Youlgreave and Hartington); "C" Squadron, Derby (detachments at Osmaston Manor, Duffield and Wirksworth); "D" Squadron, Derby (detachments at Ilkeston, Church Gresley and Repton).

Devon and Cornwall Brigade Company, Army Service Corps. See Wessex Divisional Transport and Supply Column.

Devon and Cornwall Infantry Brigade. See Wessex Division.

Devon Yeomanry, 1st. See Royal 1st Devon Yeomanry.

Devon Yeomanry, North. See Royal North Devon Hussars Yeomanry.

Devonshire Batteries, 1st, 2nd, 3rd. See 4th Wessex Brigade, Royal Field Artillery.

Devonshire Fortress Engineers. Territorial Force. Mutley Barracks, Plymouth with No.1 Works Company at Torquay (detachments at Newton Abbot and Yealmpton); Nos. 2 and 3 Works Companies in Exeter; Nos. 4 and 5 Electric Lights Companies, Mutley Barracks, Plymouth. There were two cadet companies attached designated No.1 (Yealmpton) and No.2 (Plymouth).

Devonshire Regiment. Two Regular (1st and 2nd), one Special Reserve (3rd) and four Territorial Force (4th–7th) Battalions. Depot, Exeter.

1st Battalion: Jersey.

2nd Battalion: Cairo.

3rd Battalion: Exeter.

4th Battalion: Exeter with "A" Company in Exeter (detachment at Broad Clyst); "B" and "C" Companies, Exeter; "D" Company, Exmouth (detachments at Budleigh Salterton and Lympstone); "E" Company, Tiverton (detachments at Bampton and

Devonshire Royal Garrison Artillery.
Manoeuvring 4.7 inch gun.

Dulverton); "F" Company, Sidmouth (detachments at Ottery St Mary, Newton Poppleford, Honiton and Colyton); "G" Company, Cullompton (detachments at Burlescombe and Uffculme); "H" Company, Axminster (detachments at Chardstock and Lyme Regis). The Exeter Cathedral School Cadet Company was affiliated.

5th (Prince of Wales's) Battalion: Millbay, Plymouth with "A" Company, Tavistock; "B" Company, Plymouth; "C" Company, Plymouth (detachments at Ivybridge and Kingsbridge); "D" Company, Devonport; "E" Company, Newton Abbot (detachment at Chudleigh); "F" Company, Teignmouth (detachments at Dawlish and Torquay); "G" Company, Moreton Hampstead (detachments at Bovey Tracey and Chagford); "H" Company, Totnes (detachments at Ashburton and Buckfastleigh). The Plymouth Lads' Brigade Cadet Corps at 79 Embankment Road, Plymouth, and The Haytor (Newton Abbot) Cadet Corps, headquarters at Penhurst, Newton Abbot, were affiliated.

6th Battalion: Barnstaple with "A" Company, Barnstaple (detachment at Muddiford); "B" Company, Okehampton (detachments at Hatherleigh, Bow and Sticklepath); "C" Company, Bideford (detachments at Appledore, Parkham and Hartland); "D" Company, Torrington (detachments at St Giles, Holsworthy and Ashwater); "E" Company, South Molton (detachments at Witheridge, Molland and Chittlehampton); "F" Company, Chulmleigh (detachments at Winkleigh, Kings Nympton, Burrington and Crediton); "G" Company, Combe Martin (detachments at Berrynarbor, Braunton and Croyde); "H" Company, Barnstaple.

7th (Cyclist) Battalion: Exeter with "A" Company at Torquay; "B" Company, Exeter (detachments at Topsham and Woodbury); "C" Company, Exeter; "D" Company, Cullompton (detachments at Bradninch and Silverton); "E" Company, Crediton; "F" Company, Dartmouth; "G" Company, Plymouth; "H" Company, Torquay. The Dartmouth Cadet Company at Crothers Hill, Dartmouth was affiliated.

Devonshire Royal Garrison Artillery. Territorial Force. Artillery Drill Hall, Lambhay Hill, Plymouth with No.1 Heavy Battery, Ilfracombe (detachment at Lynmouth); No.2 Heavy Battery, Devonport (detachments at Plympton and Salcombe); Nos.3 and 4 Companies, Plymouth; Nos.5 and 6 Companies, Devonport.

Division, 1st. Aldershot.

1st Infantry Brigade: Aldershot. Battalions – 1st Coldstream Guards, 1st Scots Guards, 1st Black Watch, 2nd Royal Munster Fusiliers.

2nd Infantry Brigade: Blackdown. Battalions – 2nd Royal Sussex, 1st Loyal North Lancashire, 1st Northampton, 2nd King's Royal Rifle Corps.

3rd Infantry Brigade: Bordon. Battalions – 1st Queen's, 1st South Wales Borderers, 1st Gloucestershire, 2nd Welsh.

Royal Artillery: Aldershot. XXV, XXVI, XXXIX, XLIII (Howitzer) Brigades, Royal Field Artillery; 26th Heavy Battery, Royal Garrison Artillery.

Royal Engineers: Aldershot. 23rd, 26th Field Companies; 1st Signal Company.

Division, 2nd. Aldershot.

4th Infantry Brigade (Foot Guards): London. Battalions – 2nd Grenadier Guards, 2nd, 3rd Coldstream Guards, 1st Irish Guards.

5th Infantry Brigade: Aldershot. Battalions – 2 Worcestershire, 2nd Oxfordshire and Buckinghamshire Light Infantry; 2nd Highland Light Infantry, 2nd Connaught Rangers.

6th Infantry Brigade: Aldershot. Battalions – 1st King's Liverpool, 2nd South Staffordshire, 1st Royal Berkshire, 1st King's Royal Rifle Corps.

Royal Artillery: XXXIV, XXXVI, XLI, XLIV (Howitzer) Brigades, Royal Field Artillery; 35th Heavy Battery, Royal Garrison Artillery.

Royal Engineers: 5th, 11th Field Companies; 2nd Signal Company.

3rd Division. *On manoeuvres at Farthingstone, Northamptonshire in 1912. The photo shows parcels and letters being sorted at Headquarters Post Office.*

Division, 3rd. Bulford.
7th Infantry Brigade: Tidworth. Battalions – 3rd Worcestershire, 2nd South Lancashire, 1st Wiltshire, 2nd Royal Irish Rifles.
8th Infantry Brigade: Devonport. Battalions – 2nd Royal Scots, 2nd Royal Irish Regiment, 4th Middlesex, 1st Gordon Highlanders.
9th Infantry Brigade. Potsmouth. Battalions – 1st Northumberland Fusiliers, 4th Royal Fusiliers, 1st Lincolnshire, 1st Royal Scots Fusiliers.
Royal Artillery: Bulford. XXIII, XXX (Howitzer), XL, XLII Brigades, Royal Field Artillery; 48th Heavy Battery, Royal Garrison Artillery.
Royal Engineers: 56th, 57th Field Companies; 3rd Signal Company.

Division, 4th. Woolwich.
10th Infantry Brigade: Shorncliffe. Battalions – 1st Royal Warwickshire, 2nd Seaforth, 1st Royal Irish Fusiliers, 2nd Royal Dublin Fusiliers.
11th Infantry Brigade: Colchester. Battalions – 1st Somerset Light Infantry, 1st East Lancashire, 1st Hampshire, 1st Rifle Brigade.
12th Infantry Brigade: Dover. Battalions – 1st King's Own, 2nd Lancashire Fusiliers, 2nd Royal Inniskilling Fusiliers, 2nd Essex.
Royal Artillery: Woolwich. XIV, XXIX, XXXII, XXXVII (Howitzer) Brigades, Royal Field Artillery; 31st Heavy Battery, Royal Garrison Artillery.
Royal Engineers: 7th, 9th Field Companies; 4th Signal Company.

Division, 5th. Curragh.
13th Infantry Brigade: Dublin. Battalions – 2nd King's Own Scottish Borderers, 2nd Duke of Wellington's, 1st Queen's Own Royal West Kent, 2nd King's Own Yorkshire Light Infantry.
14th Infantry Brigade: Curragh. Battalions – 2nd Suffolk, 1st East Surrey, 1st Duke of Cornwall's Light Infantry, 2nd Manchester.
15th Infantry Brigade: Belfast. Battalions – 1st Norfolk, 1st Bedfordshire, 1st Cheshire, 1st Dorsetshire.
Royal Artillery: Newbridge. VIII (Howitzer), XV, XXVII, XXVIII Brigades, Royal Field Artillery; 108th Heavy Battery, Royal Garrison Artillery.
Royal Engineers: 7th, 59th Field Companies; 5th Signal Company.

Division, 6th. Cork.
16th Infantry Brigade: Fermoy. Battalions – 1st Buffs, 1st Leicestershire, 1st King's Shropshire Light Infantry, 2nd York and Lancaster.
17th Infantry Brigade: Cork. Battalions – 1st Royal Fusiliers, 1st North Staffordshire, 2nd Leinster, 3rd Rifle Brigade.
18th Infantry Brigade: Lichfield. Battalions – 1st West Yorkshire, 1st East Yorkshire, 2nd Sherwood Foresters, 2nd Durham Light Infantry.
Royal Artillery: Mallow. II, XII (Howitzer), XXIV, XXXVIII Brigades, Royal Field Artillery; 24th Heavy Battery, Royal Garrison Artillery.
Royal Engineers: 12th, 38th Field Companies; 6th Signal Company.

Dollar Institution Officers Training Corps. One infantry company, Junior Division.

Dorchester Grammar School Officers Training Corps. One infantry company, Junior Division.

Dorset Yeomanry. See Queen's Own Dorset Yeomanry.

Dorsetshire Battery. See 3rd Wessex Brigade, Royal Field Artillery.

Dorsetshire Fortress Engineers. Territorial Force. Sidney Hall, Weymouth with No.1 Electric Lights Company. There was also a detachment at Portland.

Dorsetshire Regiment. Two Regular (1st and 2nd), one Special Reserve (3rd) and one Territorial Force (4th) battalions. Depot, Dorchester.
1st Battalion: Belfast.
2nd Battalion: Poona, India.
3rd Battalion: Dorchester.
4th Battalion: Dorchester with "A" Company, Bridport (detachments at Beaminster, Chideock and Netherbury); "B" Company, Wareham (detachments at Corfe Castle, Bere Regis and Wool); "C" Company, Dorchester (detachment at Broadway); "D" Company, Poole (detachment at Parkstone); "E" Company, Gillingham (detachments at

Dorsetshire Regiment. *Regimental button. Much of the regiment's history is shown within its badges. As the first British infantry regiment to serve in India (1754) the 39th (later 1st Battalion) were later granted the motto "Primus in Indis". The same regiment also gained the castle and key of Gibraltar (present during the siege of 1779–1783). Fort Marabout was captured from the French by the 54th Regiment (later 2nd Battalion) and this, together with the Sphinx, recalls fine service during the Egyptian Campaign of 1801.*

1st (King's) Dragoon Guards. *Cap badge. At the outbreak of war in 1914, the regiment's cap badge was the double-headed eagle of their then Colonel-in-Chief, Emperor Francis Joseph 1 of Austria. Under the circumstances the badge was quickly dropped and replaced by a simple crowned star.*

Shaftesbury and Mere); "F" Company, Wimborne (detachments at Witchampton, Broadstone and Woodlands); "G" Company, Sherborne (detachment at Milborne Port); "H" Company, Blandford (detachments at Sturminster Newton and Marnhull).

Dorsetshire Royal Garrison Artillery. Territorial Force. Lower St Albans Street, Weymouth with No.1 Company, Swanage; No.2 Company, Poole (detachment at Parkstone); No.3 Company, Portland (detachment at Weymouth).

Dover College Officers Training Corps. Two infantry companies, Junior Division.

Downside School Officers Training Corps. Near Bath, Somerset. One infantry company, Junior Division.

Dragoon Guards, 1st (King's). Lucknow, India. Depot, Dunbar.

Dragoon Guards (Queen's Bays), 2nd. Aldershot. Depot, Newport, Monmouthshire.

Dragoon Guards, 3rd (Prince of Wales's). Cairo, Egypt. Depot, Newport, Monmouthshire.

Dragoon Guards, 4th (Royal Irish). Tidworth. Depot, Newport, Monmouthshire.

Dragoon Guards, 5th (Princess Charlotte of Wales's). Aldershot. Depot, Dunbar.

Dragoon Guards (Carabiniers), 6th. Canterbury. Depot, Newport, Monmouthshire.

2nd Dragoon Guards (Queen's Bays). *Drum horse "Prince".*

3rd (Prince of Wales's) Dragoon Guards. *Wearing scarlet tunics with yellow collars, one of the party seen here (nearest camera) also shows the farriers' horseshoe badge, while in the rear rank, a sergeant wears the Prince of Wales's plumes NCOs' arm badge. The helmet plumes are a mixture of black and red.*

4th (Royal Irish) Dragoon Guards. *Tidworth, 1912. Scarlet tunics (with blue collars and cuffs) and white plumes.*

5th (Princess Charlotte of Wales's) Dragoon Guards. *Aldershot, 1913. Note white overalls, rolled great coats and NCOs' white horse arm badges.*

5th (Princess Charlotte of Wales's) Dragoon Guards. *Aldershot, 1913. Scarlet tunics (dark green collars and cuffs), red and white plumes.*

Dragoon Guards, 7th (Princess Royal's). Secunderabad, India. Depot, Newport, Monmouthshire.

Dragoons, 1st (Royal). Potchefstroom, South Africa. Depot, Dunbar.

Dragoons (Royal Scots Greys), 2nd. York. Depot, Dunbar.

2nd Dragoons (Royal Scots Greys). *Gymnastic Instructor.*

2nd Dragoons (Royal Scots Greys). *Cap badge. On 18 June, 1815, the Regiment (then known as the Royal North British Dragoons) charged with the Union Brigade at Waterloo. Sergeant Charles Ewart during the action captured with great heroism the Standard (this surmounted with an eagle) of the French 45th Regiment.*

Dragoons, 6th (Inniskilling). Muttra, India. Depot, Newport, Monmouthshire.

Drax Grammar School Cadet Company. Drax, Yorkshire.

Dublin Fusiliers. See Royal Dublin Fusiliers.

Dublin Schools Cadet Corps. 14 Dromard Terrace, Sandymount, Dublin. Two companies.

Dublin University Officers Training Corps. Three infantry companies, a transport and supply section and one section field ambulance, Senior Division.

Duke of Cambridge's Hussars. See 1st County of London Yeomanry (Middlesex, Duke of Cambridge's Hussars).

Duke of Cambridge's Own Lancers. See 17th (Duke of Cambridge's Own) Lancers.

Duke of Cambridge's Own (Middlesex Regiment). Four Regular (1st, 2nd, 3rd and 4th), two Special Reserve (5th and 6th) and four Territorial Force (7th to 10th) battalions. Depot, Mill Hill.

1st Battalion: Woolwich.

2nd Battalion: Malta.

3rd Battalion: Cawnpore, India.

4th Battalion: Devonport.

5th Battalion: Mill Hill.

6th Battalion: Mill Hill.

7th Battalion: Priory Road, Hornsey with "A" Company, Hampstead; "B" Company, Barnet; "C" Company, Hornsey; "D" Company, Highgate; "E" Company, Tottenham; "F" Company, Enfield Lock (detachment at Enfield Town); "G" Company, Tottenham; "H" Company, Hornsey. The Christ's College Cadet Company and Tollington School Cadet Company were affiliated to the 7th Battalion.

8th Battalion: 202a Hanworth Road, Hounslow with "A" Company, Twickenham; "B" Company, Brentford; "C" Company, Hounslow; "D" Company, Southall; "E" Company, Uxbridge; "F" Company, Ealing; "G" Company, Hampton; "H" Company, Staines. The Ealing Cadet Company was affiliated to the Battalion.

9th Battalion: Pound Lane, Willesden with "A" and "B" Companies, also at Pound Lane; "C" Company, Willesden (detachment at Stanmore); "D" and "E" Companies, Willesden; "F" Company, Harrow; "G" Company, Wealdstone; "H" Company, Hendon. There were three cadet units affiliated – the Harrow Cadet Company; Kilburn Grammar School Cadet Company and Sunbury House School Cadet Company.

10th Battalion: Stamford Brook Lodge, Ravenscourt Park, Hammersmith with "A" Company, St John's College, Battersea; "B" Company, St Mark's College, Chelsea; "C" to "H" Companies, Ravenscourt Park. The Bedford Park Cadet Company was affiliated.

Duke of Cambridge's Own (Middlesex Regiment). *Scarlet jackets with yellow collars and cuffs. The soldier seated wears an Army Scout badge.*

Duke of Cambridge's Own (Middlesex Regiment). *9th Battalion, Speech Day, Harrow School.*

Duke of Connaught's Own Battalion. See 6th (Duke of Connaught's Own) Battalion. Hampshire Regiment.

Duke of Connaught's Own Mounted Rifles. See Royal East Kent (The Duke of Connaught's Own) (Mounted Rifles) Yeomanry.

Duke of Cambridge's Own (Middlesex Regiment). *7th Battalion. Drums and Fifes, Falmer Camp, 1912. Note the small silver badges being worn on the right breasts of at least twelve men. Having offered to serve outside the United Kingdom in time of emergency (Territorials were only required to serve at home) individual officers and men were permitted to wear the "Imperial Service" badge (see inset). In consequence, if 90% or more from the same battalion/squadron etc. so volunteered (the 7th Middlesex was one), the words "Imperial Service" were allowed to appear in the Army List below the unit title.*

Duke of Cambridge's Own (Middlesex Regiment). *9th Battalion en route for Amballa. The Battalion, part of the Home Counties Division, had sailed for India on 30 October, 1914.*

Duke of Cambridge's Own (Middlesex Regiment). *Cap badge. Seen below the Prince of Wales's plumes, motto and coronet, the cypher of HRH the Duke of Cambridge. In 1809 the 1st Battalion (then 57th Regiment) left Gibraltar for Lisbon. It later joined Wellington's forces and on 16 May, 1811 took part in the battle of Albuhera, a bloody fight that cost the Regiment some 422 casualties out of a total strength of 570. This, in addition to the Albuhera battle honour, earned the Middlesex its well know nickname – "Diehards".*

Duke of Cornwall's Light Infantry. Two Regular (1st and 2nd), One Special Reserve (3rd) and two Territorial Force (4th and 5th) battalions. Depot, Bodmin.

1st Battalion: Curragh.

2nd Battalion: Hong Kong.

3rd Battalion: Bodmin.

4th Battalion: Truro with "A" Company, Penzance; "B" Company, Camborne; "C" Company, Falmouth; "D" Company, Helston; "E" Company, Truro; "F" Company, Hayle; "G" Company, Redruth; "H" Company, St Just (detachment at Pendeen). At Falmouth, "A" Company of the 1st Cadet Battalion of Cornwall was affiliated.

5th Battalion: Bodmin with "A" Company, Liskeard; "B" Company, Saltash (detachment at Callington); "C" Company, Launceston; "D" Company, St Austell (detachment at St Stephen); "E" Company, Bodmin (detachment at Lostwithiel); "F" Company, Camelford (detachments at Wadebridge and Delabole); "G" Company, St Columb (detachment at Newquay); "H" Company, Bude (detachments at Stratton, Kilkhampton and Morwenstow).

Duke of Cornwall's Royal Garrison Artillery. See Cornwall Royal Garrison Artillery (Duke of Cornwall's).

Duke of Edinburgh's (Wiltshire Regiment). Two Regular (1st and 2nd), one Special Reserve (3rd) and one Territorial Force (4th) battalions. Depot, Devizes.

1st Battalion: Tidworth.

2nd Battalion: Gibraltar.

3rd Battalion: Devizes.

4th Battalion: Fore Street, Trowbridge with "A" Company, Salisbury (detachment at Farley);

Duke of Cornwall's Light Infantry. *1st Battalion. Colours, Tidworth, 1912. On the left, the King's Colour, to the right the Battalion Regimental Colour.*

Duke of Cornwall's Light Infantry. *4th Battalion band, India, 1915. The Battalion sailed with the Wessex Division for India on 9 October, 1914, arriving just over a month later on 10 November.*

Duke of Cornwall's Light Infantry. *Cap badge. In recognition of its service during the defence of Lucknow during the Indian mutiny, the Light Infantry title and bugle horn badge were awarded to the 1st Battalion (then 32nd Regiment) in 1858.*

Duke of Edinburgh's (Wiltshire Regiment). *4th Battalion. Commanding Officer Lieutenant-Colonel Earl of Radnor, who took his battalion to India in October, 1914.*

Duke of Edinburgh's (Wiltshire Regiment). *Both Queen's and King's South Africa Medals are worn. The corporal also displays on his scarlet tunic (buff collars and cuffs) two awards for good shooting: best shot in company (top), best shot in battalion, junior ranks (bottom). Cap and collar badges feature a cross patée and the cypher of the Duke of Edinburgh.*

"B" Company, Wilton (detachments at Wishford and Barford); "C" Company, Trowbridge (detachment at Steeple Ashton); "D" Company, Chippenham (detachment at Calne); "E" Company, Devizes (detachments at Lavington and Bromham); "F" Company, Warminster (detachments at Westbury, Chitterne, Horningsham, Dilton Marsh and Heytesbury); "G" Company, Bradford-on-Avon (detachments at Melksham and Holt); "H" Company, Swindon (detachment at Marlborough).

Duke of Lancaster's Own Yeomanry. Territorial Force. Lancaster House, Whalley Road, Whalley Range, Manchester with "A" Squadron, Oldham (detachment at Rochdale); "B" Squadron, Bolton (detachment at Liverpool); "C" Squadron, Manchester; "D" Squadron, Preston (detachment at Blackpool).

Duke of Wellington's (West Riding Regiment). Two Regular (1st and 2nd), one Special Reserve (3rd) and four Territorial Force (4th to 7th) battalions. Depot, Halifax.

Duke of Lancaster's Own Yeomanry. *Post-marked 4 May, 1915, this postcard shows members of the Regiment training with wooden Vickers machine guns.*

Duke of Wellington's (West Riding Regiment). *5th Battalion. The scarlet jacket has white piping with bandsman's wings and lyre arm badge. The three five-pointed stars indicate that the wearer has been returned as efficient over a twelve year period. Note also the elephant and howdah collar badge. This device was granted to the 76th Regiment (later 2nd Duke of Wellington's) in recognition of its twenty year service (1787–1807) in India.*

Duke of Wellington's (West Riding Regiment). *Cap badge. Upon the death in 1852 of the Duke of Wellington – he, as Sir Arthur Wellesley, had commanded 1806–1813 – his name, crest and motto were granted to the 33rd Regiment (later 1st Battalion).*

1st Battalion: Lahore Cantonment, India.
2nd Battalion: Dublin.
3rd Battalion: Halifax.
4th Battalion: Halifax with "A", "B" and "C" Companies, also in Halifax; "D" Company, Brighouse; "E" Company, Cleckheaton; "F" Company, Halifax; "G" Company, Elland; "H" Company, Sowerby Bridge.
5th Battalion: Huddersfield with "A" Company, also Huddersfield (detachment at Meltham); "B" to "E" Companies, Huddersfield; "F" Company, Holmfirth; "G" Company, Kirkburton; "H" Company, Mirfield.
6th Battalion: Skipton-in-Craven with "A" Company, Skipton-in-Craven (detachment at Barnoldswick); "B" Company, Skipton-in-Craven; "C" Company, Guiseley; "D" and "E" Companies, Keighley; "F" Company, Settle (detachment at Ingleton); "G" Company, Haworth; "H" Company, Bingley. The Settle Cadet Battalion was affiliated.
7th Battalion: Milnsbridge with "A" and "B" Companies, also at Milnsbridge; "C" Company, Slaithwaite, "D" Company, Marsden; "E" Company, Upper Mill, "F" Company, Mossley; "G" Company, Lees; "H" Company, Mossley.

Duke of York's Own Loyal Suffolk Hussars. See Suffolk Yeomanry (The Duke of York's Own Loyal Suffolk Hussars).

Duke of York's Royal Military School. Guston near Dover.

Dulwich College Officers Training Corps. South East London. Three infantry companies, Junior Division.

Dumbartonshire Battalion. See 9th (The Dumbartonshire) Battalion, Princess Louise's (Argyll and Sutherland Highlanders).

Dumfries and Galloway Battalion. See 5th (Dumfries & Galloway) Battalion, King's Own Scottish Borderers.

Dundee Battery, City of. See 2nd Highland Brigade, Royal Field Artillery.

Dundee Fortress Engineers, City of. See City of Dundee Fortress Engineers.

Dunoon Grammar School Cadet Corps. See 8th Battalion, Princess Louise's (Argyll and Sutherland Highlanders).

Durham Batteries, 1st, 2nd, 3rd. See 3rd Northumbrian (County of Durham) Brigade, Royal Field Artillery.

Durham Batteries, 4th (Howitzer), 5th (Howitzer). See 4th Northumbrian Brigade, Royal Field Artillery (Howitzer) (County of Durham).

Durham Brigade, Royal Field Artillery County of. See 3rd Northumbrian Brigade, Royal Field Artillery (County of Durham).

Durham Fortress Engineers. Territorial Force. Western Road, Jarrow-on-Tyne with Nos. 1 and 2 Works Companies, also at Western Road, No.3 Works Company, Gateshead.

Durham Light Infantry. *"B" Company, 8th Battalion at Bede, June, 1913*

Durham Light Infantry. Two Regular (1st and 2nd), two Special Reserve (3rd and 4th) and five Territorial Force (5th to 9th) battalions. Depot, Newcastle-upon-Tyne.
1st Battalion: Nowshera, India.
2nd Battalion: Lichfield.
3rd Battalion: Newcastle-upon-Tyne.

Durham Light Infantry. *3rd Battalion. Captain A.J. Evans-Smith (centre left) is seen here with four other Special Reserve officers – two from the DLI, one Northumberland Fusiliers (front left) and one Rifle Brigade (front right).*

Durham Light Infantry. *2nd Battalion. Bandsman Walter March, Colchester, 30 October, 1912. The scarlet tunic (dark green collar and cuffs) is adorned with bandsman's wings, long service and good conduct medal and chevrons.*

Durham Royal Garrison Artillery. *This photograph shows the officers and men who manned the batteries during the bombardment of Hartlepool by German ships on 16 December, 1914.*

4th Battalion: Barnard Castle.
5th Battalion: Stockton-on-Tees with "A", "B" and "C" Companies, also in Stockton-on-Tees; "D" and "E" Companies, Darlington; "F" Company, Castle Eden (detachment at Trimdon); "G" Company, West Hartlepool; "H" Company, Darlington.
6th Battalion: Bishop Auckland with "A" Company, Bishop Auckland (detachment at Coundon); "B" Company, Bishop Auckland (detachment at West Auckland); "C" Company, Spennymoor; "D" Company, Crook (detachment at Willington); "E" Stanhope (detachments at Rookhope and Wolsingham); "F" Company, Barnard Castle (detachment at Staindrop); "G" and "H" Companies, Consett.
7th Battalion: Livingstone Road, Sunderland with "A" to "F" Companies, also in Livingstone Road; "G" and "H" Companies, South Shields.
8th Battalion: Gilesgate, Durham with "A" Company, Gilesgate (detachments at Sherburn Hill, Brandon and Sacriston); "B" Company, Gilesgate; "C" Company, Chester-le-Street; "D" Company, Birtley; "E" Company, Beamish (detachment at Burnhope); "F" Company, Stanley; "G" Company, Houghton-le-Spring (detachments at Pittington and Washington); "H" Company, Hamsteels (detachments at Langley Park and Sleetburn).
9th Battalion: Burt Terrace, Gateshead with "A" to "D" Companies, also in Burt Terrace; "E" Company, Felling; "F" Company, Chopwell; "G" Company, Blaydon (detachment at West Ryton); "H" Company, Blaydon.

Durham Light Infantry Brigade. See Northumbrian Division

Durham Light Infantry Brigade Company, Army Service Corps. See Northumbrian Divisional Transport and Supply Column.

Durham Royal Garrison Artillery. Territorial Force. The Armoury, West Hartlepool with No.1 Heavy Battery, Sunderland; Nos. 2, 3 and 4 Companies, West Hartlepool; No.5 Company, Hartlepool.

Durham University Officers Training Corps. Armstrong College, Newcastle-upon-Tyne. Four infantry companies, Senior Division.

Durham Royal Garrison Artillery. *Commanding Officer, Lieutenant-Colonel L. Robson.*

E

Ealing Cadet Company. See 8th Battalion, Duke of Cambridge's Own (Middlesex Regiment).

Earl of Carrick's Own Yeomanry. See Ayrshire Yeomanry (Earl of Carrick's Own).

Earl of Chester's Battalion. See 5th (Earl of Chester's) Battalion, Cheshire Regiment.

Earl of Chester's Yeomanry. See Cheshire Yeomanry (Earl of Chester's).

East Anglian Brigade, Royal Field Artillery, 1st. Territorial Force. The Barracks, Surrey Street, Norwich with 1st Norfolk Battery, Nelson Road, Great Yarmouth; 2nd Norfolk Battery, 3rd Norfolk Battery and Ammunition Column at Surrey Street, Norwich. The Cadet Norfolk Artillery, also at Surrey Street, was affiliated.

East Anglian Brigade, Royal Field Artillery, 2nd. Territorial Force. Artillery House, The Green, Stratford with 1st Essex Battery, Stratford; 2nd Essex Battery, 17 Victoria Road, Romford and 3rd Essex Battery, Grays. The Ammunition Column was at Stratford.

East Anglian Brigade, Royal Field Artillery (Howitzer), 3rd. Territorial Force. Great Gipping Street, Ipswich with 1st Suffolk (Howitzer) Battery, Beccles Road, Lowestoft (detachment at Beccles); 2nd Suffolk (Howitzer) Battery, Ipswich and the Ammunition Column at Arnold Road, Lowestoft. The Beccles Cadet Corps at Gillingham Rectory, Beccles was affiliated.

East Anglian Brigade, Royal Field Artillery, 4th. Territorial Force. 28 St Andrew's Street, Hertford with 1st Hertfordshire Battery, Artillery Buildings, Harpenden Road, St Albans (detachment at Hertford); 2nd Hertfordshire Battery, Clarendon Hall, Watford (detachment at Hemel Hempstead) and the Northamptonshire Battery, Queen's Street, Peterborough. The Ammunition Column was at Hertford.

East Anglian Clearing Hospital. Territorial Force. Ipswich.

East Anglian Division. Territorial Force. Claremont House, Warley.

Norfolk and Suffolk Infantry Brigade: 18a Prince of Wales's Road, Norwich. Battalions – 4th, 5th Norfolk; 4th, 5th Suffolk.

East Midland Infantry Brigade: Shire Hall, Bedford. Battalions – 5th Bedfordshire; 4th Northamptonshire; 1st Cambridgeshire; 1st Hertfordshire.

Essex Infantry Brigade: Brentwood. Battalions – 4th, 5th, 6th, 7th Essex.

Royal Artillery: Claremont House, Warley. 1st, 2nd 3rd (Howitzer), 4th East Anglian Brigades, Royal Field Artillery; East Anglian Royal Garrison Artillery.

Royal Engineers: Ashburnham Road, Bedford. 1st, 2nd East Anglian Field Companies; East Anglian Divisional Signal Company.

Army Service Corps: 156 High Road, Ilford. East Anglian Divisional Transport and Supply Column.

Royal Army Medical Corps: 1st, 2nd, 3rd East Anglian Field Ambulances.

3rd East Anglian (Howitzer) Brigade, Royal Field Artillery. *1st Suffolk (Howitzer) Battery close to their headquarters in Lowestoft, 18 March, 1911.*

East Anglian Divisional Engineers. Territorial Force. Ashburnham Road, Bedford with 1st and 2nd East Anglian Field Companies. The 2nd Field Company also had a detachment in Luton.

East Anglian Divisional Signal Company. Territorial Force. Ashburnham Road, Bedford with No.1 Section, No.2 (Norfolk and Suffolk) Section, No.3 (East Midland) Section and No.4 (Essex) Section.

East Anglian Divisional Transport and Supply Column. Territorial Force. 156 High Road, Ilford with Headquarters Company, also at 156 High Road (detachments at Ballingdon and Woolwich); Norfolk and Suffolk Brigade Company, King's Lynn (detachment at Downham Market); East Midland Brigade Company, Northampton and Essex Brigade Company, Bay Lodge, The Green, Stratford (detachment at Woolwich).

East Anglian Field Ambulance, 1st. Territorial Force. Woodbridge Road, Ipswich. There were also detachments at Woodbridge, Needham Market and Trimley.

East Anglian Field Ambulance, 2nd. Territorial Force. 44 Bethel Street, Norwich. There were also detachments at Dereham and Lowestoft.

East Anglian Field Ambulance, 3rd. Territorial Force. Walthamstow Lodge, Church Hill, Walthamstow with "A" and "B" Sections, Southend-on-Sea; "C" Section, Silvertown (detachment at Prittlewell).

East Anglian Field Companies, 1st, 2nd. See East Anglian Divisional Engineers.

East Anglian Royal Garrison Artillery (Essex). Territorial Force. Artillery House, The Green, Stratford.

East Kent Regiment. See Buffs (East Kent Regiment)

East Kent Yeomanry. See Royal East Kent (The Duke of Connaught's Own) (Mounted Rifles) Yeomanry.

East Lancashire Divisional Royal Army Medical Corps.

East Lancashire Brigade Company, Army Service Corps. See East Lancashire Divisional Transport and Supply Column.

East Lancashire Brigade, Royal Field Artillery, 1st. Territorial Force. 50 King Street, Blackburn with 4th Lancashire Battery, also at King Street; 5th Lancashire Battery, Church; 6th Lancashire Battery, Burnley and Ammunition Column, Blackburn.

East Lancashire Brigade, Royal Field Artillery (The Manchester Artillery), 2nd. Territorial Force. Hyde Road, Manchester with 15th, 16th, 17th Lancashire Batteries and Ammunition Column.

East Lancashire Brigade, Royal Field Artillery (The Bolton Artillery), 3rd. Territorial Force. Bolton with 18th, 19th, 20th Lancashire Batteries and Ammunition Column.

East Lancashire Brigade, Royal Field Artillery (Howitzer) (The Cumberland Artillery), 4th. Territorial Force. Workington with 1st Cumberland (Howitzer) Battery, Carlisle and 2nd Cumberland (Howitzer) Battery, Workington. The Ammunition Column was also at Workington (detachments at Maryport and Whitehaven).

East Lancashire Clearing Hospital. Territorial Force. Manchester.

East Lancashire Division. Territorial Force. National Buildings, St Mary's Parsonage, Manchester.

Lancashire Fusiliers Infantry Brigade: 5 Chapel Street, Preston. Battalions – 5th, 6th, 7th, 8th Lancashire Fusiliers.

East Lancashire Infantry Brigade: 15 Piccadilly, Manchester. Battalions – 4th, 5th East Lancashire; 9th, 10th Manchester.

Manchester Infantry Brigade: 3 Stretford Road, Manchester. Battalions – 5th, 6th, 7th, 8th Manchester.

Royal Artillery: Nantwich. 1st, 2nd, 3rd, 4th (Howitzer) East Lancashire Brigades, Royal Field Artillery; 2nd Lancashire Royal Garrison Artillery.

Royal Engineers: 73 Seymour Grove, Old Trafford, Manchester. 1st, 2nd East Lancashire Field Companies; East Lancashire Divisional Signal Company.

Army Service Corps: Hulme Barracks, Manchester. East Lancashire Divisional Transport and Supply Column.

Royal Army Medical Corps: 1st, 2nd, 3rd East Lancashire Field Ambulances.

Attached: 4th, 5th Border Regiment; No. 18 Field Ambulance Royal Army Medical Corps (Special Reserve).

East Lancashire Regiment. *5th Battalion Signal Section. At least one aspect of this photograph suggests that it was taken during war time. Look at the third soldier from the left, back row. The second button down on his service dress jacket has been covered with black cloth. A custom adopted by some to indicate that a relative had been killed in action.*

East Lancashire Divisional Engineers. Territorial Force. 73 Seymour Grove, Old Trafford, Manchester with 1st and 2nd East Lancashire Field Companies.

East Lancashire Divisional Signal Company. Territorial Force. 73 Seymour Grove, Old Trafford, Manchester with No.1 Section, No.2 (Lancashire Fusiliers) Section, No.3 (East Lancashire) Section, No.4 (Manchester) Section.

East Lancashire Divisional Transport and Supply Column. Territorial Force. Hulme Barracks, Manchester with Headquarters Company, also at Hulme Barracks; Lancashire Fusiliers Brigade Company, Hulme Barracks; East Lancashire Brigade Company, Rawtenstall and Manchester Brigade Company, Hulme Barracks.

East Lancashire Field Ambulance, 1st. Territorial Force. Upper Chorlton Road, Manchester. "C" Section was in Bolton.

East Lancashire Field Ambulance, 2nd. Territorial Force. Upper Chorlton Road, Manchester. "C" Section was in Burnley.

East Lancashire Divisional Engineers. *No. 2 Field Company at camp.*

East Lancashire Field Ambulance, 3rd. Territorial Force. Upper Chorlton Road, Manchester. "C" Section was in Bury.

East Lancashire Field Companies, 1st, 2nd. See East Lancashire Divisional Engineers.

East Lancashire Infantry Brigade. See East Lancashire Division.

East Lancashire Regiment. Two Regular (1st and 2nd), one Special Reserve (3rd) and two Territorial Force (4th and 5th) battalions. Depot, Preston.
1st Battalion: Colchester.
2nd Battalion: Wynberg, South Africa.
3rd Battalion: Preston.

East Riding of Yorkshire Yeomanry. *The regimental badge – a fox in full cry – can be seen here being worn on the collars. The maroon tunic with its light blue facings follows lancer style.*

4th Battalion: Blackburn with "A" to "E" Companies, also Blackburn; "F" and "G" Companies, Darwen; "H" Company, Clitheroe.
5th Battalion: Burnley with "A" Company, also Burnley; "B" Company, Burnley (detachment at Padiham); "C" and "D" Companies, Burnley; "E" Company, Padiham; "F" Company, Accrington; "G" Company, Haslingden (detachment at Ramsbottom); "H" Company, Bacup.

East Midland Brigade Company, Army Service Corps. See East Anglian Divisional Transport and Supply Column.

East Midland Infantry Brigade. See East Anglian Division.

East Riding Batteries, 1st, 2nd. See 2nd Northumbrian Brigade, Royal Field Artillery.

East Riding Fortress Engineers. Territorial Force. Colonial Street, Hull with No.1 Works Company and No.2 Electric Lights Company.

East Riding of Yorkshire Yeomanry. Territorial Force. Railway Street, Beverley with "A" Squadron, Hull; "B" Squadron, Beverley (detachments at North Cave, Hornsea and Patrington); "C" Squadron, Fulford (detachment at Dunnington); "D" Squadron, Driffield (detachments at Hunmanby, Pocklington, Settrington and Bridlington).

East Riding Royal Garrison Artillery. Territorial Force. Park Street, Hull with Nos. 1,2,3 and 4 Companies.

East Surrey Regiment. Two Regular (1st and 2nd), two Special Reserve (3rd and 4th) and two Territorial Force (5th and 6th) battalions.
1st Battalion: Dublin.
2nd Battalion: Chaubattia, India.
3rd Battalion: Kingston-upon-Thames.
4th Battalion: Kingston-upon-Thames.
5th Battalion: 17 St George's Road, Wimbledon with "A" Company, Streatham; "B" Company, Leatherhead (detachments at Bookham and Walton-on-the-Hill); "C" Company, Sutton; "D" Company, Mitcham; "E", "F" and "G" Companies, Wimbledon; "H" Company, Epsom.
6th Battalion: Orchard Road, Kingston-upon-Thames with "A" Company, Esher (detachments at Cobham and Hersham); "B" and "C" Companies, Richmond; "D", "E" and "F" Companies, Kingston-upon-Thames; "G" Company, Chertsey (detachment at Weybridge); "H" Company, Egham. The Richmond County School Cadet Corps was affiliated.

East Surrey Regiment. *Cap badge. In the centre, the arms of Guildford. Adopted by the Regiment in 1881.*

East Surrey Regiment. *5th Battalion Band, India. With the Home Counties Division, the Battalion embarked at Southampton for India on 29 October, 1914, arriving Bombay on the following 2 December.*

East Surrey Regiment. *Sergeant, 5th Battalion. Scarlet tunic, white facings.*

East Surrey Regiment. *6th Battalion. Another battalion having gained 90% Imperial Service commitment (see 7th Duke of Cambridge's Own Middlesex Regiment photograph), almost all men wear the Imperial Service brooch. As a battalion that continued its rifle regiment dress customs, the 6th East Surrey wear black buttons, badges and shoulder titles.*

East Yorkshire Regiment. Two Regular (1st and 2nd), one Special Reserve (3rd) and two Territorial Force (4th and 5th) battalions. Depot, Beverley.
1st Battalion: York.
2nd Battalion: Kamptee, India.
3rd Battalion: Beverley.
4th Battalion: Londesborough Barracks, Hull with "A" to "F" Companies, also at Londesborough Barracks; "G" and "H" Companies, East Hull.
5th (Cyclist) Battalion: Park Street, Hull with "A" to "D" Companies, also at Park Street; "E" Company, Howden (detachments at North Cave and Staddlethorpe); "F" Company, Beverley (detachments at Hessle, Market Weighton and Pocklington); "G" Company, Bridlington (detachments at Driffield, Hunmanby and Filey); "H" Company, Hornsea (detachments at Hedon and Withernsea).

East Yorkshire Yeomanry. See East Riding of Yorkshire Yeomanry.

Eastbourne College Officers Training Corps. Two infantry companies, Junior Division.

Eastern General Hospital, 1st. Territorial Force. 39 Green Street, Cambridge.

Eastern General Hospital, 2nd. Territorial Force. 117 Gloucester Road, Brighton.

Eastern Mounted Brigade. Territorial Force. Belchamp Hall, Sudbury. Included Suffolk, Norfolk and Essex Yeomanries; Essex Royal Horse Artillery. The Hertfordshire, Bedfordshire and Northamptonshire Yeomanries were attached for training.

Eastern Mounted Brigade Ammunition Column. See Essex Royal Horse Artillery.

Eastern Mounted Brigade Field Ambulance. Territorial Force. Grove Road, Luton with "A" Section, Luton (detachment at Dunstable); "B" Section, Bedford.

Eastern Mounted Brigade Signal Troop. Territorial Force. 8 Head Street, Colchester.

Eastern Mounted Brigade Transport and Supply Column. Territorial Force. Market Road, Chelmsford.

Eastern Telegraph Reserve. Special Reserve.

Edinburgh Academy Officers Training Corps. One infantry company, Junior Division.

Edinburgh Batteries, 1st, 2nd City of. See 1st Lowland Brigade, Royal Field Artillery.

Edinburgh Fortress Engineers, City of. See City of Edinburgh Fortress Engineers.

Edinburgh, Royal Garrison Artillery, City of. See Lowland Royal Garrison Artillery (City of Edinburgh).

Edinburgh University Officers Training Corps. One battery of field artillery, a company of engineers, three infantry companies and two sections field ambulance, Senior Division.

Elizabeth College Officers Training Corps. Guernsey. One engineer company, Junior Division.

Ellesmere College Officers Training Corps. One infantry company, Junior Division.

Elstow School Officers Training Corps. One engineer company, Junior Division.

Emanuel School Officers Training Corps. Wandsworth Common, London. One infantry company, Junior Division.

Empress of India's Lancers. See 21st (Empress of India's) Lancers.

Engineer and Railway Staff Corps. Territorial Force. 15 Dean's Yard, Westminster.

Epsom College Officers Training Corps. Two infantry companies, Junior Division.

Essex and Suffolk Royal Garrison Artillery. Territorial Force. Main Road, Dovercourt with No.1 Company, Harwich (detachment at Felixstowe);

Essex and Suffolk Royal Garrison Artillery. No. 4 Company.

East Yorkshire Regiment. *4th Battalion at camp, Louth, July, 1910.*

Essex Regiment. *1st Battalion shooting team, Banglor, India 1909. All nine men wear medals for service in South Africa (1899–1902) and (on the right breast and arm) awards for good shooting. The tunics are scarlet with white collars and piping.*

Essex Regiment. *6th (Cyclist) Battalion.*

Essex Regiment. *4th Battalion Colours and cap badge. This postcard serves to illustrate how, although allowed to used regimental badges, Territorials were not permitted to include battle honours gained by the regulars. Therefore, any scrolls or tablets so inscribed were required to be left blank. Hence, on this occasion, the space (it would normally bear the word "Egypt" in recognition of service by the 1st Battalion in 1801) below the Sphinx. The Sphinx itself, not to mention the Castle and Key of Gibraltar (2nd Battalion), although a device conferred in recognition of service, was permitted. On occasion, and we see an example here, additional scrolls were added bearing the South Africa battle honour won by the Volunteers during the Second Boer War.*

Essex Regiment. *Collar badge. Three notched swords (seaxes) from the arms of Essex.*

Essex Regiment. *7th Battalion. This postcard is dated 18 August, 1913. Almost two years to the day later, the Battalion would land at Suvla Bay, Gallipoli.*

No.2 Company, Stratford; No.3 Company, Southend-on-Sea; No.4 Company, Ipswich.

Essex Batteries, 1st, 2nd, 3rd. See 2nd East Anglian Brigade, Royal Field Artillery.

Essex Brigade Company, Army Service Corps. See East Anglian Divisional Transport and Supply Column.

Essex Fortress Engineers. Territorial Force. Market Road, Chelmsford with No.1 Electric Lights Company.

Essex Infantry Brigade. See East Anglian Division.

Essex Regiment. Two Regular (1st and 2nd), one Special Reserve (3rd) and five Territorial Force (4th to 8th) battalions. Depot, Warley.

1st Battalion: Mauritius.

2nd Battalion: Chatham.

3rd Battalion: Warley.

4th Battalion: Brentwood with "A" Company, Romford; "B" Company, Manor Park; "C" Company, Ilford; "D" Company, Barking; "E" Company, Loughton (detachments at Abridge and Woodford); "F" Company, Southminster (detachments at Wickford, Billericay, Althorne, Bradwell, Burnham-on-Crouch, Mountnessing and Tillingham); "G" Company, Ongar (detachments at Epping and Harlow); "H" Company, Hornchurch (detachments at Dagenham, Rainham and Harold Wood). There were four cadet units affiliated – the Cranbrook College (Ilford) Cadets; Manor Park Cadet Company, at 63 Carlyce Road; Ongar Grammar School Cadets and Warley Garrison Cadets.

5th Battalion: Association Buildings, Market Road, Chelmsford with "A" Company, Chelmsford (detachments at Broomfield, Writtle and Waltham); "B" Company, Chelmsford (detachments at Boreham, Hatfield and Danbury); "C" Company, Colchester; "D" Company, Manningtree (detachments at Dedham and Bradfield); "E" Company, Halstead (detachments at Hedingham, Yeldham, Pebmarch, Earls Colne and Maplestead); "F" Company, Braintree (detachments at Bocking, Dunmow, Thaxted, Great Bardfield, Felstead and Coggeshall); "G" Company, Maldon (detachments at Wickham Bishops, Witham, Terling, Tiptree and Tollesbury); "H" Company, Clacton-on-Sea (detachments at Wyvenhoe and Walton-on-the-Naze). The King Edward VI School, Chelmsford Cadet Corps and Colchester Royal Grammar School Cadets were affiliated.

6th Battalion: West Ham with "A" to "G" Companies, also West Ham; "H" Company, Prittlewell (detachment at Grays). The Palmer's School Cadet Corps at Grays and Southend High School Cadet Corps were affiliated.

7th Battalion: Walthamstow Lodge, Church Hill, Walthamstow. "H" Company also had a detachment at Chingford.

8th (Cyclist) Battalion: Colchester with "A" Company, Leyton; "B" Company, West Ham; "C" Company, Colchester (detachments at Braintree, Dunmow and Maldon); "D" Company, Saffron Walden (detachment at Stansted); "E" Company, East Ham; "F" Company, Ilford; "G" Company, Brentwood; "H" Company, Coggeshall.

1st Cadet Battalion: Headquarters at 1 Wellington Street, Canning Town and affiliated to the 6th Battalion. Two companies made up of boys from the West Ham Cadet Corps; St Gabriel's, Canning

Essex Royal Garrison Artillery. *4.7 inch gun at Thetford camp, 1911.*

Essex Royal Horse Artillery. *The guns being fired at Lydd artillery range in Kent.*

Town Cadet Corps; St Matthew's Cadets at Custom House and the Church of the Ascension Cadet Corps.

Essex Royal Garrison Artillery. See East Anglian Royal Garrison Artillery (Essex).

Essex Royal Horse Artillery. Territorial Force. Market Road, Chelmsford. No.1 Section, Colchester; No.2 Section, Chelmsford (detachment at Ingatestone). Included the Eastern Mounted Brigade Ammunition Column located "A" Sub-Section, Colchester, "B" Sub-Section, Chelmsford.

Essex Yeomanry. Territorial Force. 17 Sir Isaac's Walk, Colchester with "A" Squadron, Colchester (detachments at Clackton-on-Sea, Harwich, Walton-on-the-Naze and Ardleigh); "B" Squadron, Braintree (detachments at Halstead, Chelmsford and Tiptree); "C" Squadron, Waltham Abbey (detachments at Loughton, Bishop's Stortford and Dunmow); "D" Squadron, Southend-on-Sea (detachments at Brentwood, Grays, Stratford and Orsett).

Eton College Officers Training Corps. One infantry battalion, Junior Division.

Exeter Cathedral School Cadet Company. See 4th Battalion, Devonshire Regiment.

Exeter School Officers Training Corps. One infantry company, Junior Division.

Essex Royal Horse Artillery. *Brass shoulder title.*

Essex Yeomanry. *This postcard, published after 1914, provides much information regarding the regiment's history. Both full dress – dark blue with scarlet facings and helmet plume – and service dress are shown.*

F

Felstead School Officers Training Corps. Two infantry companies, Junior Division.

Fettes College Officers Training Corps. Edinburgh. Two infantry companies, Junior Division.

Fife and Forfar Yeomanry. Territorial Force. Kirkcaldy with "A" Squadron, Cupar (detachments at Kirkcaldy, Ladybank and St Andrews); "B" Squadron, Dunfermline (detachments at Balfron, Stirling, Kippen, Kelty, Kinross and Alloa); "C" Squadron, Dundee; "D" Squadron, Forfar (detachments at Arbroath, Edzell, Montrose and Laurencekirk).

Fife Battalion. See 7th (Fife) Battalion, Black Watch (Royal Highlanders).

Fifeshire Battery. See 2nd Highland Brigade, Royal Field Artillery.

Fifeshire Royal Garrison Artillery. See Highland Royal Garrison Artillery (Fifeshire).

Finsbury Rifles. See 11th Battalion, London Regiment.

First Surrey Rifles. See 21st Battalion, London Regiment.

Flintshire Battalion. See 5th (Flintshire) Battalion, Royal Welsh Fusiliers.

Forest School Officers Training Corps. Walthamstow, London. One infantry company, Junior Division.

Forfarshire Battery. See 2nd Highland Brigade, Royal Field Artillery.

Felstead School Officers Training Corps. *Various shooting badges are worn (left arm) and the lozenge (right arm) award for efficiency.*

Forth Royal Garrison Artillery. Territorial Force. Easter Road Barracks, Edinburgh with Nos. 1, 2, 3 and 4 Companies, also at Easter Road; No.5 Company, Kirkcaldy (detachment at Kinghorn); No.6 Company, Burntisland (detachment at Inverkeithing).

Framlingham College Officers Training Corps. One infantry company, Junior Division.

Frimley and Camberley Cadet Corps. See 5th Battalion, Queen's (Royal West Surrey Regiment).

Fusiliers, Royal. See Royal Fusiliers (City of London Regiment).

Fife and Forfar Yeomanry. *The cap badge shows a knight mounted on a galloping horse. Known as the "Thane of Fife", the device has long been associated with Fife (it was used on the seal of Duncan, Earl of Fife as early as 1360) and as a military badge once used by the old Fife Fencible Cavalry (disbanded, 1797).*

G

Gambia Company. Bathurst.

Gentlemen-at-Arms. See His Majesty's Body Guard of the Honourable Corps of Gentlemen-at-Arms.

George Heriot's School Officers Training Corps. Edinburgh. One infantry company, Junior Division.

George Watson's Boys' College Officers Training Corps. Edinburgh. Two infantry companies, Junior Division.

Giggleswick School Officers Training Corps. Near Settle, Yorkshire. One infantry company, Junior Division.

Glamorgan Batteries, 1st (Howitzer), 2nd (Howitzer). See 1st Welsh Brigade, Royal Field Artillery (Howitzer).

Glamorgan Batteries, 3rd, 4th. See 2nd Welsh Brigade, Royal Field Artillery.

Glamorgan Battalion. See 6th (Glamorgan) Battalion, Welsh Regiment.

Glamorgan Fortress Engineers. Territorial Force. Park Street, Cardiff with No.1 Works Company, also at Park Street; No.2 Works Company, Gladstone Road, Barry (detachment at Barry Island); No.3 Electric Lights Company, Park Street, Cardiff.

Glamorgan Royal Garrison Artillery. Territorial Force. Cardiff with Nos. 1, 2 and 3 Companies, also at Cardiff; No.4 Company, Penarth; No.5 Company, Barry.

Glamorgan Royal Horse Artillery. Territorial Force. Port Talbot. Including the South Wales Mounted Brigade Ammunition Column.

Glamorgan Yeomanry. Territorial Force. Bridgend with "A" Squadron, Swansea (detachments at Neath, Port Talbot and Reynoldston); "B" Squadron, Bridgend (detachments at Maesteg, Cowbridge and Porthcawl); "C" Squadron, Cardiff; "D" Squadron, Pontypridd (detachments at Nelson, Llwynypia, Caerphilly, Mountain Ash, Aberdare and Merthyr Tydfil).

Glasgow Academy Officers Training Corps. Two infantry companies, Junior Division.

Glasgow Batteries, 1st, 2nd, 3rd City of. See 3rd Lowland Brigade, Royal Field Artillery.

Glasgow Batteries, 4th (Howitzer), 5th (Howitzer) City of. See 4th Lowland Brigade, Royal Field Artillery (Howitzer).

Glasgow High School Officers Training Corps. Two infantry companies, Junior Division.

Glasgow Highland Battalion. See 9th (Glasgow Highland) Battalion, Highland Light Infantry.

Glasgow Highland Cadet Company, 1st. See 9th (Glasgow Highland) Battalion, Highland Light Infantry.

Glasgow Highlanders. See 9th (Glasgow Highland) Battalion, Highland Light Infantry.

__Glamorgan Royal Horse Artillery.__ "A" Sub-Section at camp, 1914.

Gloucestershire Regiment. *2nd Battalion. "G" Company, winners of Inter- Company Cricket Shield, 1912.*

Gloucestershire Regiment. *4th Battalion. Sergeants, Morfu Camp, Conway, August, 1911. Scarlet tunics with white collars cuffs and piping.*

Gloucestershire Regiment. *5th Battalion. Cyclists.*

Glamorgan Yeomanry.

Glasgow Postal Telegraph Messengers' Cadet Corps. See 9th Battalion, Highland Light Infantry.

Glasgow University Officers Training Corps. One engineer and three infantry companies, Senior Division.

Glasgow Yeomanry. See Queen's Own Royal Glasgow and Lower Ward of Lanarkshire Yeomanry.

Glenalmond College Officers Training Corps. Two infantry companies, Junior Division.

Gloucester and Worcester Brigade Company, Army Service Corps. See South Midland Divisional Transport and Supply Column.

Gloucester and Worcester Infantry Brigade. See South Midland Division.

Gloucestershire Batteries, 1st, 2nd, 3rd. See 1st South Midland Brigade, Royal Field Artillery (Gloucestershire).

Gloucestershire Brigade, Royal Field Artillery. See 1st South Midland Brigade, Royal Field Artillery (Gloucestershire).

Gloucestershire Regiment. Two Regular (1st and 2nd), one Special Reserve (3rd) and three Territorial Force (4th, 5th and 6th) battalions. Depot, Bristol.

1st Battalion: Bordon.

2nd Battalion: Tientsin, China.

3rd Battalion: Bristol.

4th (City of Bristol) Battalion: Queen's Road, Clifton

with "A" to "E" Companies, also at Queen's Road; "F" Company, St George, Bristol; "G" and "H" Companies, Bristol.
5th Battalion: Gloucester with "A" and "B" Companies, also in Gloucester; "C" Company, Stroud (detachment at Cirencester); "D" Company, Tewkesbury (detachment at Kemerton); "E" and "F" Companies, Cheltenham; "G" Company, Dursley (detachment at Wotton-under-Edge); "H" Company, Campden (detachments at Blockley, Shipton-on-Stour and Moreton-in-Marsh).
6th Battalion: St Michael's Hill, Bristol. There were two cadet companies, numbered 1st and 2nd, attached.

Gloucestershire Yeomanry. See Royal Gloucestershire Hussars Yeomanry.

Gold Coast Regiment. Headquarters at Kumasi and comprising one artillery battery and an infantry battalion.

Gordon Boys' Home Cadet Corps. West End, Chobam, Surrey. Two companies.

Gordon Brigade Company, Army Service Corps, 3rd. See Highland Divisional Transport and Supply Column.

Gordon Highlanders. Two Regular (1st and 2nd), one Special Reserve (3rd) and four Territorial Force (4th to 7th) battalions. The Regiment also had attached, two companies from the Shetland Islands. Depot, Aberdeen.
1st Battalion: Plymouth.
2nd Battalion: Cairo.

Gloucestershire Regiment. *Cap badge (left), Back Badge (right). Both 1st and 2nd Battalions (as 28th and 61st Regiments) served in Egypt during the 1801 campaign and gained the Sphinx, superscribed "Egypt", honour. In addition, the 28th earned for the Regiment the privilege of wearing a second head-dress badge. Known as the "Back Badge", and worn as the name suggests, at the back of the cap, the badge signifies how during the fighting at Alexandria the men fought back-to-back as the French attacked from both front and rear.*

Gloucestershire Regiment. *6th Battalion. Drummer Robert Harper. The same basic full-dress uniform as seen in the 4th Battalion photograph with the additional lace and wings of a drummer. Note also Robert Harper's Imperial Service badge, bugle cords and his two awards (lower left arm) for good shooting – best shot in band (top), best shot (junior ranks) in battalion (bottom).*

Gordon Highlanders. *Private in marching order 1914.*

Gordon Highlanders. *Sergeant (Territorial battalion). The scarlet doublet has yellow collar and cuffs with Royal Tiger collar badges. Authorized in July, 1807, these commemorate the services of the old 75th Regiment (later 1st Battalion) in India between 1787 and 1806. The kilt is of Gordon pattern tartan and the subject is identified as a Territorial by the three-tier white metal shoulder title, and two efficiency stars on lower right arm.*

3rd Battalion: Aberdeen.
4th Battalion: Aberdeen.
5th (Buchan and Formartin) Battalion: Peterhead with "A" Company, Strichen (detachments at New Pitsligo, New Aberdour, New Dear and Maud); "B" Company, Peterhead (detachments at Longside and St Fergus); "C" Company, Peterhead (detachments at Boddam and Hatton); "D" Company, Turriff (detachments at Fyvie and Cuminestown); "E"

Gordon Highlanders. *6th Battalion.*

Gordon Highlanders. *Cap badge. Raised by George Marques of Huntly (later Duke of Gordon) the 92nd Regiment (later 2nd Battalion) wore from his Crest, the ducal coronet, stag's head and motto "Bydand". The latter interpreted in Adam's* The Clans, Septs and Regiments of the Scottish Highlands *as "Abiding or Lasting".*

Company, Ellon (detachments at Auchnagatt, Methlick, Skilmafilly and Newburgh); "F" Company, Old Meldrum (detachments at Tarves, Newmachar and Pitmedden); "G" Company, Fraserburgh (detachment at Rosehearty); "H" Company, Fraserburgh (detachment at Lonmay).

6th (Banff and Donside) Battalion: Keith with "A" Company, Banff (detachments at Aberchirder, Cornhill and Portsoy); "B" Company, Dufftown (detachments at Aberlour, Chapelton, Glenrinnes and Minmore); "C" Company, Keith (detachment at Grange); "D" Company, Buckie (detachments at Findochty and Cullen); "E" Company, Inverurie (detachment at Pitcaple); "F" Company, Alford (detachments at Cushnie, Lumsden, Glenbuckat, Strathdon, Corgarff and Towie); "G" Company, Bucksburn (detachment at Dyce); "H" Company, Huntly (detachments at Insch and Rhynie).

7th (Deeside Highland) Battalion: Banchory with "A"

Grenadier Guards. *Colour-Sergeants (note arm badges mounted on chevrons). The back of this photograph identifies the soldier first from left as Pay-Sergeant Oakley.*

Company, Banchory (detachments at Durris and Torphins); "B" Company, Portlethen; "C" Company, Stonehaven, "D" Company, Laurencekirk (detachments at Auchenblae, Bervie, Fettercairn, Fordoun and Marykirk); "E" Company, Ballater (detachments at Crathie and Braemar); "F" Company, Aboyne (detachments at Tarland, Finzean and Logie Coldstone); "G" Company, Kemnay (detachments at Skene, Blackburn, Monymusk and Echt); "H" Company, Peterculter (detachment at Countesswells).

The Shetland Companies: Lerwick with "A" Company, also at Lerwick; "B" Company, Lerwick (detachment at Scalloway).

Gordon Infantry Brigade. See Highland Division.

Greenwich Naval Cadet Unit. 160 Annandale Road, East Greenwich, London. Three companies.

Grenadier Guards. Three Regular battalions.

1st Battalion: Warley.

2nd Battalion: Chelsea Barracks, London.

3rd Battalion: Wellington Barracks, London.

Gresham's School Officers Training Corps. Holt, Norfolk. Two infantry companies, Junior Division.

Grimsby Municipal College Officers Training Corps. One infantry company, Junior Division.

Guernsey Militia. See Royal Guernsey Militia.

Grenadier Guards. *1st Battalion. Seen here (second from left) is HRH the Prince of Wales. The back of the photograph notes that this was the first occasion in which he "mounted his first duty..." and that the Battalion was shortly to move to the front. 1st Grenadier Guards joined 20th Brigade, 7th Division at Lyndhurst in September, and on 5 October, 1914 left Southampton for France.*

Grenadier Guards. *Dated April, 1912, this postcard shows Private H. Barter, of Totnes, Devon, who at six foot-eight-and-a-half inches is noted as "the tallest soldier in the British Army". He is seen here with a drummer boy of the Coldstream Guards.*

Grenadier Guards. *Drill order.*

Grenadier Guards. *Guard changing at Windsor Castle.*

H

Hackney Battalion. See 10th Battalion, London Regiment.

Haddington Cadet Corps. See 8th Battalion, Royal Scots (Lothian Regiment).

Haileybury College Officers Training Corps. Four infantry companies, Junior Division.

Hallamshire Battalion. See 4th (Hallamshire) Battalion, York and Lancaster Regiment.

Haltwhistle Cadets. See 4th Battalion, Northumberland Fusiliers.

Hampshire Batteries, 1st, 2nd, 3rd. See 1st Wessex Brigade, Royal Field Artillery.

Hampshire Batteries, 4th (Howitzer), 5th (Howitzer). See 2nd Wessex Brigade, Royal Field Artillery (Howitzer).

Hampshire Battery, 6th. See 3rd Wessex Brigade, Royal Field Artillery.

Hampshire Brigade Company, Army Service Corps. See Wessex Divisional Transport and Supply Column.

Hampshire Fortress Engineers. Territorial Force. Commercial Road, Portsmouth with Nos.1 and 2 Works Companies, Hampshire Terrace, Portsmouth; No.3 Works Company, Eastleigh; No.4 Electric Lights Company, Hampshire Terrace, Portsmouth; No.5 Electric Lights Company, Freshwater, Isle of Wight (detachments at Lymington and East Cowes); No.6 Electric Lights Company, Gosport.

Hampshire Infantry Brigade. See Wessex Division.

Hampshire Regiment. Two Regular (1st and 2nd), one Special Reserve (3rd) and six Territorial Force (4th to 9th) battalions. Depot, Winchester.

1st Battalion: Colchester.

2nd Battalion: Mhow, India.

3rd Battalion: Winchester.

4th Battalion: Winchester with "A" and "B" Companies, also Winchester; "C" Company, Botley (detachments at Chandler's Ford, Bishop's Waltham, Hursley, Mottisfont, Twyford, East Tytherley and Newtown); "D" Company, Andover (detachments at Tidworth, Highclere, Burghclere, Kingsclere, Woodhay, Whitchurch and Cholderton); "E" Company, Aldershot (detachments at Farnborough, Fleet, Cove and Redfields); "F" Company, Yateley (detachments at Crowthorne, Blackwater and Eversley); "G" Company, Basingstoke (detachments at Hartley Wintney, Silchester, Odiham and Strathfieldsaye); "H" Company, Alton (detach-

Hampshire Regiment. *2nd Battalion football teams, Roberts' Heights, Transvaal, 1910.*

ments at Alresford and Selborne). The Peter Symonds School Cadet Corps at Winchester and Basingstoke and Eastrop Cadet Corps were affiliated.
5th Battalion: Southampton with "A" to "E" Companies, also Southampton (detachments at Sarisbury, Woolston, Bitterne, Shirley and Westend); "F" Company, Eastleigh (detachment at Fair Oak); "G" Company, Southampton; "H" Company, Southampton (detachment at Bursledon).
6th (Duke of Connaught's) Battalion: Connaught Hall, Portsmouth with "A" to "D" Companies, also at Connaught Hall; "E" Company, Gosport (detachment at Lee-on-Solent); "F" Company, Havant (detachments at Waterlooville, South Hayling and Rowlands Castle); "G" Company, Petersfield (detachments at Greatham, Liphook, Headley and Clanfield); "H" Company, Fareham (detachments at Titchfield, Swanwick, Wickham and Portchester).
7th Battalion: 177 Holdenhurst Road, Bournemouth with "A" Company, Lymington (detachments at East Boldre, Milford-on-Sea, Brockenhurst and Baddesley); "B" Company, Christchurch (detachments at Highcliffe and Milton); "C" Company, Ringwood (detachments at Burley and Fordingbridge); "D" Company, Totton (detachments

Hampshire Regiment. *7th Battalion. The badge of this battalion featured the gauge once used to measure dogs in the New Forest. Said to be a stirrup once belonging to King Rufus, any dog that could not pass through it had, to prevent it running fast enough to chase deer, the three middle claws of its front paws removed.*

Hampshire Regiment. *8th (Isle of Wight Rifles "Princess Beatrice's") Battalion. Green uniforms (with black collars and cuffs) and black fur caps. The officers (far left and front) wear black patent leather pouch belts with silver whistle and chains.*

at Hythe, Fawley and Marchwood); "E" to "H" Companies, Bournemouth. The Lymington Cadet Corps was affiliated.

8th (Isle of Wight Rifles, "Princess Beatrice's") Battalion: Newport with "A" Company, Ryde (detachments at Havenstreet, Binstead and Fishbourne); "B" Company, St Helens (detachments at Bembridge, Seaview and Brading); "C" Company, Newport (detachments at Calbourne and Yarmouth); "D" Company, Newport (detachments at Wootton and Lock's Green); "E" Company, Sandown (detachments at Shanklin and Newchurch); "F" Company, Ventnor (detachment at Wroxall); "G" Company, Newport (detachments at Niton, Whitwell, Godshill, Chillerton and Brightstone); "H" Company, Cowes (detachment at Northwood). The Ventnor Cadet Company was affiliated.

9th (Cyclist) Battalion: Hamilton House, Commercial Road, Southampton with "A" Company, Southampton (detachment at Swanwick); "B" Company, Bournemouth (detachment at Dorchester); "C" Company, Romsey; "D" Company, Portsmouth; "E" Company, Horndean (detachment at Petersfield); "F" Company, West Meon; "G" Company, Basingstoke (detachment at Herriard); "H" Company, Whitchurch.

1st Cadet Battalion: 41a Union Street, Aldershot and affiliated to the 6th Battalion. "G" (Surrey) and "H" (Surrey) Companies at Farnham, however, were affiliated to the 5th Battalion, Queen's (Royal West Surrey Regiment).

2nd Cadet Battalion: Connaught Drill Hall, Portsmouth. Twelve companies affiliated to 6th Battalion.

Hampshire Regiment. *8th (Isle of Wight Rifles "Princess Beatrice's") Battalion. Cap badge. The tower of Carisbrooke Castle features with the battle honour awarded for service during the Second Boer War.*

Hampshire Royal Garrison Artillery. *No. 4 Company. This photo taken at Cliff End Camp, 1909, shows both full and service dress (the latter worn with dress helmets) uniforms. The white buff equipment worn is 1888 pattern.*

Hampshire Royal Garrison Artillery. Territorial Force. St Mary's Road, Southampton with No.1 Heavy Battery, Southampton (detachment at Eastleigh); No.2 Company, Southampton; No.3 Company, Eastleigh (detachment at Bishop's Waltham); No.4 Company, Portsmouth; No.5 Company, Southampton; No.6 Company, Woolston and Bitterne; No.7 Company, Southampton; No.8 Company, Eastleigh.

Hampshire Royal Garrison Artillery (Heavy). See Wessex Royal Garrison Artillery (Hampshire).

Hampshire Royal Horse Artillery. Territorial Force. Southampton. Included the 1st South Western Mounted Brigade Ammunition Column at Basingstoke.

Hampshire Yeomanry (Carabiniers). Territorial Force. Hyde Close, Winchester with "A" Squadron, Portsmouth (detachments at Freshwater, Newport, Ryde, Petersfield and Titchfield); "B" Squadron, Winchester (detachments at Alton, Aldershot, Basingstoke and Bishop's Waltham); "C" Squadron, Southampton (detachments at Eastleigh, Andover and Romsey); "D" Squadron, Bournemouth (detachments at Stuckton, Highcliffe, Burley and Beaulieu).

Hampshire Yeomanry (Carabiniers). *Cap badge. The Hampshire Rose backed by crossed carbines.*

Herefordshire Regiment. *Cap badge. A lion holding a sword is the crest of Hereford.*

Handsworth Grammar School Officers Training Corps. One infantry company, Junior Division.

Harrow Cadet Company. See 9th Battalion, Duke of Cambridge's Own (Middlesex Regiment).

Harrow School Officers Training Corps. Harrow-on-the-Hill, Middlesex. Three infantry companies, Junior Division.

Haytor (Newton Abbot) Cadet Corps, The. See 5th (Prince of Wales's) Battalion, Devonshire Regiment.

Hereford Cathedral School Officers Training Corps. One infantry company, Junior Division.

Herefordshire Regiment. Territorial Force. The Barracks, Hereford.
1st Battalion: "A" Company, Hereford (detachments at Peterchurch, Madley, Marden and Burghill); "B" Company, Ross-on-Wye (detachment at Upton Bishop); "C" Company, Ledbury (detachments at Colwall, Much Marcle and Bosbury); "D" Company, Kington (detachments at Presteigne and Eardisley); "E" Company, Ruardean (detachment at Littledean); "F" Company, Leominster (detachment at Bromyard); "G" Company, Rhayader (detachments at Knighton, Chapel Lawn, Newbridge, Bucknell and Llandrindod Wells); "H" Company, Hereford.

Herne Bay College Cadet Corps. See 4th Battalion, Buffs (East Kent Regiment).

Hertford Grammar School Officers Training Corps. One infantry company, Junior Division.

Hertfordshire Batteries, 1st, 2nd. See 4th East Anglian Brigade, Royal Field Artillery.

Hertfordshire Cadet Company, 2nd. See Hertfordshire Regiment.

Hertfordshire Cadets, 3rd. See Hertfordshire Regiment.

Hertfordshire Cadets, 4th. See Hertfordshire Regiment.

Hertfordshire Regiment. Territorial Force. Hertford.
1st Battalion: "A" Company, Hertford (detachments at Watton, Hatfield and Berkhamsted); "B" Company, St Albans (detachments at London Colney and Harpenden); "C" Company, Bishop's Stortford (detachments at Sawbridgeworth, Braughing, Widford, Ware and Wadesmill); "D" Company, Watford (detachment at Chorley Wood); "E" Company, Royston (detachments at

Hertfordshire Regiment. *Knighton Detachment of "G" Company. Scarlet tunics with grass-green facings and white piping are being worn with brown belts. The officer (centre) wears the full-dress "Universal Pattern" home service helmet.*

Letchworth, Baldock and Ashwell); "F" Company, Hemel Hempstead (detachments at Great Berkhamsted, Ashridge, Tring and Ivinghoe); "G" Company, Hitchin (detachments at Welwyn, Stevenage and Whitwell); "H" Company, Waltham Cross (detachments at Wormley, Cheshunt and Hoddesdon). Three cadet units were affiliated – 2nd Hertfordshire (Watford Scouts) Cadet Company at Clarendon Hall, Watford; 3rd Hertfordshire Cadets (Stortford School), Bishop's Stortford, and 4th Hertfordshire Cadets (St George's School) at Harpenden. Note: Recognition of the 1st Hertfordshire Cadets (Chorley Wood) had been withdrawn in December, 1913.

Hertfordshire Yeomanry. Territorial Force. Hertford with "A" Squadron, Watford (detachments at St John's Wood and Berkhamstead); "B" Squadron, Hertford (detachments at Broxbourne, Enfield Lock and Sawbridgeworth); "C" Squadron, St Albans (detachments at Harpenden, Hendon, Westminster, Islington and Hemel Hempstead); "D" Squadron, High Barnet (detachments at Enfield, Harringay, Hitchin and Islington).

Highgate School Officers Training Corps. One infantry company, Junior Division.

Highland Brigade, Royal Field Artillery, 1st. Territorial Force. North Street, Aberdeen with 1st City of Aberdeen, 2nd City of Aberdeen, 3rd City of Aberdeen Batteries and Ammunition Column.

Highland Brigade, Royal Field Artillery, 2nd. Territorial Force. Dudhope Drill Hall, Brown Street, Dundee with the Forfarshire Battery, Arbroath; Fifeshire Battery, Leven (detachment at East Wemyss) and the City of Dundee Battery. The Ammunition Column was also in Dundee.

Highland Brigade, Royal Field Artillery (Howitzer), 3rd. Territorial Force. 8 South Street, Greenock with 1st and 2nd Renfrewshire (Howitzer) Batteries, also at South Street. There were two Ammunition Columns, both at Cathcart, one being designated as the Renfrewshire Small Arm Section Ammunition Column.

Highland Brigade, Royal Garrison Artillery (Mountain), 4th. Territorial Force. Russell Street, Rothesay with the Argyllshire (Mountain) Battery, Campbeltown (detachments at Oban and Tobermory); Ross and Cromarty (Mountain) Battery, Lochcarron (detachments at Kishorn, Kyle of Lochalsh, Applecross, Plockton, Dornie and Stornoway); Buteshire (Mountain) Battery, Rothesay (detachments at Largs and Kilchattan). The Ammunition Column was located – Headquarters and "A" Sub-Section, Tarbert; "B" Sub-Section, Millport and "C" Sub-Section, Dingwall.

4th Highland (Mountain) Brigade, Royal Garrison Artillery. *Buteshire Battery.*

Highland Clearing Hospital. Territorial Force. Aberdeen.

Highland Cyclist Battalion. Territorial Force. Kirkcaldy with "A" Company, also at Kirkcaldy; "B" Company, Cowie; "C" Company, Tayport; "D" Company, Forfar; "E" Company, Dunfermline; "F" Company, New Scone; "G" Company, East Wemyss; "H" Company, Bannockburn.

Highland Division. Territorial Force. 2 Charlotte Street, Perth.

Seaforth and Cameron Infantry Brigade: Margaret Street, Inverness. Battalions – 4th, 5th, 6th Seaforth Highlanders; 4th Cameron Highlanders.

Gordon Infantry Brigade: Fonthill Road, Aberdeen. Battalions – 4th, 5th, 6th, 7th Gordon Highlanders.

Argyll and Sutherland Infantry Brigade: Princess Street, Stirling. Battalions – 6th, 7th, 8th, 9th Argyll and Sutherland Highlanders.

Royal Artillery: Dunhope Drill Hall, Dundee. 1st, 2nd, 3rd Highland (Howitzer) Brigades, Royal Field Artillery; 4th Highland (Mountain) Brigade, Royal Garrison Artillery; Highland Royal Garrison Artillery.

Royal Engineers: 80 Hardgate Street, Aberdeen. 2nd Highland Field Company, Highland Divisional Signal Company.

Army Service Corps: Tay Street, Perth. Highland Divisional Transport and Supply Column.

Royal Army Medical Corps: 1st, 2nd, 3rd Highland Field Ambulances.

Attached: The Shetland Companies, Gordon Highlanders.

Highland Divisional Engineers. Territorial Force. 80 Hardgate, Aberdeen with 1st Highland Field Company, at 21 Jardine Street, Glasgow and 2nd Highland Field Company, 80 Hardgate.

Highland Divisional Signal Company. Territorial Force. 80 Hardgate, Aberdeen with No.1 Section, No.2 (Seaforth and Cameron) Section, No.3 (Gordon) Section, No.4 (Argyll and Sutherland) Section.

Highland Divisional Transport and Supply Column. Territorial Force. Tay Street, Perth with 1st (Headquarters) Company, also at Tay Street; 2nd Company, St John Street, Stirling (detachment at Grangemouth); 3rd (Gordon Brigade) Company, Fonthill Road, Aberdeen and 4th Company, Dundee.

Highland Field Ambulance, 1st. Territorial Force. Fonthill Road, Aberdeen.

Highland Field Ambulance, 2nd. Territorial Force. Fonthill Road, Aberdeen.

Highland Divisional Engineers. *Piper.*

Highland Field Ambulance, 3rd. Territorial Force. Dunhope Drill Hall, Brown Street, Dundee.

Highland Field Companies, 1st, 2nd. See Highland Divisional Engineers.

Highland Light Infantry. Two Regular (1st and 2nd), two Special Reserve (3rd and 4th) and five Territorial Force (5th to 9th) battalions. Depot, Hamilton.

1st Battalion: Ambala, India.

2nd Battalion: Maida Barracks, Aldershot.

3rd Battalion: Hamilton.

4th Battalion: Hamilton.

5th (City of Glasgow) Battalion: 24 Hill Street, Garnethill, Glasgow.

6th (City of Glasgow) Battalion: 172 Yorkhill Street, Glasgow.

7th (Blythswood) Battalion: 69 Main Street, Bridgeton, Glasgow.

8th (Lanark) Battalion: Lanark with "A" Company, Lesmahagow (detachments at Stonehouse, Coalburn and Blackwood); "B" Company, Lanark (detachments at Biggar, Ponfeigh and Douglas); "C" Company, Shotts (detachments at Cleland, Salsburgh and Harthill); "D" Company, Carluke; "E" Company, Forth (detachment at Tarbrax); "F" Company, Law (detachment at Overtown); "G" Company, Newmains; "H" Company, Wishaw.

9th (Glasgow Highland) Battalion: 81 Greendyke Street, Glasgow. There was a cadet company, designated 1st (Glasgow Highland) Cadet Company, affiliated at the Head Post Office, Glasgow. Formally known as the Glasgow Postal Telegraph Messengers' Cadet Corps.

Highland Light Infantry. *5th (City of Glasgow) Battalion. Many Territorial Force efficiency stars adorn regimental pattern uniforms – scarlet doublets, buffs collars and cuffs, white piping, MacKenzie tartan.*

Highland Light Infantry Brigade. See Lowland Division.

Highland Light Infantry Brigade Company, Army Service Corps. See Lowland Divisional Transport and Supply Column.

Highland Mounted Brigade. Territorial Force. Academy Street, Inverness. Included Fife and Forfar, 1st and 2nd Lovat's Scouts Yeomanries; Inverness-shire Royal Horse Artillery.

Highland Mounted Brigade Ammunition Column. See Inverness-shire Royal Horse Artillery.

Highland Mounted Brigade Field Ambulance. Territorial Force. Rose Street, Inverness.

Highland Mounted Brigade Signal Troop. Territorial Force. Academy Street. Inverness.

Highland Mounted Brigade Transport and Supply Column. Territorial Force. One company at Academy Street, Inverness.

Highland Royal Garrison Artillery (Fifeshire). Territorial Force. Elgin Street, Dunfermline. There were also detachments at Charlestown (Battery) and Culcross (Ammunition Column).

Highlanders Battalion. See 9th Battalion, Royal Scots (Lothian Regiment).

Hillhead High School Officers Training Corps. Glasgow. One infantry company, Junior Division.

His Majesty's Body Guard of the Honourable Corps of Gentlemen-at-Arms. London.

Home Counties Brigade, Royal Field Artillery, 1st. Territorial Force. Church Street, Brighton with 1st and 2nd Sussex Batteries, also at Church Street, and 3rd Sussex Battery at Marmion Road, Hove (detachment at Shoreham). The Ammunition Column was at Worthing. Affiliated to the Brigade were the Steyne School Cadet Corps at Worthing and the Brighton Brigade, Sussex Cadets. A third unit, headquarters at 35 Temple Street, Brighton, was designated 1st Cadet Battalion, 1st Home Counties Brigade (Imperial Service Cadet Corps).

Home Counties Brigade, Royal Field Artillery, 2nd. Territorial Force. The Goffs, Eastbourne with 4th Sussex Battery, also at The Goffs (detachment at Hailsham); 5th Sussex Battery, Hatherly Road, St Leonards-on-Sea (detachment at Hastings), and 6th Sussex Battery, The Downs, Bexhill (detachments at Pevensey and Ninfield). The Ammunition Column was at Hailsham. The St Leonards Collegiate School Cadet Company and Imperial Service Cadet Corps, Eastbourne were affiliated.

1st Home Counties Brigade, Royal Field Artillery. *Steyne School Cadet Corps. The uniform seen here – dark blue hat, shirt and trousers – was worn by the Corps from its recognition by the War Office in April, 1913, until 1916 and the introduction that year of khaki service dress.*

Home Counties Divisional Transport and Supply Column. *Trumpeters, Seaford. Uniforms are blue with white collars, piping and trouser strips.*

2nd Home Counties Field Ambulance. *Bass drummer.*

Home Counties Brigade, Royal Field Artillery (Cinque Ports), 3rd. Territorial Force. Liverpool Street, Dover with 1st Kent Battery, also at Liverpool Street; 2nd Kent Battery, Shellon Street, Folkestone and 3rd Kent Battery, High Street, Ramsgate (detachment at Margate). The Ammunition Column was located – Gun Section, Deal; Small Arm Section, Sandwich.

Home Counties Brigade, Royal Field Artillery (Howitzer), 4th. Territorial Force. "Trevethan", Bexley Road, Erith with 4th Kent (Howitzer), 5th Kent (Howitzer) Batteries and Ammunition Column.

Home Counties Clearing Hospital. Territorial Force. Surbiton.

Home Counties Division. Territorial Force. Hounslow.

Surrey Infantry Brigade: Caxton House, Westminster. Battalions – 4th, 5th Queen's Royal West Surrey; 5th, 6th East Surrey.

Kent Infantry Brigade: 1 Bank Street, Tonbridge. Battalions – 4th, 5th Buffs, East Kent; 4th, 5th Queen's Own Royal West Kent.

Middlesex Infantry Brigade: 15 Pall Mall East, London. Battalions – 7th, 8th, 9th, 10th Middlesex.

Royal Artillery: 14 Nightingale Place, Woolwich. 1st, 2nd, 3rd, 4th (Howitzer) Home Counties Brigades, Royal Field Artillery; Home Counties Royal Garrison Artillery.

Royal Engineers: Ordnance Yard, Eastbourne. 1st, 2nd Home Counties Field Companies; Home Counties Divisional Signal Company.

Army Service Corps: Hounslow. Home Counties Divisional Transport and Supply Column.

Royal Army Medical Corps: 1st, 2nd, 3rd Home Counties Field Ambulances.

Attached: 4th, 5th Royal Sussex Regiment.

Home Counties Divisional Engineers. Territorial Force. Ordnance Yard, Eastbourne with 1st Home Counties Field Company, also at Ordnance Yard (detachment at Brighton); 2nd Home Counties Field Company, Tower Road West, St Leonards-on-Sea (detachment at Bexhill). The University School Cadet Company at Hastings was affiliated.

Home Counties Divisional Signal Company. Territorial Force. 23 Gloucester Place, Brighton with No.1 Section, No.2 (Surrey) Section, No.3 (Kent) Section, No.4 (Middlesex) Section.

Home Counties Divisional Transport and Supply Column. Territorial Force. Hounslow with Headquarters Company at 117 Gloucester Road, Brighton; Surrey Brigade Company, 259 Walton Road, Woking; Kent Brigade Company, Union Street, Maidstone and Middlesex Brigade Company, Barnet (detachment at Teddington).

Home Counties Field Ambulance, 1st. Territorial Force. The Palace, Maidstone with "A" Section, also in Maidstone; "B" Section, Snodland; "C" Section, Chatham.

Home Counties Field Ambulance, 2nd. Territorial Force. Ashford with "A" Section, Canterbury; "B" Section, Ashford (detachment in Folkestone); "C" Section, Whitstable.

Home Counties Field Ambulance, 3rd. Territorial Force. 24 Claremont Road, Surbiton.

Home Counties Royal Garrison Artillery (Kent).

Home Counties Field Companies, 1st, 2nd. See Home Counties Divisional Engineers.

Home Counties Royal Garrison Artillery (Kent). Territorial Force. Faversham. There were also detachments at Chatham (Battery) and Chatham (Ammunition Column).

Honourable Artillery Company. The senior member of the Territorial Force, the HAC comprised two batteries of horse artillery, each with an ammunition column, and an infantry section of four companies. Headquarters at Armoury House, Finsbury. The batteries were designated "A" (1st City of London Horse Artillery) and "B" (2nd City of London Horse Artillery). Ammunition columns were – London Mounted Brigade Ammunition Column (with "A" Battery) and South Eastern Mounted Brigade Ammunition Column (with "B" Battery).

Honourable Corps of Gentlemen. See His Majesty's Body Guard of the Honourable Corps of Gentlemen-at-Arms.

Honourable Artillery Company. *Cap badge, infantry section.*

Honourable Artillery Company. *"A" Battery. The cap badge is that of the Royal Artillery, but the letters HAC replace "Ubique" on the upper scroll. The lower scroll also differs in that the motto "Arma Pacis Fulcra" (Arms the Mainstay of Peace) is substituted for the usual "Quo Fas et Gloria Ducunt" (Wherever right and glory lead). "B" Battery wear a similar brass shoulder title.*

Honourable Artillery Company. *Drummers, infantry section. The uniform is based on that of the Grenadier Guards, but with white metal (instead of brass) buttons and badges.*

***Huntingdonshire* Cyclists.** *Cap badge.*

Hugh Myddelton School Cadet Corps. Headquarters at the Guildhall, London. Two companies.

Hull Cadet Company, St Mark's Church Scouts. St Mark's Vicarage, Hull.

Huntingdonshire Cyclist Battalion. St Mary's Street, Huntingdon.

Hurstpierpoint College Officers Training Corps. One infantry company, Junior Division.

Hussars, 3rd (King's Own). Shorncliffe. Depot, Bristol.

Hussars, 4th (Queen's Own). Curragh. Depot, Dublin.

Hussars, 7th (Queen's Own). Bangalore, India. Depot, Bristol.

Hussars, 8th (King's Royal Irish). Ambala, India. Depot, Dublin.

3rd (King's Own) Hussars. *Cap badge. The White Horse of Hanover.*

3rd (King's Own) Hussars. *On 27 June, 1743, the 3rd Hussars (then Bland's Dragoons) drove the enemy from the field at Dettingen and in doing so took as trophies two silver kettle-drums. Note that no drum banners are used, battle honours and other distinctions being engraved instead on the drums themselves. Seen also in this photo is the kettle-drummer's silver collar. Just over three inches in height, this distinction was presented by Lady Southampton (Lord Southampton had become Colonel of the Regiment) in 1772. Uniforms are blue with scarlet collars and yellow cord and the Royal Artillery line the way.*

4th (Queen's Own) Hussars. *Cap badge. Authorized in 1906, the motto means with "heart and hand".*

7th (Queen's Own) Hussars. *Cap badge.*

8th (King's Royal Irish) Hussars. *Cap badge. The harp was authorized, along with the title "King's Royal Irish", in 1777.*

11th (Prince Albert's Own) Hussars. *Both cap and collar badge feature the crest and motto – Treu und Fest (Faithful and Firm) – of Prince Albert. This, together with the title "Prince Albert's Own", was granted in 1840 in commemoration of the Regiment that year having escorted the Prince from Dover to London prior to his marriage to Queen Victoria. The blue jacket has yellow cord and is worn with crimson trouser stripes.*

Hussars, 10th (Prince of Wales's Own Royal). Potchefstroom, South Africa. Depot, Scarborough.

Hussars, 11th (Prince Albert's Own). Aldershot. Depot, Dublin.

Hussars, 13th. Meerut, India. Depot, Dublin.

Hussars, 14th (King's). Mhow, India. Depot, Scarborough.

Hussars, 15th (The King's). Longmoor. Depot, Bristol.

14th (King's) Hussars. *A Prussian eagle (seen here on the collar), the regimental badge, was replaced, due to anti-German feeling, in 1915. The same device, but a larger version, can also be seen above the chevrons.*

18th (Queen Mary's Own) Hussars. *Major E.C. Haag, Commander of "C" Squadron at Tidworth, 1914. Blue uniform adorned by gold lace and cord, white over red plume.*

Hussars, 18th (Queen Mary's Own). Tidworth. Depot, Scarborough.

Hussars, 19th (Queen Alexandra's Own Royal). Hounslow. Depot, Bristol.

Hussars, 20th. Colchester. Depot, Scarborough.

Hutcheson's Grammar School Cadet Corps. See 7th Battalion, Cameronians (Scottish Rifles).

Hymers College Officers Training Corps. Hull. One infantry company, Junior Division.

19th (Queen Alexandra's Own Royal) Hussars. *Taken at Hounslow in 1914, this photo shows one of the regiment's badges – the cypher, coronet and cross (Dannebrog or Dane's cross) of HRH Alexandra Princess of Wales. The tunic is blue with yellow cord.*

20th Hussars. *Blue uniforms, crimson busby-bag, yellow plumes, cord and piping.*

I

Ilford Church Cadets. 193 Mortlake Road, Ilford. Two companies.

Imperial Cadet Yeomanry (City of London). 118–122 Holborn.

Imperial Cadet Yeomanry, Yorkshire Squadron. See Yorkshire Hussars Yeomanry (Alexandra, Princess of Wales's Own)

Imperial Service Cadet Corps, Brighton. See 1st Home Counties Brigade, Royal Field Artillery.

Imperial Service Cadet Corps, Eastbourne. See 2nd Home Counties Brigade, Royal Field Artillery.

Imperial Service College Officers Training Corps. Windsor. One infantry company, Junior Division.

Indian Central Flying School. See Royal Flying Corps.

Infantry. Under this heading are included the four regiments (Welsh not formed until 1915) of Foot Guards – Grenadier, Coldstream, Scots and Irish (the Guards Depot was at Caterham) – and the Infantry of the Line. The latter formed the bulk of the infantry arm and comprised sixty-nine regiments – forty-eight English, ten Scottish, eight Irish and three Welsh. These followed a strict order of precedence (based on formation date, or in some cases, when brought onto the British establishment) which ran (shortened titles only) as follows: Royal Scots, Queen's, Buffs, King's Own, Northumberland Fusiliers, Royal Warwickshire, Royal Fusiliers, King's Liverpool, Norfolk, Lincolnshire, Devonshire, Suffolk, Somerset Light Infantry, West Yorkshire, East Yorkshire, Bedfordshire, Leicestershire, Royal Irish Regiment, Yorkshire, Lancashire Fusiliers, Royal Scots Fusiliers, Cheshire, Royal Welsh Fusiliers, South Wales Borderers, King's Own Scottish Borderers, Cameronians, Royal Inniskilling Fusiliers, Gloucestershire, Worcestershire, East Lancashire, East Surrey, Duke of Cornwall's Light Infantry, Duke of Wellington's, Border, Royal Sussex, Hampshire, South Staffordshire, Dorsetshire, South Lancashire, Welsh, Black Watch, Oxfordshire and Buckinghamshire Light Infantry, Essex, Sherwood Foresters, Loyal North Lancashire, Northamptonshire, Royal Berkshire, Queen's Own Royal West Kent, King's Own Yorkshire Light Infantry, King's Shropshire Light Infantry, Middlesex, King's Royal Rifle Corps, Wiltshire, Manchester, North Staffordshire, York and Lancaster, Durham Light Infantry, Highland Light Infantry, Seaforth Highlanders, Gordon Highlanders, Cameron Highlanders, Royal Irish Rifles, Royal Irish Fusiliers, Connaught Rangers, Argyll and Sutherland Highlanders, Leinster, Royal

Inns of Court Officers Training Corps. Band, Berkhamsted, 1914.

Inns of Court Officers Training Corps. *The badge of the Regiment shows four sets of arms arranged in the form of a cross – Lincolns Inn (top), Inner Temple (right), Grays Inn (bottom), Middle Temple (left). The battle honour "South Africa 1900–1901 is also featured.*

Inns of Court Officers Training Corps. *This postcard, after an illustration by M. Wood, shows the regimental button. It was at a review in 1803 that King George III, having learnt that the Regiment, then the Inns of Court Volunteers, was made up of lawyers, dubbed them "The Devil's Own".*

Munster Fusiliers, Royal Dublin Fusiliers and Rifle Brigade.

Territorial Force battalions were included in most regiments – there were none in the Guards and Irish regiments, or within the framework of the Royal Fusiliers, King's Royal Rifle Corps and Rifle Brigade (TF battalions affiliated to these three regiments were included in the London Regiment) – and these varied from one or two (in most) and as many as seven in some. They were generally numbered on from the Special Reserve, but two, the Breconshire and Buckinghamshire, were known by name only. Also within the Territorial Force were a number of independent regiments – Honourable Artillery Company, Monmouthshire, Cambridgeshire, London, Inns of Court, Hertfordshire, Herefordshire and several Cyclist battalions. Territorial Force battalions were each made up of eight companies lettered "A" to "H".

Inniskilling Dragoons. See 6th (Inniskilling) Dragoons.

Inniskilling Fusiliers. See Royal Inniskilling Fusiliers.

Inns of Court Officers Training Corps. Territorial Force. 10 Stone Buildings, Lincoln's Inn. Holborn, London with three companies ("A", "B" and "C") and a cavalry squadron.

Inverness-shire Royal Horse Artillery. Territorial Force. Market Street, Inverness. Included the Highland Mounted Brigade Ammunition Column at King Street, Nairn.

Ipswich School Officers Training Corps. One infantry company, Junior Division.

Irish Fusiliers. See Princess Victoria's (Royal Irish Fusiliers).

Irish Guards. One Regular battalion.
1st Battalion: Wellington Barracks, London.

Irish Horse. See North Irish Horse and South Irish Horse.

Irish Lancers. See 5th (Royal Irish) Lancers.

Irish Regiment. See Royal Irish Regiment.

Irish Rifles. See Royal Irish Rifles.

Isle of Man Volunteers. See 7th Volunteer Battalion, King's (Liverpool Regiment).

Isle of Wight Rifles. See 8th (Isle of Wight Rifles "Princess Beatrice's") Battalion, Hampshire Regiment.

Irish Guards. *Cap badge. The Star of the Order of St Patrick. The motto "Quis Separabit (Who shall separate us) appears above the date MDCCLXXXIII – 1783 being the year when the Order was instigated.*

Above: Irish Guards. *Drums and Fifes with Irish Wolfhound regimental pet.*

Left: Irish Guards. *Regimental-Sergeant-Major. Note tunic and cuff buttons arranged in groups of four and shamrock collar badges.*

Below: Irish Guards. *Drill order.*

J

Jersey Militia. See Royal Jersey Militia

K

Kelly College Officers Training Corps. Tavistock. One infantry company, Junior Division.

Kelvinside Academy Officers Training Corps. Glasgow. One infantry company, Junior Division.

Kensington Battalion. See 13th Battalion, London Regiment.

Kensington and Hammersmith Navy League Boys' Brigade. See 13th London Regiment.

Kent Batteries, 1st, 2nd, 3rd. See 3rd Home Counties Brigade, Royal Field Artillery.

Kent Batteries, 4th (Howitzer), 5th (Howitzer). See 4th Home Counties Brigade, Royal Field Artillery (Howitzer).

Kent Brigade Company, Army Service Corps. See Home Counties Divisional Transport and Supply Column.

Kent Cyclist Battalion. Territorial Force. Tonbridge with "A" Company, Bromley; "B" Company, Tonbridge (detachment at Pembury); "C" Company, Beckenham; "D" Company, Maidstone (detachment at Chatham); "E" Company, Tunbridge Wells; "F" Company, Canterbury (detachments at Ashford and Whitstable); "G" Company, Ramsgate (detachments at Margate and Sandwich); "H" Company, Sandgate (detachments at Hythe, Dover and Folkestone).

Kent (Fortress) Cadet Battalion. See Kent Fortress Engineers.

Kent Cyclist Battalion. *Clearly seen in this photograph, and taken from the arms of Kent, is the battalion's rampant horse and motto "Invicta" ("unconquered") cap badge.*

Kent Fortress Engineers. Territorial Force. Submarine Mining School, Gillingham with No.1 Works Company, Tonbridge (detachment at Southborough); No.2 Works Company, Ashford; No.3 Works Company, Southborough; No.4 Electric Lights Company, Submarine Mining School, Gillingham; No.5 Electric Lights Company, Gravesend. The Kent (Fortress) Cadet Battalion, four companies at Broomhill, Southborough, Tunbridge Wells, was attached.

Kent Infantry Brigade. See Home Counties Division.

Kent Royal Garrison Artillery. Territorial Force. Sheerness with No.1 Company, Fort Clarence, Rochester (detachment at Sheerness); No.2 Company, Gravesend (detachment at Northfleet); No.3 Company, Dover (detachment at Folkestone).

Kent Royal Garrison Artillery. *Cliff End Camp, 1912.*

Kent Royal Garrison Artillery (Heavy). See Home Counties Royal Garrison Artillery (Kent).

Kent Yeomanry, East. See Royal East Kent Yeomanry.

Kent Yeomanry, West. See Queen's Own West Kent Yeomanry

Kilburn Grammar School Cadet Company. See 9th Battalion, Duke of Cambridge's Own (Middlesex Regiment).

King Alfred's School Officers Training Corps. Wantage, Berkshire. One infantry company, Junior Division.

King Edward VI School, Chelmsford Cadet Corps. See 5th Battalion, Essex Regiment.

King Edward VII School Officers Training Corps. Sheffield. One infantry company, Junior Division.

King Edward's Grammar School Officers Training Corps. Bury St Edmunds. One infantry company, Junior Division.

King Edward's Horse (The King's Oversea Dominions Regiment). Special Reserve. Duke of York's Headquarters, Chelsea, London.

King Edward's School, Bath Officers Training Corps. One infantry company, Junior Division.

King Edward's School, Birmingham Officers Training Corps. Two infantry companies, Junior Division.

King Edward's School, Witley Cadet Corps. Four companies.

King William's College Officers Training Corps. Isle of Man. One infantry company, Junior Division.

King's African Rifles.

1st (Central Africa) Battalion: Zomba, Nyasaland.
3rd (East Africa) Battalion: Nairobi, Kenya.
4th (Uganda) Battalion: Bombo.

King's Body Guard for Scotland. Edinburgh. Also known as Royal Company of Archers.

King's Body Guard of the Yeoman of the Guard. Tower of London. Also known as Yeoman Warders of the Tower and "Beefeaters".

King's College Officers Training Corps. Taunton. One infantry company, Junior Division.

King's College School Officers Training Corps. Wimbledon. One infantry company, Junior Division.

King's Dragoon Guards. See 1st (King's) Dragoon Guards.

King's Hussars. See 14th (King's) Hussars and 15th (The King's) Hussars.

King's (Liverpool Regiment). Two Regular (1st and 2nd), two Special Reserve (3rd and 4th) and six Territorial Force (5th–10th) battalions. Depot, Seaforth. The Regiment also had attached the former members of the Volunteer Force on the Isle of Man.

1st Battalion: Talavera Barracks, Aldershot.

2nd Battalion: Peshawar, India.

3rd Battalion: Seaforth.

4th Battalion: Seaforth.

5th Battalion: 65 St Anne Street, Liverpool.

6th (Rifle) Battalion: Prince's Park Barracks, Liverpool.

7th Battalion: 99 Park Street, Bootle with "A" to "D" Companies, also at 99 Park Street; "E" Company was at Crosby; "F" Company, Bootle; "G" Company, Southport. "H" Company was also in Southport (detachment at Formby). The Southport Cadet Corps at 60 Scarisbrick New Road, Southport was affiliated.

8th (Irish) Battalion: 75 Shaw Street, Liverpool.

9th Battalion: 57–61 Everton Road, Liverpool with "A" to "E" Companies, also at 57–61 Everton Road;. "F" Company was at Ormskirk; "G" Company, Liverpool; "H" Company, Ormskirk.

10th (Scottish) Battalion: 7 Fraser Street, Liverpool.

7th (Isle of Man) Volunteer Battalion: In a Special Army Order dated 18 March, 1908 dealing with the transfer of the Volunteers to the Territorial Force, Section 88 reads as follows: "The Isle of Man Volunteers (7th V.B. Liverpool Regiment) will not be included in the Territorial Force, but will remain subject to Volunteer conditions." This was to place the 7th VB King's Liverpools – a title which it retained – in a unique position for the next six years, the formation being the only volunteer unit in the British Isles until the formation of the Volunteer Training Corps after war was declared in 1914.

King's (Liverpool Regiment). *7th Battalion leaving their Colours for safekeeping at Bootle Town Hall, 15 August, 1914.*

King's (Liverpool Regiment). *9th Battalion Drums and Bugles at camp near Lancaster, 1910.*

King's (Liverpool Regiment). *8th (Irish) Battalion, blackened-brass shoulder title.*

King's (Liverpool Regiment). *10th (Scottish) Battalion at Denbigh, 1913. The kilts and trews are Forbes pattern tartan.*

King's Oversea Dominions Regiment. See King Edward's Horse (The King's Oversea Dominions Regiment).

King's Own Hussars. See 3rd (King's Own) Hussars.

King's Own Malta Regiment of Militia. Two battalions.

King's Own (Royal Lancaster Regiment). Two Regular (1st and 2nd), one Special Reserve (3rd) and two Territorial Force (4th and 5th) battalions. Depot, Lancaster.

1st Battalion: Dover.

2nd Battalion: Lebong, India.

3rd Battalion: Lancaster.

4th Battalion: Ulverston with "A" Company was in

Left: King's Oversea Dominions Regiment. *Regimental-Quarter-Master-Sergeant D. Fegan. A member of the Regiment since its formation in 1901, RQMS Fegan wears the regimental khaki uniform. The facings are scarlet and the headdress plume black cock-feathers. As a member of the Canadian Squadron (prior to 1909 the Regiment was made up of squadrons named British Asian, Canadian, Australasian and South African) his collar badge is a beaver on a maple-leaf backing.*

Below: King's Oversea Dominions Regiment. *The NCOs in this photograph, seen here with a sergeant of the 20th Hussars, wear the elephant collar badges of the British Asian Squadron.*

Ulverston (detachment at Grange); "B" Company, Ulverston (detachments at Greenodd, Haverthwaite and Lakeside); "C", "D", "E" and "F" Companies, Barrow-in-Furness; "G" Company, Dalton-in-Furness (detachment at Askam); "H" Company, Millom (detachments at Broughton-in-Furness, Coniston and Hawkshead).

5th Battalion: Lancaster with "A" Company in Lancaster (detachment at Galgate); "B", "C" and "D" Companies, Lancaster; "E" Company, Morecambe; "F" Company, Carnforth (detachments at Arnside, Silverdale and Caton); "G" Company, Fleetwood (detachments at Poulton, Garstang and Blackpool); "H" Company, Fleetwood (detachments at Preesall and Thornton).

King's Own (Royal Lancaster Regiment). *Inspection by Field-Marshal Lord Roberts.*

King's Own (Royal Lancaster Regiment). *4th Battalion, Kirkham Camp (near Preston), 1912.*

King's Own (Royal Lancaster Regiment). *5th Battalion. The corporal seen here wears on his lower right arm (regulations direct left arm) the star and crossed rifles awarded to best shot in company. The regimental badge of the Lion of England (awarded by William III) is seen on both cap and collar.*

King's Own Royal Regiment. See Norfolk Yeomanry (The King's Own Royal Regiment).

King's Own Scottish Borderers. Two Regular (1st and 2nd), one Special Reserve (3rd) and two Territorial Force (4th and 5th) battalions. Depot, Berwick-upon-Tweed.

1st Battalion: Lucknow, India.

2nd Battalion: Dublin.

3rd Battalion: Dumfries.

4th (The Border) Battalion: Galashiels with "A" Company, Kelso (detachment at Jedburgh); "B" Company, Hawick; "C" Company, Hawick (detachment at Newcastleton); "D" Company, Duns (detachments at Greenlaw, Lauder and Earlston); "E" Company, Coldstream (detachments at Ayton,

Eyemouth, Chirnside, Swinton and Coldingham); "F" and "G" Companies, Galashiels; "H" Company, Selkirk (detachments at Melrose and St Boswells). *5th (Dumfries & Galloway) Battalion:* Dumfries with "A" Company, Dumfries (detachment at Moniaive); "B" Company, Annan (detachments at Langholm and Canonbie); "C" Company, Lockerbie (detachments at Ecclefechan and Moffat); "D" Company, Sanquhar (detachments at Thornhill and Kirkconnel); "E" Company, Maxwell Town; "F" Company, Dalbeattie; "G" Company, Castle Douglas (detachments at Corsock, Gatehouse and Kirkcudbright); "H" Company, Newton Stewart (detachments at Wigtown, Creetown, Kirkcowan, Whithorn and Garlieston).

Above: King's Own Scottish Borderers. *2nd Battalion. The Quarter-Master (left) and Regimental-Quarter-Master-Sergeant.*

Above left: King's Own Scottish Borderers. *Raised in the city in 1689, the Castle of Edinburgh is seen here on the blue collar. The scarlet doublet is worn with Leslie pattern tartan trews.*

Left: King's Own Scottish Borderers. *Captain P.A.V. Stewart. Both he and his men wear regimental full-dress Kilmarnock bonnets with black-cock's feathers.*

King's Own Scottish Borderers. *4th Battalion. The pipers of the Battalion wore Buccleugh tartan.*

King's Own (Yorkshire Light Infantry). Two Regular (1st and 2nd), one Special Reserve (3rd) and two Territorial Force (4th and 5th) battalions. Depot, Pontefract.

1st Battalion: Singapore.

2nd Battalion: Dublin.

3rd Battalion: Pontefract.

4th Battalion: Wakefield with "A" and "B" Companies, also at Wakefield; "C" Company, Normanton; "D" Company, Ossett; "E" and "F" Companies, Dewsbury; "G" Company, Batley; "H" Company, Morley.

5th Battalion: French Gate, Doncaster with "A" Company, Pontefract; "B" and "C" Companies, Doncaster; "D" Company, Goole; "E" Company, Featherstone; "F" Company, Doncaster; "G" Company, Conisbrough; "H" Company, Castleford.

King's Royal Irish Hussars. See 8th (King's Royal Irish) Hussars.

King's Own (Yorkshire Light Infantry). *2nd Battalion seen here at Aldershot celebrating Minden Day. At the Battle of Minden (1 August, 1759) roses blossomed on the heath close to the town and while advancing the troops plucked the flowers and with them adorned their hats, coats, equipment and drums.*

King's Royal Rifle Corps. *"G" Company, 1st Cadet Battalion, Browndown Camp, Hampshire, August, 1913. The uniforms seen here follow closely those of the regular battalions – green with scarlet collars and piping, rifle-pattern fur caps. The officer and sergeants (centre row) have black patent leather pouch-belts with Maltese Cross ornaments. The embroidered (scarlet) shoulder designation is 1 over C over KRR and the fur caps have silver crowned bugle horns mounted on a scarlet cord-boss.*

King's Royal Rifle Corps. Four Regular (1st, 2nd, 3rd and 4th) and two Special Reserve (5th and 6th) battalions. Depot, Winchester.

1st Battalion: Salamanca Barracks, Aldershot.

2nd Battalion: Blackdown, Farnborough.

3rd Battalion: Meerut, India.

4th Battalion: Gharial, India.

5th Battalion: Winchester.

6th Battalion: Winchester.

1st Cadet Battalion: 42–44 Sun Street, Finsbury Square, London.

King's School, Bruton Officers Training Corps. One infantry company, Junior Division.

King's School, Canterbury Officers Training Corps. Two infantry companies, Junior Division.

King's (Shropshire Light Infantry). *2nd Battalion Band, Trimulgherry, India, 1912.*

King's School, Grantham Officers Training Corps. One infantry company, Junior Division.

King's School, Peterborough Cadet Corps. See 4th Battalion, Northamptonshire Regiment.

King's School, Rochester Officers Training Corps. One infantry company, Junior Division.

King's School, Warwick Officers Training Corps. One infantry company, Junior Division.

King's School, Worcester Officers Training Corps. One infantry company, Junior Division.

King's (Shropshire Light Infantry). Two Regular (1st and 2nd), one Special Reserve (3rd) and one Territorial Force (4th) battalions. Depot, Shrewsbury.

1st Battalion: Tipperary.

2nd Battalion: Secunderabad, India.

3rd Battalion: Shrewsbury:

4th Battalion: Shrewsbury with "A" Company, also at Shrewsbury; "B" Company, Whitchurch (detachment at Wem); "C" Company, Wellington (detachments at Market Drayton and Hodnet); "D" Company, Ironbridge (detachment at Much Wenlock); "E" Company, Shifnal (detachments at Oakengates and Newport); "F" Company, Bridgnorth (detachment at Highley); "G" Company, Ludlow (detachments at Craven Arms, Clee Hills and Cleobury Mortimer); "H" Company, Oswestry (detachment at Ellesmere). The Bridgnorth Cadet Company at Eimslea, Bridgnorth, was affiliated.

Kirkby Lonsdale Cadet Company. See 4th Battalion, Border Regiment.

Kirkcaldy High School Officers Training Corps. One infantry company, Junior Division.

Kirkcudbrightshire Battery. See 2nd Lowland Brigade, Royal Field Artillery.

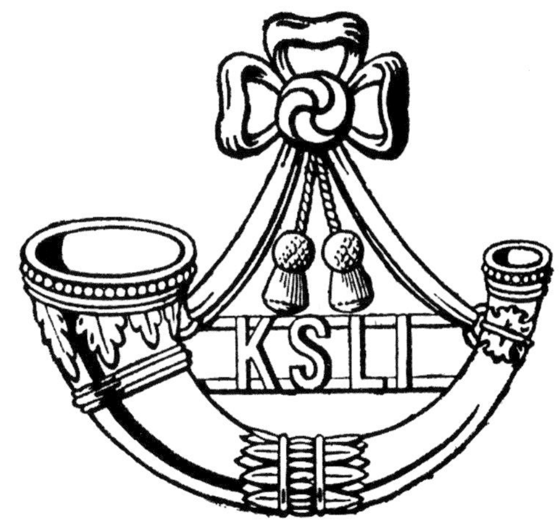

King's (Shropshire Light Infantry). *Cap badge.*

L

Lanark Battalion. See 8th (Lanark) Battalion, Highland Light Infantry.

Lanarkshire Yeomanry. Territorial Force. Lanark with "A" Squadron, Douglas (detachments at Auchinheath, Lesmahagow, Douglas Water and Coalburn); "B" Squadron, Lanark (detachments at Carluke, Carstairs, Wishaw, Peebles and Biggar); "C" Squadron, Coatbridge (detachment at Glasgow); "D" Squadron, Dumfries (detachments at Lockerbie, Langholm, Annan, Moffat, Thornhill and Sanquhar).

Lancashire and Cheshire Royal Garrison Artillery. Territorial Force. 19 Low Hill, Liverpool with Nos 1, 2, 3 and 4 Companies, also at Low Hill; Nos. 5 and 6 Companies, Riverview Road, Seacombe; Nos. 7 and 8 Companies, Barrow-in-Furness.

Lancashire Batteries, 1st, 2nd, 3rd. See 1st West Lancashire Brigade, Royal Field Artillery.

Lancashire Batteries, 4th, 5th, 6th. See 1st East Lancashire Brigade, Royal Field Artillery.

Lancashire Batteries, 7th (Howitzer), 8th (Howitzer). See 4th West Lancashire Brigade, Royal Field Artillery (Howitzer).

Lancashire Batteries, 9th, 10th, 11th. See 2nd West Lancashire Brigade, Royal Field Artillery.

Lanarkshire Yeomanry. *Clearly seen in this photograph is the regimental cap badge of a double-headed eagle.*

Lancashire Batteries, 12th, 13th, 14th. See 3rd West Lancashire Brigade, Royal Field Artillery.

Lancashire Batteries, 15th, 16th, 17th. See 2nd East Lancashire Brigade, Royal Field Artillery (The Manchester Artillery).

Lancashire Batteries, 18th, 19th, 20th. See 3rd East Lancashire Brigade, Royal Field Artillery (The Bolton Artillery).

Lancashire Brigade, Royal Garrison Artillery. Territorial Force. Sefton Barracks, Upper Warwick Street, Toxteth Park, Liverpool and comprising 1st and 2nd Lancashire Heavy Batteries, each with its own ammunition column.

Lancashire Fortress Engineers. Territorial Force. Tramway Road, Aigburth, Liverpool with No.1 Works Company; Nos.2 and 3 Electric Lights Companies.

Lancashire Fusiliers. Two Regular (1st and 2nd), two Special Reserve (3rd and 4th) and four Territorial Force (5th–8th) battalions. Depot, Bury.

1st Battalion: Karachi, India.

2nd Battalion: Dover.

3rd Battalion: Bury.

4th Battalion: Bury.

5th Battalion: Castle Armoury, Bury with "A" and "B" Companies, also at Castle Armoury; "C" and "D" Companies, Heywood; "E" and "F" Companies, Bury; "G" Company, Radcliffe; "H" Company, Bury.

Lancashire Fusiliers. *In marching order, the soldiers left and right wear service dress and equipment. Both the colour-sergeant (left) and officer (right) are in full dress – scarlet tunics with white collars and cuffs.*

Lancashire Fusiliers. *Cap badge.*

6th Battalion: Rochdale with "A" Company, Middleton; "B", "C" and "D" Companies, Rochdale; "E" Company, Middleton; "F" Company, Rochdale; "G" and "H" Companies, Todmorden.

7th Battalion: Cross Lane, Salford.

8th Battalion: Cross Lane, Salford. The Battalion also included a cadet company, designated 1st Cadet Company, which was formally known as the Broughton Lads' Brigade.

Lancashire Fusiliers Brigade Company, Army Service Corps. See East Lancashire Divisional Transport and Supply Column.

Lancashire Fusiliers Infantry Brigade. See East Lancashire Division.

Lancashire Hussars Yeomanry. Territorial Force. Prince Alfred Road, Liverpool with "A" Squadron, Ashton-in-Makerfield (detachments at Wigan and Liverpool); "B" Squadron, St Helens; "C" Squadron, Newton-le-Willows; "D" Squadron, Rainhill.

Lancashire Royal Garrison Artillery, 1st, 2nd. See Lancashire Brigade, Royal Garrison Artillery.

Lancaster Regiment. See King's Own (Royal Lancaster Regiment).

Lancers, 5th (Royal Irish). Dublin. Depot, Woolwich.

9th (Queen's Royal) Lancers. *Photograph taken after the presentation on silver kettle-drums at Tidworth, 1913. The drum banners bearing regimental battle honours are seen below and the blue uniforms have scarlet collars and plastron (chest covering). The plumes are black and white*

Lancers, 9th (Queen's Royal). Tidworth. Depot, Woolwich.

Lancers, 12th (Prince of Wales's Royal). Norwich. Depot, Woolwich.

Lancers, 16th (The Queen's). Curragh. Depot, Woolwich.

16th (The Queen's) Lancers. *The uniform here comprises scarlet tunic, with blue collar and plastron, blue trousers, black plume.*

12th (Prince of Wales's Royal) Lancers. *The Regiment is identified here by the collar badge – crossed lances, Prince of Wales's plumes, the Roman numerals "XII" – and brass shoulder title 12L. Note also the Trumpeters' arm badge.*

17th (Duke of Cambridge's Own) Lancers. *Cap badge. The skull, crossed bones and words represent the motto "Death or Glory".*

Lancers, 17th (Duke of Cambridge's Own). Sialkot, India. Depot, Woolwich.

Lancers, 21st (Empress of India's). Rawal Pindi, India. Depot, Woolwich.

Lancing College Officers Training Corps. Shoreham, Sussex and comprising three infantry companies.

Leeds Grammar School Officers Training Corps. One infantry company, Junior Division.

Leeds Postal Telegraph Messengers' Cadet Company. See Northern Command Signal Companies (Army Troops).

Leeds Rifles. See 7th and 8th Battalions, Prince of Wales's Own (West Yorkshire Regiment).

Leeds University Officers Training Corps. One infantry company, Senior Division.

Leicestershire Regiment. Two Regular (1st and 2nd), one Special Reserve (3rd) and two Territorial Force (4th and 5th) battalions. Depot, Leicester.
1st Battalion: Fermoy.
2nd Battalion: Ranikhet, India.
3rd Battalion: Leicester.
4th Battalion: Oxford Street, Leicester with "A" Company, also at Oxford Street; "B" Company, Leicester (detachment at Anstey); "C" Company, Leicester (detachment at Syston); "D", "E", "F" and "G" Companies, Leicester; "H" Company, Wigston.
5th Battalion: Loughborough with "A" Company, Ashby-de-la-Zouch (detachment at Coalville); "B" Company, Oakham (detachments at Cottesmore, Whissendine and Uppingham); "C" Company, Melton Mowbray (detachments at Bottesford, Harby and Wymodham); "D" Company, Hinckley; "E" Company, Market Harborough (detachments at Kibworth and Fleckney); "F" Company, Mountsorrel (detachment at Woodhouse Eaves); "G" Company, Shepshed (detachments at Barrowden, Bisbrooke and Ketton); "H" Company, Loughborough.

Leicestershire Royal Horse Artillery. Territorial Force. 1 Magazine Square, Leicester. Included the North Midland Mounted Brigade Ammunition Column.

Leicestershire Yeomanry (Prince Albert's Own). Territorial Force. Leicester with "A" Squadron, Melton Mowbray (detachments at Uppingham, Rearsby, Harby and Oakham); "B" Squadron, Leicester; "C" Squadron, Loughborough (detachments at Whitwick, Mountsorrel and Leicester); "D" Squadron, Lutterworth (detachments at Market Bosworth, Market Harborough, Wigston, Ibstock and Hinckley).

Leinster Regiment. See Prince of Wales's Leinster Regiment (Royal Canadians).

Leicestershire Regiment. *1st Battalion, Aldershot, 1911. The scarlet tunics have white collars and cuffs. Two officers (on the right, front rank) wear full-dress helmets.*

Leicestershire Yeomanry (Prince Albert's Own).

Lewisham Cadet Battalion. Hill View, Grove Park, Lewisham, London.

Leys School Officers Training Corps. Cambridge. Two infantry companies, Junior Division.

Life Guards, 1st. Hyde Park, London.

Life Guards, 2nd. Regent's Park Barracks, London.

Lincoln and Leicester Brigade Company, Army Service Corps. See North Midland Divisional Transport and Supply Column.

Lincoln and Leicester Infantry Brigade. See North Midland Division.

Lincolnshire Batteries, 1st, 2nd, 3rd. See 1st North Midland Brigade, Royal Field Artillery.

Lincolnshire Regiment. Two Regular (1st and 2nd), one Special Reserve (3rd) and two Territorial Force (4th and 5th) battalions. Depot, Lincoln.

1st Battalion: Portsmouth.

2nd Battalion: Bermuda.

3rd Battalion: Lincoln.

4th Battalion: Lincoln with "A" Company, also at Lincoln; "B" Company, Grantham; "C" Company, Boston; "D" Company, Stamford; "E" Company, Lincoln; "F" Company, Spalding (detachments at Bourne and Sleaford); "G" Company, Horncastle (detachment at Woodhall Spa); "H" Company, Lincoln.

5th Battalion: Grimsby with "A" and "B" Companies, also at Grimsby; "C" Company, Spilsby (detachment at Skegness); "D" Company, Louth (detachment at North Thoresby); "E" Company, Barton; "F" Company, Alford; "G" Company, Frodingham (detachment at Brigg); "H" Company, Gainsborough.

2nd Life Guards. *Cyclist section.*

Life Guards. *In the 1st Life Guards the cord (flask-cord) running through the shoulder-belt is red. The 2nd have blue.*

Lincolnshire Yeomanry.

Lincolnshire Yeomanry. Territorial Force. Old Barracks, Lincoln with "A" Squadron, Grantham (detachments at Stamford, Bourne and Holbeach); "B" Squadron, Louth (detachments at Spilsby, Horncastle, Alford, Skegness and Boston); "C" Squadron, Lincoln (detachments at Sleaford, Gainsborough, Market Rasen and Wragby); "D" Squadron, Grimsby (detachments at Barton, Brigg, Scunthorpe and Ulceby).

Liverpool Brigade Company, Army Service Corps. See West Lancashire Divisional Transport and Supply Column.

Liverpool College Officers Training Corps. One infantry company, Junior Division.

Liverpool Infantry Brigade. See West Lancashire Division.

Liverpool Institute Officers Training Corps. One infantry company, Junior Division.

Liverpool Irish. See 8th (Irish) Battalion, King's (Liverpool Regiment).

Liverpool Regiment. See King's (Liverpool Regiment).

Liverpool Scottish. See 10th (Scottish) Battalion, King's (Liverpool Regiment).

London Airline Signal Company. See London District Signal Companies (Army Troops)

London Batteries, 1st, 2nd, 3rd (City of London). See 1st London Brigade, Royal Field Artillery (City of London).

London Batteries, 4th, 5th, 6th (County of London). See 2nd London Brigade, Royal Field Artillery.

London Batteries, 7th, 8th, 9th (County of London). See 3rd London Brigade, Royal Field Artillery.

London Batteries, 10th (Howitzer), 11th (Howitzer) (County of London). See 4th London Brigade, Royal Field Artillery (Howitzer).

London Batteries, 12th, 13th, 14th (County of London). See 5th London Brigade, Royal Field Artillery.

London Batteries, 15th, 16th, 17th (County of London). See 6th London Brigade, Royal Field Artillery.

London Batteries, 18th, 19th, 20th (County of London). See 7th London Brigade, Royal Field Artillery.

London Batteries, 21st (Howitzer), 22nd (Howitzer) (County of London). See 8th London Brigade, Royal Field Artillery (Howitzer).

London Brigade Companies, Army Service Corps, 1st, 2nd, 3rd. See 1st London Divisional Transport and Supply Column.

London Brigade Companies, Army Service Corps, 4th, 5th, 6th. See 2nd London Divisional Transport and Supply Column.

1st London (City of London) Brigade, Royal Field Artillery. *Commanding- Officer Lieutenant-Colonel J. Stollery.*

London Brigade, Royal Field Artillery (City of London), 1st. Territorial Force. Handel Street, Bloomsbury and comprising 1st City of London, 2nd City of London, 3rd City of London Batteries and Ammunition Column.

London Brigade, Royal Field Artillery, 2nd. Territorial Force. Royal Arsenal, Woolwich with 4th County of London and 5th County of London Batteries at Beresford Street, Woolwich; 6th County of London Battery, Eltham and Ammunition Column, Beresford Street. The 1st Woolwich Cadet Corps at High Street, Plumstead was affiliated.

London Brigade, Royal Field Artillery, 3rd. Territorial Force. Leonard Street, Finsbury with 7th County of London, 8th County of London, 9th County of London Batteries and Ammunition Column.

4th London Brigade, Royal Field Artillery. *Drivers and trumpeters at camp in Kent, 1910. Note the leather and steel leg-protectors worn on the right legs of the drivers when mounted.*

London Brigade, Royal Field Artillery (Howitzer), 4th. Territorial Force. Ennersdale Road, Lewisham with 10th County of London (Howitzer), 11th County of London (Howitzer) Batteries and Ammunition Column.

London Brigade, Royal Field Artillery, 5th. Territorial Force. 76 Lower Kennington Lane, Lambeth with 12th County of London and 13th County of London Batteries, also at 76 Lower Kennington Lane; 14th County of London Battery, Porteous Road, Paddington and Ammunition Column, 76 Lower Kennington Lane.

London Brigade, Royal Field Artillery, 6th. Territorial Force. 105 Holland Road, Brixton with 15th County of London, 16th County of London, 17th County of London Batteries and Ammunition Column.

5th London Brigade, Royal Field Artillery. *Cap badge.*

6th London Brigade, Royal Field Artillery. *"B" Sub-Section, 16th County of London Battery on Salisbury Plain*

London Brigade, Royal Field Artillery, 7th. Territorial Force. High Street, Fulham with 18th County of London Battery, also at High Street, Fulham; 19th County of London Battery, Wood Lane, Shepherd's Bush; 20th County of London Battery and Ammunition Column, High Street, Fulham.

London Brigade, Royal Field Artillery (Howitzer) 8th. Territorial Force. "Oaklands", St Margaret's Road, Woolwich with 21st County of London (Howitzer); 22nd County of London (Howitzer) Batteries and Ammunition Column.

London District Signal Companies. *The London Wireless Signal Company in camp at Worthing, 1913.*

London Brigade, Royal Garrison Artillery. Territorial Force. Offord Road, Islington with 1st and 2nd London Heavy Batteries, each with its own ammunition column.

London Cable Signal Company. See London District Signal Companies (Army Troops).

London Clearing Hospitals, 1st, 2nd. Territorial Force. Duke of York's Headquarters, Chelsea.

London District Signal Companies (Army Troops). Territorial Force. Palmers Street, Westminster with London Wireless Signal Company, London Cable Signal Company and London Airline Signal Company.

London Division, 1st. Territorial Force. Frier's House, New Broad Street.

1st London Infantry Brigade: Frier's House, New Broad Street. Battalions – 1st, 2nd, 3rd, 4th London.

2nd London Infantry Brigade: Buckingham Gate, Westminster. Battalions – 5th, 6th, 7th, 8th London.

3rd London Infantry Brigade: Buckingham Gate, Westminster. Battalions – 9th, 10th, 11th, 12th London.

Royal Artillery: Frier's House, New Broad Street. 1st, 2nd, 3rd, 4th (Howitzer) London Brigades, Royal Field Artillery. 1st London Royal Garrison Artillery.

Royal Engineers: 10 Victoria Park Square, Bethnal Green. 1st, 2nd London Field Companies; 1st London Divisional Signal Company.

Army Service Corps: Charles Street, Plumstead. 1st London Divisional Transport and Supply Column.

Royal Army Medical Corps: 1st, 2nd, 3rd London Field Ambulances.

Attached: London Wireless, Cable and Airline Signal Companies; Honourable Artillery Company (Infantry).

London Division, 2nd. Territorial Force. Duke of York's Headquarters, Chelsea.
4th London Infantry Brigade: Buckingham Gate, Westminster. Battalions – 13th, 14th, 15th, 16th London.
5th London Infantry Brigade: Buckingham Gate, Westminster. Battalions – 17th, 18th, 19th, 20th London.
6th London Infantry Brigade: Duke of York's Headquarters, Chelsea. Battalions – 21st, 22nd, 23rd, 24th London.
Royal Artillery: Duke of York's Headquarters, Chelsea. 5th, 6th, 7th, 8th (Howitzer) London Brigades, Royal Field Artillery; 2nd London Royal Garrison Artillery.
Royal Engineers: Duke of York's Headquarters, Chelsea. 3rd, 4th London Field Companies; 2nd London Divisional Signal Company.
Army Service Corps: Duke of York's Headquarters. 2nd London Divisional Transport and Supply Column.
Royal Army Medical Corps: 4th, 5th, 6th London Field Ambulances.
Attached: 28th London Regiment.

London Divisional Engineers, 1st. Territorial Force. 10 Victoria Park Square, Bethnal Green with 1st and 2nd London Field Companies.

London Divisional Engineers, 2nd. Territorial Force. Duke of York's Headquarters, Chelsea with 3rd and 4th London Field Companies. A cadet unit designated Royal Engineer Cadets (2nd London Division) was affiliated.

London Divisional Signal Company, 1st. Territorial Force. 10 Victoria Park Square, Bethnal Green with No. Section, No.2 (1st London) Section, No.3 (2nd London) Section, No.4 (3rd London) Section.

London Divisional Signal Company, 2nd. Territorial Force. Duke of York's Headquarters, Chelsea with No.1 Section, No.2 (4th London) Section, No.3 (5th London) Section, No.4 (6th London) Section.

London Divisional Transport and Supply Column, 1st. Territorial Force. Charles Street, Plumstead with Headquarters, 1st, 2nd and 3rd London Brigade Companies.

London Divisional Transport and Supply Column, 2nd. Territorial Force. Duke of York's Headquarters, Chelsea with Headquarters Company, 4th, 5th and 6th London Brigade Companies.

London Electrical Engineers. Territorial Force. Six companies at 46 Regency Street, Westminster.

London Field Ambulances (City of London), 1st, 2nd, 3rd. Territorial Force. Duke of York's Headquarters, Chelsea.

***2nd London Divisional Signal Company.** Prior to 1913, each of the fourteen Territorial Force Divisional Engineer formations included a Telegraph Company. In that year these were removed and organised separately as Divisional Signal Companies.*

***1st London Divisional Transport and Supply Column.** Seen here at annual camp, the vehicle in the photograph has been hired, complete with civilian driver.*

London Field Ambulance, 4th. Territorial Force. School of Ambulance, Brookhill Road, Woolwich. There were also detachments at Dartford and Erith.

London Field Ambulance, 5th. Territorial Force. 159 Greenwich Road, Greenwich.

London Field Ambulance, 6th. Territorial Force. Duke of York's Headquarters, Chelsea.

London Field Companies, 1st, 2nd. See 1st London Divisional Engineers.

London Field Companies, 3rd, 4th. See 2nd London Divisional Engineers.

London General Hospitals (City of London), 1st, 2nd. Territorial Force. Duke of York's Headquarters, Chelsea.

London General Hospital, 3rd. Territorial Force. 3 Henry Street, Holborn.

London General Hospital, 4th. Territorial Force. Duke of York's Headquarters, Chelsea.

London Horse Artillery, 1st and 2nd City of. See Honourable Artillery Company.

London Infantry Brigade, 1st, 2nd, 3rd. See 1st London Division.

London Infantry Brigade, 4th, 5th, 6th. See 2nd London Division.

London Irish Rifles. See 18th Battalion, London Regiment.

London Mounted Brigade. Territorial Force. Duke of York's Headquarters, Chelsea. Included City of London, 1st and 3rd County of London Yeomanries; "A" Battery, Honourable Artillery Company. The 2nd County of London Yeomanry and "B" Battery, Honourable Artillery Company were attached for training.

London Mounted Brigade Ammunition Column. See Honourable Artillery Company.

London Mounted Brigade Field Ambulance. Territorial Force. 3 Henry Street, Gray's Inn Road, Holborn.

London Mounted Brigade Signal Troop. Territorial Force. Duke of York's Headquarters, Chelsea.

London Mounted Brigade Transport and Supply Column. Territorial Force. 51 Calthorpe Street, Holborn.

London Regiment. Territorial Force. Recruited within the City and Greater (County of) London areas, this Territorial Force regiment comprised twenty-six battalions, largest peace-time infantry formation within the British Army. However, each battalion constituted an independent regiment. This was recognised in 1922 when "Battalion" was replaced by "Regiment" within each regimental title. When the London Regiment was created in 1908, it was intended to include the Honourable Artillery Company (*qv*) and Inns of Court Volunteers (*qv*) as 26th and 27th Battalions respectively. But this was not acceptable and these, certainly in the case of the HAC, ancient regiments, remained outside (note vacant numbers) of the new formation. The first eight battalions were administered by the City of London Territorial Force Association, and those from 9th to 28th, by the County TFA. The full title for each battalion included "City/County of

1st (City of London) Battalion, London Regiment (Royal Fusiliers). *Officers, Malta. The Battalion had sailed from Southampton on 4 September, 1914.*

2nd (City of London) Battalion, London Regiment (Royal Fusiliers). *Colours outside the battalion's Tufton Street headquarters. The uniform – scarlet tunics, blue collars and cuffs, fur racoon-skin caps with white hackles – and badges are those of the Royal Fusiliers.*

London" in brackets, after the battalion's numerical designation. Sub-titles, if any, were placed at the end – eg: 1st (City of London) Battalion, The London Regiment (Royal Fusiliers). As with other independent Territorial Force regiments and battalions, the London Regiment had no direct affiliation to any regular formation. Although all, having prior to 1908 been part of a Regimental system, retained a strong association, badges, uniform, traditions etc. with their former parent formation.

1st (City of London) Battalion (Royal Fusiliers): Handel Street, Bloomsbury with "A", "B" and "C" Companies, also at Handel Street; "D" and "E" Companies, 15 Battersea Square; "F", "G" and "H" Companies, Handel Street.

2nd (City of London) Battalion (Royal Fusiliers): 9 Tufton Street, Westminster.

3rd (City of London) Battalion (Royal Fusiliers): 21 Edward Street, St Pancras. There was also a detachment at 207 Harrow Road, Paddington.

4th (City of London) Battalion (Royal Fusiliers): 112 Shaftesbury Street, Shoreditch.

5th (City of London) Battalion (London Rifle Brigade): 130 Bunhill Row, Finsbury. The Coopers' Company School Cadet Corps at The Guildhall was affiliated.

6th (City of London) Battalion (Rifles): 57a Farringdon Road, Finsbury. The Battalion also had a cadet company, designated 1st Cadet Company, at 67a Farringdon Street.

7th (City of London) Battalion: 24 Sun Street, Finsbury Square with "A", "B" and "C" Companies, also at 24 Sun Street; "D" and "E" Companies, 36

7th (City of London) Battalion, London Regiment. *Cap badge. The white-metal number seven on a brass grenade is the source of the battalion's nickname "The Shiny Seventh".*

8th (City of London) Battalion, London Regiment (Post Office Rifles). *The cap badge includes two battle honours unique within the Territorial Force. The Battalion (as 24th Middlesex Rifle Volunteer Corps) provided postal workers for the Army Post Office during the Egyptian Campaign of 1882 and as early as 1899 in South Africa.*

Elm Grove, Hammersmith; "F", "G" and "H" Companies, 24 Sun Street.

8th (City of London) Battalion (Post Office Rifles): 130 Bunhill Row, Finsbury.

9th (County of London) Battalion (Queen Victoria's Rifles): 56 Davies Street, Westminster.

10th (County of London) Battalion (Hackney): 49 The Grove, Hackney. The Rutland Street School (LCC) Cadet Corps in Stepney, and another unit of three companies at the LCC School, Homerton Row, Homerton were affiliated.

11th (County of London) Battalion (Finsbury Rifles): 17 Penton Street, Pentonville.

12th (County of London) Battalion (The Rangers): Chenies Street, Bedford Square, Holborn.

13th (County of London) Battalion (Kensington): Iverna Gardens, Kensington. The St Peter's Cadet Company at 69 Ladbroke Grove, Holland Park and Kensington and Hammersmith Navy League Boys' Brigade at 34 Scarsdale Villas, Kensington were affiliated.

14th (County of London) Battalion (London Scottish): 59 Buckingham Gate, Westminster.

15th (County of London) Battalion (Prince of Wales's Own Civil Service Rifles): Somerset House, Strand, Westminster. There was also a cadet unit, the 2nd (Civil Service) Cadet Battalion, with headquarters in the East Wing, Somerset House.

16th (County of London) Battalion (Queen's Westminster Rifles): Queen's Hall, 58 Buckingham Gate, Westminster. There was also a cadet corps designated Queen's Westminster Cadet Corps at Westminster City School, Palace Street.

17th (County of London) Battalion (Poplar and Stepney Rifles): 66 Tredegar Road, Bow.

18th (County of London) Battalion (London Irish Rifles): Duke of York's Headquarters, Chelsea.

19th (County of London) Battalion (St Pancras): 76 High Street, Camden Town.

20th (County of London) Battalion (Blackheath and Woolwich): Holly Hedge House, Blackheath. There was also a detachment at Woolwich.

21st (County of London) Battalion (First Surrey Rifles): 4 Flodden Road, Camberwell. The South London Cadets at Arch 338, Medlar Street, Camberwell was affiliated.

22nd (County of London) Battalion (The Queen's): 2 Jamaica Road, Bermondsey.

23rd (County of London) Battalion: 27 St John's Hill, Clapham Junction. The St Thomas's (Wandsworth) Cadet Corps at West Hill, Wandsworth was affiliated.

24th (County of London) Battalion (The Queen's): 71 New Street, Southwark.

25th (County of London) Cyclist Battalion: Fulham House, Putney Bridge.

28th (County of London) Battalion (Artists Rifles): Duke's Road, St Pancras.

1st Cadet Battalion: 31 Union Street, Southwark. Seven companies.

10th (County of London) Battalion, London Regiment (Hackney). *Cap badge. The tower seen in the centre of the badge is that of St Augustine's Church and the motto means Justice in our Tower. Both are from the seal (later arms) of Hackney.*

13th (County of London) Battalion, London Regiment (Kensington). *The Battalion lines the road during a royal visit to South London in 1911. The uniforms are grey with scarlet facings.*

13th (County of London) Battalion, London Regiment (Kensington). *The cap badge featured the arms of Kensington.*

14th (County of London) Battalion, London Regiment (London Scottish). *The uniform is grey (known as Elcho grey) with blue facings.*

14th (County of London) Battalion, London Regiment (London Scottish). *Cap badge. Scotland is well represented in St Andrew's Cross, Lion of Scotland and thistles, and the Regiment by its South Africa 1900–02 battle honour and motto Strike Sure.*

15th (County of London) Battalion, London Regiment (Prince of Wales's Own Civil Service Rifles). *The band wear full-dress uniforms – grey with blue facings.*

22nd (County of London) Battalion, London Regiment (The Queen's). *The cap badge is the Paschal Lamb of the Queen's (Royal West Surrey Regiment).*

23rd (County of London) Battalion, London Regiment. *Cap badge. Associated with the Regiment since 1873, the battalion's badge was based on that of the East Surrey Regiment.*

24th (County of London) Battalion, London Regiment (The Queen's). *Badges and uniform – scarlet tunic with blue facings – are those of the Queen's (Royal West Surrey Regiment).*

25th (County of London) Cyclist Battalion, London Regiment. *Clearly marked with the battalion's designation, this vehicle returning from annual camp in 1913 carries cycles and stretchers.*

London Rifle Brigade. See 5th Battalion, London Regiment.

London Royal Garrison Artillery, 1st, 2nd. See London Brigade, Royal Garrison Artillery.

London Sanitary Company (City of London), 1st. Territorial Force. Duke of York's Headquarters, Chelsea.

London Sanitary Company, 2nd. Territorial Force. Duke of York's Headquarters, Chelsea.

London Scottish. See 14th Battalion, London Regiment.

London Wireless Signal Company. See London District Signal Companies (Army Troops).

London Yeomanry, City of. See City of London Yeomanry (Rough Riders).

London Yeomanry, 1st County of. See 1st County of London Yeomanry (Middlesex, Duke of Cambridge's Hussars).

London Yeomanry, 2nd County of. See 2nd County of London Yeomanry (Westminster Dragoons).

London Yeomanry, 3rd County of. See 3rd County of London Yeomanry (Sharpshooters).

Lord Robert's Boys. See 1st City of London Cadet Battalion (Lord Robert's Boys).

Loretto School Officers Training Corps. Musselburgh. Two infantry companies, Junior Division.

Lothian Infantry Brigade. Territorial Force. 23 Rutland Square, Edinburgh. Battalions – 4th, 5th, 8th, 9th Royal Scots with 6th, 7th Royal Scots and 8th Highland Light Infantry attached.

Lothian Regiment. See Royal Scots (Lothian Regiment).

Lothians and Border Horse. Territorial Force. 7 Wemyss Place, Edinburgh with "A" Squadron, Dunbar (detachments at Earlston, Greenlaw, North Berwick, Musselburgh, Lauder, Kelso, Berwick, Haddington, Tranent, East Linton, Duns and Coldstream); "B" Company, Edinburgh (detachments at Musselburgh, Dalkeith, Eskbank, Penicuik, Gorebridge, Lasswade and Loanhead); "C" Company, Hawick (detachments at Galashiels, Jedburgh, Innerleithen, Kelso, Melrose, Newcastleton, Peebles, Selkirk, Stow, Yetholm and St Boswells); "D" Squadron, Edinburgh (detachments at Linlithgow, Bathgate, Broxburn, Hopetoun, Mid Calder, South Queensferry, Ratho and Winchburgh).

Lovat's Scouts Yeomanry. *The regimental badge of a buck's head (from the crest of Lord Lovat) is being worn here in the bonnets, on the collars, sporrans and Pipe-Major's cross-belt.*

***Lothians and Border Horse.** The cap badge – a garb, or wheat-sheaf – is said to be symbolic of the Border farmlands where the Regiment recruited.*

Louth School Officers Training Corps. One infantry company, Junior Division.

Lovat's Scouts Yeomanry, 1st. Territorial Force. Beauly with "A" Squadron, Roy Bridge (detachments at Fort Augustus, Loch Laggan, Spean Bridge, Glenfinnan, Sheil Bridge and Fort William); "B" Squadron, Lochmaddy (detachments at Bayhead, Sollas, Craegorry, Clachan, Torlam and Daliburgh); "C" Squadron, Skeabost (detachments at Uig, Portree, Duntulm, Staffin, Glendale, Waternish, Dunvegan and Braes); "D" Squadron, Beauly (detachments at Struy, Convinth, Clunes, Beaufort, Dores, Errogie, Whitebridge and Glenurquhart).

Lovat's Scouts Yeomanry, 2nd. Territorial Force. Beauly with "E" Squadron, Kyle of Lochalsh (detachments at Armadale, Aultbea, Glenelg, Strathcarron, Dundonnell, Strathcannaird, Ullapool, Achiltibuie and Achnasheen); "F" Squadron, Dornoch (detachments at Brora, Helmsdale, Scourie, Tongue, Melness, Bettyhill, Dunbeath, Latheron and Berriedale); "G" Squadron, Alness (detachments at Bonar Bridge, Lairg, Ardgay, Rosehall, Fearn, Edderton, Tain and Contin); "H" Squadron, Inverness (detachments at Nairn, Laggan Bridge, Aviemore, Nethy Bridge, Munlochy, Cawdor, Glenferness and Tomatin).

Lowland Brigade, Royal Field Artillery, 1st. Territorial Force. 30 Grindlay Street, Edinburgh with 1st and 2nd City of Edinburgh Batteries, Midlothian Battery and Ammunition Column.

Lowland Brigade, Royal Field Artillery, 2nd. Territorial Force. Irvine with 1st Ayrshire Battery, also at Irvine; 2nd Ayrshire Battery, Kilmarnock; Kirkcudbrightshire Battery, Kirckudbright and Ammunition Column, Ardrossan.

Lowland Brigade, Royal Field Artillery, 3rd. Territorial Force. 8 Newton Terrace, Charing Cross, Glasgow with 1st City of Glasgow Battery, Berkeley Street, Glasgow; 2nd City of Glasgow Battery, Percy Street, Maryhill, Glasgow; 3rd City of Glasgow Battery, Keppochhill, Springburn, Glasgow and Ammunition Column, Percy Street, Maryhill, Glasgow.

Lowland Brigade, Royal Field Artillery (Howitzer), 4th. Territorial Force. 8 Newton Terrace, Charing Cross, Glasgow with 4th City of Glasgow (Howitzer) Battery, Butterbiggins Road, Govanhill, Glasgow; 5th City of Glasgow (Howitzer) Battery, Elder Street, Govan, Glasgow and Ammunition Column, Butterbiggins Road, Govanhill, Glasgow.

Lowland Clearing Hospital. Territorial Force. Glasgow.

Lowland Division. Territorial Force. 7 West George Street, Glasgow.

South Scottish Infantry Brigade: 7 Wellington Square, Ayr. Battalions – 4th, 5th Royal Scots Fusiliers; 4th, 5th King's Own Scottish Borderers.

Scottish Rifle Brigade: 34 Robertson Street, Glasgow. Battalions – 5th, 6th, 7th, 8th Cameronians.

Highland Light Infantry Brigade: 34 Robertson Street, Glasgow. Battalions – 5th, 6th, 7th, 8th Highland Light Infantry.

Royal Artillery: Newton Terrace, Charing Cross, Glasgow. 1st, 2nd, 3rd, 4th (Howitzer) Lowland Brigades, Royal Field Artillery; Lowland Royal Garrison Artillery.

Royal Engineers: Rutherglen. 1st, 2nd Lowland Field Companies; Lowland Divisional Signal Company.

Army Service Corps: 22 Lochburn Road, Maryhill, Glasgow. Lowland Divisional Transport and Supply Column.

Royal Army Medical Corps: 1st, 2nd, 3rd Lowland Field Ambulances.

Attached: Scottish Wireless, Cable and Airline Signal Companies; 1st Highland Field Company.

Lowland Divisional Engineers. Territorial Force. Rutherglen with 1st Lowland Field Company at Coatdyke, Coatbridge (detachment at Airdrie), 2nd Lowland Field Company, Rutherglen (detachments at Shettleston and Motherwell).

Lowland Divisional Signal Company. Territorial Force. Rutherglen with No.1 Section, No.2 (Scottish Rifle) Section, No.3 (Highland Light Infantry) Section, No.4 (South Scottish) Section.

Lowland Divisional Transport and Supply Column. Territorial Force. 22 Lochburn Road, Maryhill,

Glasgow with 1st (Headquarters) Company, also at 22 Lochburn Road; 2nd Company, Brandon Terrace, Edinburgh; 3rd (Scottish Rifle Brigade) Company, Motherwell (detachment at Rutherglen) and 4th (Highland Light Infantry Brigade) Company, Gilbert Street, Yorkhill, Glasgow.

Lowland Field Ambulances, 1st, 2nd. Territorial Force. Yorkhill Parade, Yorkhill, Glasgow.

Lowland Field Ambulance, 3rd. Territorial Force. Easter Road Barracks, Edinburgh.

Lowland Field Companies, 1st, 2nd. See Lowland Divisional Engineers.

Lowland Mounted Brigade. Territorial Force. 10 Dublin Street, Edinburgh. Included Ayrshire, Lanarkshire, Lothians and Border Horse Yeomanries; Ayrshire Royal Horse Artillery. The Royal Glasgow Yeomanry was attached for training.

Lowland Mounted Brigade Ammunition Column. See Ayrshire Royal Horse Artillery.

Lowland Mounted Brigade Field Ambulance. Territorial Force. Yorkhill Parade, Yorkhill, Glasgow.

Lowland Mounted Brigade Signal Troop. Territorial Force. 10 Dublin Street, Edinburgh.

Lowland Mounted Brigade Transport and Supply Column. Territorial Force. Brandon Terrace, Edinburgh.

Lowland Royal Garrison Artillery (City of Edinburgh). Territorial Force. McDonald Road, Edinburgh.

Loyal North Lancashire Regiment. Two Regular (1st and 2nd), one Special Reserve (3rd) and two Territorial Force (4th and 5th) battalions. Depot, Preston.

1st Battalion: Tournay Barracks, Aldershot.

2nd Battalion: Bangalore, India.

3rd Battalion: Preston.

4th Battalion: 97 Avenham Lane, Preston with "A" Company, also at 97 Avenham Lane; "B" Company, Longridge; "C" Company, Preston (detachment at Bamber Bridge); "D" Company, Preston (detachment at Leyland); "E" Company, Lytham; "F" Company, Horwich; "G" and "H" Companies, Chorley. The Arnold House School Cadet Corps at South Shore, Blackpool was affiliated.

5th Battalion: Bolton with "A", "B" and "C" Companies, also at Bolton; "D" Company, Farnworth; "E" Company, Bolton; "F" Company, Astley Bridge; "G" Company, Hindley; "H" Company, Little Hulton.

Loyal Suffolk Hussars. See Suffolk Yeomanry (The Duke of York's Own Loyal Suffolk Hussars).

Lymington Cadet Corps. See 7th Battalion, Hampshire Regiment.

Lowland Mounted Brigade Transport and Supply Column. *Ashkirk, Selkirkshire, 1911.*

M

Macclesfield Grammar School Cadet Corps. See 7th Battalion, Cheshire Regiment.

Macclesfield Industrial School Cadet Corps. See 7th Battalion, Cheshire Regiment.

Magdalene Cadet Company. Magdalene College Club, Wyndham Road, Camberwell, London.

Maidstone Grammar School Officers Training Corps. One infantry company, Junior Division.

Malta Artillery. See Royal Malta Artillery.

Malta Regiment of Militia. See King's Own Malta Regiment of Militia.

Malvern College Officers Training Corps. Three infantry companies, Junior Division.

Manchester Artillery. See 2nd East Lancashire Brigade, Royal Field Artillery (The Manchester Artillery).

Manchester Brigade Company, Army Service Corps. See East Lancashire Divisional Transport and Supply Column.

Manchester Grammar School Officers Training Corps. One infantry company, Junior Division.

Manchester Infantry Brigade. See East Lancashire Division.

Manchester Regiment. Two Regular (1st and 2nd), two Special Reserve (3rd and 4th) and six Territorial Force (5th to 10th) battalions. Depot, Ashton-under-Lyne.

1st Battalion: Jullundur, India.

2nd Battalion: Curragh.

3rd Battalion: Ashton-under-Lyne.

4th Battalion: Ashton-under-Lyne.

5th Battalion: Bank Street, Wigan with "A" to "E" Companies, also at Bank Street; "F" Company, Patricroft; "G" Company, Leigh; "H" Company, Atherton.

6th Battalion: 3 Stretford Road, Hulme, Manchester.

7th Battalion: Burlington Street, Manchester.

8th (Ardwick) Battalion: Ardwick.

9th Battalion: Ashton-under-Lyne.

10th Battalion: Oldham.

1st Cadet Battalion: Poplar Street, Viaduct Street, Ardwick. Affiliated to the Manchester Infantry Brigade.

2nd Cadet Battalion: Coldhurst, Oldham. Affiliated to 10th Battalion.

Manchester University Officers Training Corps. One signal section and three companies of infantry, Senior Division.

Manor Park Cadet Company. See 4th Battalion, Essex Regiment.

Manchester Regiment. *7th Battalion.*

Manchester Regiment. *7th Battalion. Although the Regiment as a whole took into use the fleur-de-lys as a cap badge in 1922 – this in commemoration of the services of the old 63rd (later 1st Battalion) in the West Indies – the 7th had itself adopted the device many years before. The jacket is scarlet with white facings.*

Manchester Regiment. 9th Battalion. Although shoulder titles are clear in most cases, confirmation that this photo is of the 9th Manchesters (the cap badge places the Regiment) is the chalked billet-markings on the wall to the right.

Marlborough College Officers Training Corps. Six infantry companies, Junior Division.

Marner School (LCC) Cadet Company. Headquarters at the Guildhall, London.

Merchant Taylors' School Officers Training Corps. Charterhouse Square, London. Two infantry companies, Junior Division.

Merchiston Castle School Officers Training Corps. Edinburgh. Two infantry companies, Junior Division.

Merioneth and Montgomery Battalion. See 7th (Merioneth & Montgomery) Battalion, Royal Welsh Fusiliers.

Middlesex Brigade Company, Army Service Corps. See Home Counties Divisional Transport and Supply Column.

Middlesex Infantry Brigade. See Home Counties Division.

Middlesex Regiment. See Duke of Cambridge's Own (Middlesex Regiment).

Middlesex Yeomanry. See 1st County of London Yeomanry (Middlesex, Duke of Cambridge's Hussars).

Midlothian Battery. See 1st Lowland Brigade, Royal Field Artillery.

Military Foot Police. Aldershot.

Military Knights of Windsor. The August, 1914 *Army List* records eleven officers under the heading of "Royal Foundation" and four under "Lower Foundation".

Military Mounted Police. Aldershot.

Military Provost Staff Corps. Attached to military prisons.

Mill Hill School Officers Training Corps. Mill Hill, North-West London. Two infantry companies, Junior Division.

Monkton Combe School Officers Training Corps. Near Bath, Somerset. One infantry company, Junior Division.

Monmouthshire Batteries, 1st, 2nd, 3rd. See 4th Welsh Brigade, Royal Field Artillery.

Monmouthshire Regiment. Territorial Force. Comprised three battalions.

1st Battalion: Stow Hill, Newport with "A"

Above: 1st Life Guards.

Right: 6th Dragoon Guards (Carabiniers).

Below: 1st (King's) Dragoon Guards.

Above: 7th (Princess Royal's) Dragoon Guards.

Above right: 1st (Royal) Dragoons.

Right 2nd Dragoons (Royal Scots Greys).

Harry Payne
The 7th Hussars entering London for road duty on the occasion of a Royal Visit

Above left: 3rd (King's Own) Hussars.

Above: 5th (Royal Irish) Lancers.

Left: 7th (Queen's Own) Hussars.

Above left: 8th (King's Royal Irish) Hussars.

Above: 10th (Prince of Wales's Own Royal) Hussars.

Left: 11th (Prince Albert's Own) Hussars.

12th LANCERS (Prince of Wales's).

Above: 12th (Prince of Wales's Royal) Lancers.

Above right: 17th (Duke of Cambridge's Own) Lancers.

Right: 21st (Empress of India's) Lancers.

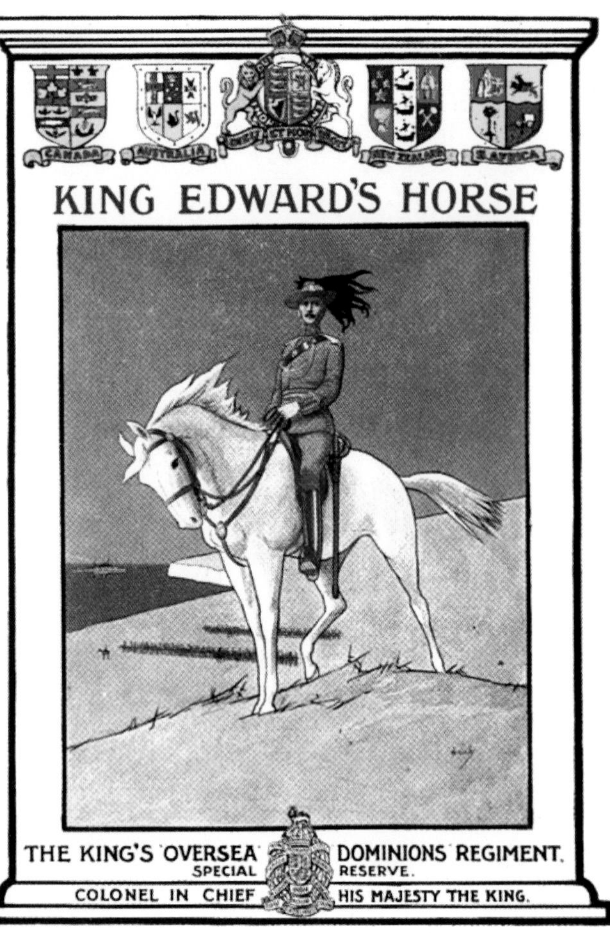

THE GRENADIER GUARDS,
"Good Bye, and Good Luck"

Above left: King Edward's Horse (The King's Oversea Dominions Regiment).

Left: Royal Flying Corps.

Above: Grenadier Guards.

Above left: Coldstream Guards.

Above right: Scots Guards.

Left: Irish Guards.

Below: 7th London Brigade, Royal Field Artillery.

Above: Royal Horse Artillery.

Below: Royal Field Artillery.

Above: Royal Scots (Lothian Regiment).

Below: Royal Fusiliers (City of London Regiment).

THE ROYAL WARWICKSHIRE REGIMENT.
The Drum-Major in Review Order.
Arthur Chidley

Above: Royal Warwickshire Regiment.

Above right: King's (Liverpool Regiment).

Right: Prince of Wales's Own (West Yorkshire Regiment).

Below: Bedfordshire Regiment.

THE LANCASHIRE FUSILIERS.
The Guard.

Above: *Lancashire Fusiliers.*

Left: Royal Welsh Fusiliers.

Below: Royal Scots Fusiliers.

Top left: South Wales Borderers.

Top right: Gloucestershire Regiment.

Above: King's Own Scottish Borderers.

Left: King's Royal Rifle Corps.

Above: 4th Battalion, King's Own (Yorkshire Light Infantry).

Right: Black Watch (Royal Highlanders).

Below: The Honourable Artillery Company.

Above: 1st Cadet Battalion, King's Royal Rifle Corps.

Below left: Seaforth Highlanders (Ross-shire Buffs, the Duke of Albany's).

Below right: Rifle Brigade (The Prince Consort's Own).

THE SEAFORTH HIGHLANDERS.
Harry Payne
Piper and Bandsman
Review order.

THE MANCHESTER REGIMENT,
Changing Guard.

Above: Manchester Regiment.

Below: Queen's Own Cameron Highlanders.

THE QUEEN'S OWN,
CAMERON HIGHLANDERS.

A Charge up the hill.

THE QUEEN'S

Hoping you receive this

A Few Smart Men Wanted for
The LONDON
CYCLISTS
25th (C. OF L.) CYCLIST BN.
THE LONDON REGIMENT
ERNEST IBBETSON '12
HEADQUARTERS AT
Fulham House, Putney Bridge, S.W.
Local Companies in North and South-East London.
For Particulars, apply to the Orderly Room, Fulham House, Putney Bridge.
GOD SAVE THE KING

Top: 24th (County of London) Battalion, the London Regiment (The Queen's).

Above: 14th (County of London) Battalion, the London Regiment (London Scottish).

Left: 25th (County of London) Cyclist Battalion, the London Regiment.

Company, Newport (detachment at Caerleon; "B" Company, Newport; "C" Company, Newport (detachment at Rogerstone); "D" Company, Newport; "E" Company, Chepstow (detachments at Sudbrook and Itton Court); "F" Company, Aberbargoed; "G" Company, Rhymney (detachment at New Tredegar); "H" Company, Blackwood (detachment at Ynysddu).

2nd Battalion: Osborne Road, Pontypool with "A" Company, Pontypool (detachment at Goytre); "B" Company, Pontypool; "C" Company, Pontypool (detachment at Garndiffaith); "D" Company, Abercarn; "E" Company, Blaenavon; "F" Company, Llanhilleth; "G" Company, Coleford (detachment at Usk); "H" Company, Crumlin.

3rd Battalion: Abergavenny with "A" Company, also at Abergavenny; "B" Company, Ebbw Vale; "C" Company, Cwm; "D" Company, Sirhowy; "E" and "F" Companies, Abertillery; "G" Company, Tredegar; "H" Company, Blaina.

1st Cadet Battalion: Headquarters at Tal-y-Coed. Comprised six companies affiliated: 1st Battalion (one, Chepstow), 2nd Battalion (three, Abercarn, Monmouth Grammar School and Usk) and 3rd Battalion (two, Abergavenny and Ebbw Vale).

Manchester Regiment. *The cap badge for all battalions except the 7th prior to 1922 was the arms of the City of Manchester. Seen here as it appeared in the centre of the officers' full-dress blue-cloth helmets, the badge was unpopular among the men who thought it gave them the appearance of "corporation tram drivers".*

Monmouthshire Regiment. *1st Battalion at Bow Street, near Aberystwyth in 1910. The uniforms are green with black facings and the cap badges white metal Dragons.*

Monmouthshire Royal Engineers Militia. See Royal Monmouthshire Royal Engineers Militia.

Montgomeryshire Yeomanry. Territorial Force. Welshpool with "A" Squadron, Llanfyllin (detachments at Meifod, Llanrhaiadr, Llanfihangel, Llangedwyn, Trefonen, Llanfair and Llansantffraid); "B" Squadron, Welshpool (detachments at Guilsfield, Castle Caereinion, Four Crosses, Chirbury, Berriew, Trewern and Forden); "C" Squadron, Newtown (detachments at Church Stoke, Caersws, New Mills, Llanbrynmair, Montgomery, Trefeglwys, Bettws, Cemmes Road, Dolfor and Llangurig) "D" Squadron, Llandrindod Wells (detachments at Llanidloes, Builth Wells, Rhayader, Llanbister, Knighton and Hay-on-Wye).

Morayshire Battalion. See 6th (Morayshire) Battalion, Seaforth Highlanders (Ross-shire Buffs, The Duke of Albany's).

Morpeth Grammar School Cadet Company. See 7th Battalion, Northumberland Fusiliers.

Morrison's Academy Officers Training Corps. Crieff. One infantry company, Junior Division.

Munster Fusiliers. See Royal Munster Fusiliers.

Monmouthshire Regiment. *1st Battalion. Recruits outside "H" Company Headquarters at Blackwood in the early months of the war. The building has changed little and today the Red Dragon and battalion name can still be seen above the entrance.*

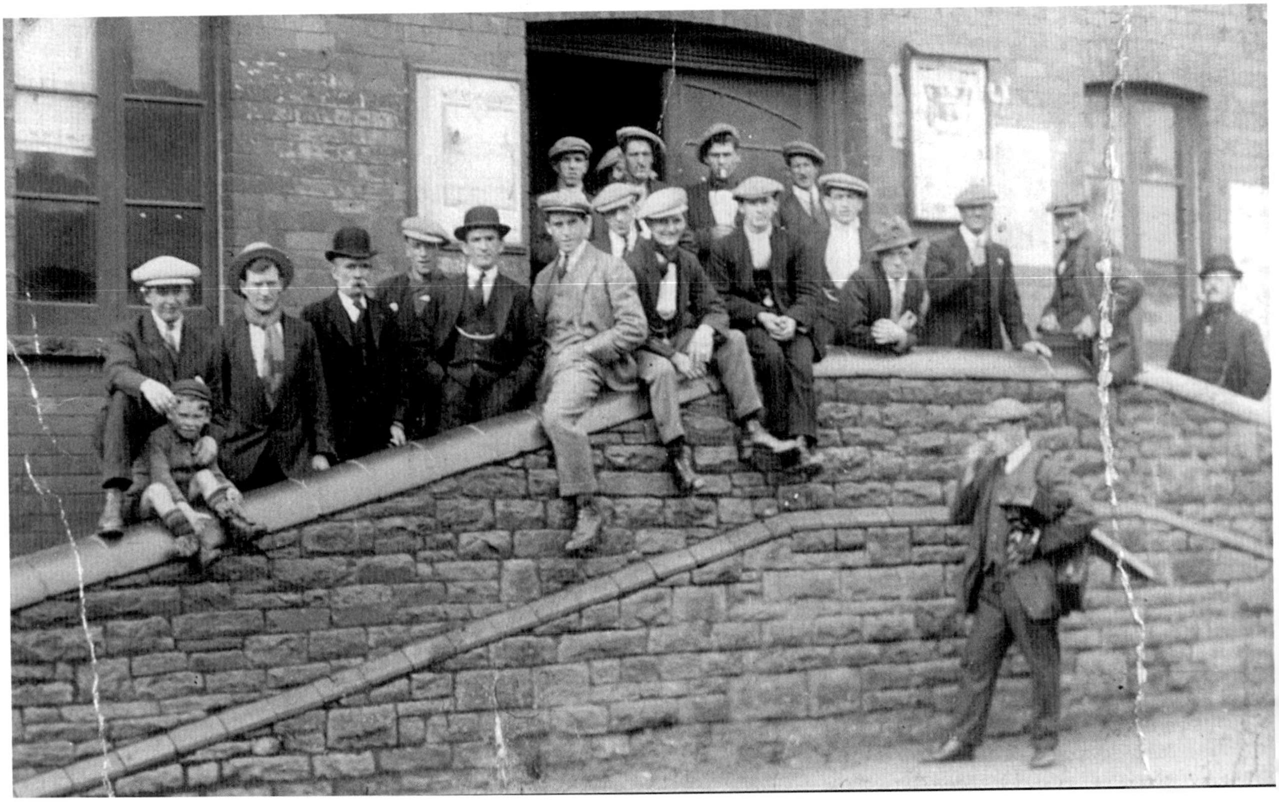

Monmouthshire Regiment. *2nd Battalion. Seen here is the cap badge worn by officers. Other ranks had the same Dragon device, but without the title scroll.*

Monmouthshire Regiment. *3rd Battalion officers' cap badge.*

N

New Brighton Cadet Corps, 1st. See 4th Battalion, Cheshire Regiment.

New Brighton Cadet Corps, 2nd. See 4th Battalion, Cheshire Regiment.

New College (Herne Bay) Cadet Corps. See 4th Battalion, Buffs (East Kent Regiment).

Newcastle Divisional Signal Company. See Northumbrian Divisional Signal Company (The Newcastle).

Newcastle-under-Lyme High School Officers Training Corps. One infantry company, Junior Division.

Newport Cadet Corps. See 4th Welsh Brigade, Royal Field Artillery.

Newport Market School Cadet Corps. 74 Coburg Row, Westminster, London. One company.

Nigeria Regiment. Headquarters Kaduna and comprising two artillery batteries, four infantry and one mounted infantry battalions.

Artillery: No.1 Battery, Kaduna; No.2 Battery, Calabar.

1st Battalion: Kaduna.

2nd Battalion: Lukoia.

3rd Battalion: Calabar.

4th Battalion: Lagos.

5th Battalion (Mounted Infantry): Kano.

Norfolk and Suffolk Brigade Company, Army Service Corps. See East Anglian Divisional Transport and Supply Column.

Norfolk and Suffolk Infantry Brigade. See East Anglian Brigade.

Norfolk Batteries, 1st, 2nd, 3rd. See 1st East Anglian Brigade, Royal Field Artillery.

Norfolk Regiment. Two Regular (1st and 2nd), one Special Reserve (3rd) and three Territorial Force (4th, 5th and 6th) battalions. Depot, Norwich.

1st Battalion: Hollywood, Belfast.

2nd Battalion: Belgaum, India.

3rd Battalion: Norwich.

4th Battalion: St Giles, Norwich with "A" and "B" Companies, also at St Giles; "C" Company, Long Stratton (detachments at Mulbarton and Saxlingham); "D" Company, Diss (detachments at Harleston and Tivetshall); "E" Company, Attleborough (detachments at East Harling, Kenninghall, Banham, Old Buckenham and Watton); "F" Company, Wymondham (detachments at Hethersett, Swardeston, Colney and Hingham); "G" Company, Brandon (detachments at Thetford, Methwold and Feltwell); "H" Company, Thorpe St Andrew (detachments at Loddon, Blofield, Acle, Burgh St Margaret, Framingham Pigot and Coltishall).

5th Battalion: East Dereham with "A" Company at King's Lynn; "B" Company, Downham (detachments at Hunstanton, Thornham, Hilgay and Stoke Ferry); "C" Company, Fakenham (detachments at Wells, Syderstone, Aylsham and Corpusty); "D" Company, Dereham (detachments at Castle Acre and Swaffham); "E" Company, Sandringham (detachments at Dersingham, Wolferton, Hillington and West Newton); "F" Company, Cromer (detachments at Melton Constable, Holt, Sheringham, North Walsham and Gunton); "G" and "H" Companies, Great Yarmouth.

Norfolk Regiment. *Musicians' wings and lace are worn, one man (right) having also the "Best Shot in Band" award on his lower left arm. The uniforms are scarlet with yellow facings and the collar badges feature the figure of Britannia.*

Norfolk Regiment. *Britannia, this time on the cap badges, and two proficiency awards – Machine Gunner (MG) and Rangefinder (R).*

Norfolk Yeomanry (The King's Own Royal Regiment). *Seen clearly here is the King George V Cypher cap badge and brass shoulder title KORR.*

6th (Cyclist) Battalion: Cattle Market Street, Norwich with "A" Company, also at Cattle Market Street; "B" Company, Great Yarmouth; "C" Company, King's Lynn (detachment at Terrington); "D" Company, Thetford (detachment at Attleborough); "E" Company, Fakenham (detachments at Walsingham, Holkham, Wells and Ryburgh); "F" Company, Ditchingham; "G" Company, Watton (detachment at Swaffham); "H" Company, Norwich (detachment at Great Yarmouth).

Norfolk Yeomanry (The King's Own Royal Regiment). Territorial Force. Cattle Market Street, Norwich with "A" Squadron, Norwich (detachments at Attleborough, Long Stratton, Loddon, Diss and Harleston); "B" Squadron, North Walsham (detachments at Brandiston, Blofield, Coltishall, Cromer, Hanworth, Holt, Marsham, Reepham, Stalham and Great Yarmouth); "C" Squadron, Fakenham (detachments at Barwick, Bircham, Brisley, Dersingham, East Dereham, Fransham, Hardingham, Huntstanton, Massingham, Quarles, Summerfield, Swaffham, Watton, Wells, Wymondham and Walsingham); "D" Squadron, King's Lynn (detachments at Downham, Thetford and Wisbech).

North Berwick Cadet Corps. See 8th Battalion, Royal Scots (Lothian Regiment).

North Devon Yeomanry. See Royal North Devon Hussars Yeomanry.

North Eastern County School Officers Training Corps. Barnard Castle. Two infantry companies, Junior Division.

Norfolk Yeomanry (The King's Own Royal Regiment). *Blue jacket with yellow collar and cuffs – Royal Arms collar badge.*

North Eastern County School Officers Training Corps.

North Irish Horse. Special Reserve. Skegoniel Avenue, Belfast. Shown in the *Army List*, together with the South Irish Horse, under the collective heading of Irish Horse.

North Lancashire Brigade Company, Army Service Corps. See West Lancashire Divisional Transport and Supply Column.

North Lancashire Infantry Brigade. See West Lancashire Division.

North Lancashire Regiment. See Loyal North Lancashire Regiment.

North Midland Brigade, Royal Field Artillery, 1st. Territorial Force. Artillery Drill Hall, Grimsby with 1st and 2nd Lincolnshire Batteries, also at Grimsby; 3rd Lincolnshire Battery, Louth (detachment at Grimsby), and Ammunition Column, Grimsby.

North Midland Brigade, Royal Field Artillery, 2nd. Territorial Force. Victoria Square, Shelton, Stoke-on-Trent with 1st and 2nd Staffordshire Batteries, also at Victoria Square; 3rd Staffordshire Battery, Leek and Ammunition Column, Victoria Square.

North Midland Brigade, Royal Field Artillery, 3rd. Territorial Force. West Park, Wolverhampton with 4th Staffordshire Battery, also West Park; 5th Staffordshire Battery, West Bromwich; 6th Staffordshire Battery, Bailey Street, Stafford and Ammunition Column, Wolverhampton.

North Midland Brigade, Royal Field Artillery (Howitzer), 4th. Territorial Force. Siddal's Road, Derby with 1st Derbyshire (Howitzer) Battery; 2nd Derbyshire (Howitzer) Battery and Ammunition Column. The 1st Battery also had a detachment at West Hallam.

North Midland Clearing Hospital. Territorial Force. Leicester.

North Midland Division. Territorial Force. Lichfield.

Lincoln and Leicester Infantry Brigade: Culverthorpe, Grantham. Battalions – 4th, 5th Lincolnshire; 4th, 5th Leicestershire.

Staffordshire Infantry Brigade: Market Square, Stafford. Battalions – 5th, 6th South Staffordshire; 5th, 6th North Staffordshire.

Notts & Derby Infantry Brigade: Derby Road, Nottingham. Battalions – 5th, 6th, 7th, 8th Sherwood Foresters.

Royal Artillery: 5 Market Square, Stafford. 1st, 2nd, 3rd, 4th (Howitzer) North Midland Brigades, Royal Field Artillery; North Midland Royal Garrison Artillery.

Royal Engineers: Norton Hall, Norton Canes, Cannock. 1st, 2nd North Midland Field Companies;

North Midland Divisional Signal Company.
Army Service Corps: 7 Magazine Square, Leicester. North Midland Divisional Transport and Supply Column.
Royal Army Medical Corps: 1st, 2nd, 3rd North Midland Field Ambulances.

North Midland Divisional Engineers. Territorial Force. Norton Hall, Norton Canes, Cannock with 1st North Midland Field Company in Smethwick, 2nd North Midland Field Company, Norton Canes, Cannock.

North Midland Divisional Signal Company. Territorial Force. Booth Street, Stoke-on-Trent with No.1 Section, No.2 (Staffordshire) Section, No.3 (Notts and Derby) Section, No.4 (Lincoln and Leicester) Section.

North Midland Divisional Transport and Supply Column. Territorial Force. 7 Magazine Square, Leicester with Headquarters Company, Handsworth; Lincoln and Leicester Brigade Company, 19 Magazine Square, Leicester (detachment at Market Harborough); Staffordshire Brigade Company, Handsworth and Notts & Derby Brigade Company, Derby Road, Nottingham.

North Midland Field Ambulance, 1st. Territorial Force. 91 Siddals Road, Derby.

North Midland Field Ambulance, 2nd. Territorial Force. Oxford Street, Leicester.

North Midland Field Ambulance, 3rd. Territorial Force. The Deanery, Stafford Street, Wolverhampton. There was also a detachment at Penkridge.

North Midland Field Companies, 1st, 2nd. See North Midland Divisional Engineers.

North Midland Mounted Brigade. Territorial Force. 7 Magazine Square, Leicester. Included Staffordshire, Leicestershire, Lincolnshire Yeomanries; Leicestershire Royal Horse Artillery.

North Midland Mounted Brigade Ammunition Column. See Leicestershire Royal Horse Artillery.

North Midland Mounted Brigade Field Ambulance. Territorial Force. Nineveh Road, Handsworth, Birmingham.

North Midland Mounted Brigade Signal Troop. Territorial Force. 7 Magazine Square, Leicester.

North Midland Mounted Brigade Transport and Supply Column. Territorial Force. 11 The Magazine, Leicester. There was also a detachment at Coalville.

North Midland Royal Garrison Artillery (Staffordshire). Territorial Force. Wilfred Place, Hartshill, Stoke-on-Trent.

North Midland Royal Garrison Artillery (Staffordshire). *Sergeants, Barr Camp, Morecambe, August, 1910.*

North Paddington Cadets, 1st. Pember Hall, Pember Road. Three companies.

North Riding Battery. See 2nd Northumbrian Brigade, Royal Field Artillery.

North Riding Fortress Engineers. Territorial Force. Bright Street, Middlesbrough with No.1 Electric Lights Company.

North Riding Royal Garrison Artillery. See Northumbrian Royal Garrison Artillery (North Riding).

North Scottish Royal Garrison Artillery. Territorial Force. Broughty Ferry with No.1 Company, Fonthill Road, Aberdeen; No.2 Company, Cromarty (detachments at Jemimaville, Newhall and Davidston); No.3 Company, Broughty Ferry; No.4 Company, Montrose.

North Somerset Yeomanry. Territorial Force. Bath with "A" Squadron, Bath (detachments at Bathampton, Farmborough, Frome, Mells and Road); "B" Squadron, Weston-super-Mare (detachments at Axbridge, Clevedon, Langford and Nailsea); "C" Squadron, Shepton Mallet (detachments at Queen Camel, Ston Easton, Wells, Wincanton and Castle Cary); "D" Squadron, Bristol (detachments at Queen Charlton, Barrow Gurney and Keynsham).

North Staffordshire Regiment. See Prince of Wales's (North Staffordshire Regiment).

North Wales Brigade Company, Army Service Corps. See Welsh Divisional Transport and Supply Column.

North Wales Infantry Brigade. See Welsh Division.

Northampton School Cadet Corps. See 4th Battalion, Northamptonshire Regiment.

Northamptonshire Battery. See 4th East Anglian Brigade, Royal Field Artillery.

Northamptonshire Regiment. Two Regular (1st and 2nd), one Special Reserve (3rd) and one Territorial Force (4th) battalions. Depot, Northampton.

1st Battalion: Blackdown, Farnborough.

2nd Battalion: Alexandria, Egypt.

3rd Battalion: Northampton.

4th Battalion: Clare Street, Northampton with "A" Company, also at Clare Street; "B" Company, Northampton (detachments at Daventry and Weedon); "C" Company, Northampton (detachments at Althorp Park, Long Buckby and Harpole); "D" Company, Northampton; "E" Company, Wellingborough (detachment at Finedon); "F" Company, Kettering; "G" Company, Desborough (detachment at Rothwell); "H" Company, Higham Ferrers (detachments at Rushden and Irthlingborough). The King's School, Peterborough

North Somerset Yeomanry. *Trumpeters.*

Northamptonshire Regiment. *1st Battalion. Bandmaster A.A. Weyer, Poona, 1908.*

Northamptonshire Regiment. *1st Battalion. Machine Gun Section, Poona, 1908.*

Northamptonshire Regiment. *Scarlet tunics with white facings, the drummer (extreme right) wears the full-dress home service helmet.*

Northamptonshire Regiment. *Cap badge. The Castle and Key of Gibraltar were awarded to the 2nd Battalion (then 58th Regiment) for the defence of the rock 1779–83. The battle honour "Talavera" was gained during the Peninsular War by the old 48th Regiment (later 1st Battalion).*

Cadet Corps and Northampton School Cadet Corps at Billing Road, Northampton, were affiliated.

Northamptonshire Yeomanry. Territorial Force. Clare Street, Northampton with "A" Squadron, Northampton (detachment at Cottesbrooke); "B" Squadron, Peterborough (detachments at Oundle, Glinton and Thrapston); "C" Squadron, Kettering (detachments at Wellingborough, Rushden and Clipston); "D" Squadron, Daventry (detachments at Weedon, Blisworth, Blakesley and West Haddon).

Northern Airline Signal Company. See Northern Command Signal Companies (Army Troops).

Northern Command Signal Companies (Army Troops). Territorial Force. Leeds with Northern Wireless Signal Company, Northern Cable Signal Company and Northern Airline Signal Company. The Leeds Postal Telegraph Messengers' Cadet Company was affiliated.

Northern Cable Signal Company. See Northern Command Signal Companies (Army Troops).

Northern Cyclist Battalion. Territorial Force. Hutton Terrace, Sandyford Road, Newcastle-upon-Tyne with "A" and "B" Companies, Sunderland; "C" Company, West Hartlepool; "D" Company, Chester-le-Street; "E" Company, Newcastle-upon-Tyne; "F" Company, Blyth; "G" Company, Whitley Bay; "H" Company, Newcastle-upon-Tyne.

Northern General Hospital, 1st. Territorial Force. Hutton Terrace, Newcastle-upon-Tyne.

Northern General Hospital, 2nd. Territorial Force. Harewood Barracks, Leeds.

Northern General Hospital, 3rd. Territorial Force. Sheffield.

Northern General Hospital, 4th. Territorial Force. 6b Guildhall Street, Lincoln.

Northern General Hospital, 5th. Territorial Force. Leicester.

Northern Wireless Signal Company. See Northern Command Signal Companies (Army Troops).

Northumberland Batteries, 1st, 2nd, 3rd. See 1st Northumbrian Brigade, Royal Field Artillery.

Northumberland Brigade Company, Army Service Corps. See Northumbrian Divisional Transport and Supply Column.

Northumberland Fusiliers. Two Regular (1st and 2nd), one Special Reserve (3rd) and four Territorial Force (4th–7th) battalions. Depot, Newcastle-upon-Tyne.

1st Battalion: Portsmouth.

2nd Battalion: Sabathu, India.

3rd Battalion: Newcastle-upon-Tyne.

4th Battalion: Hexham with "A" Company, also in Hexham (detachment at Acomb); "B" Company, Bellingham (detachments at Plashetts, Otterburn and Woodburn); "C" Company, Haydon Bridge (detachments at Allendale, Langley and Newbrough); "D" Company, Prudhoe (detachment at Mickley); "E" Company, Corbridge; "F" Company, Haltwhistle; "G" Company, Newburn (detachment at Whorlton); "H" Company, Prudhoe. The Haltwhistle Cadets at Scardeburg, Haltwhistle were affiliated.

5th Battalion: Walker, Newcastle-upon-Tyne with "A", "B" and "C" Companies, also in Walker; "D", "E" and "F" Companies, Wallsend; "G" Company, Gosforth (detachments at West Moor and Seaton Burn); "H" Company, Gosforth.

Northumberland Fusiliers. *Firing salute at Dover on the occasion of the King's Birthday Parade, 26 June, 1908. Scarlet tunics, gosling-green facings, red-over-white cap hackles.*

6th Battalion: Northumberland Road, Newcastle-upon-Tyne. The Allan's School Cadet Unit at Allan's Endowed School, Northumberland Road was affiliated.

7th Battalion: Alnwick with "A" Company was in Morpeth; "B" Company, Ashington; "C" Company, Belford (detachments at Ford, Wooler and Chatton); "D" Company, Alnwick; "E" Company, Amble (detachments at Broomhill and Warkworth); "F" Company, Alnwick (detachment at Rothbury); "G" Company, Berwick-upon-Tweed; "H" Company, Berwick-upon-Tweed (detachment at Scremerston.) The Morpeth Grammar School Cadet Company was affiliated.

Northumberland Hussars Yeomanry. Territorial Force. Northumberland Road, Newcastle-upon-Tyne with "A" Squadron, also at Northumberland Road; "B" Squadron, South Shields (detachments at Sunderland, Darlington, Spennymoor and West Hartlepool); "C" Squadron, Morpeth (detachments at Alnwick, Ashington, Rothbury, North Shields and Eglingham); "D" Squadron, Hexham (detachments at Stanley, Prudhoe, Allendale and Wark-on-Tyne).

Northumberland Hussars Yeomanry. *Lieutenant (and Bandmaster) H.G. Amers. Blue jacket with silver cord and lace. Also worked in silver wire is the cap badge. Said to represent Alnwick Castle.*

Northumberland Infantry Brigade. See Northumbrian Division.

Northumbrian Brigade, Royal Field Artillery, 1st. Territorial Force. Barrack Road, Newcastle-upon-Tyne with 1st, 2nd, 3rd Northumberland Batteries and Ammunition Column.

Northumbrian Brigade, Royal Field Artillery, 2nd. Territorial Force. Wenlock Barracks, Anlaby Road, Hull with 1st and 2nd East Riding Batteries, Park Street, Hull; North Riding Battery, Scarborough (detachment at Whitby) and Ammunition Column, Park Street, Hull.

Northumbrian Brigade, Royal Field Artillery (County of Durham), 3rd. Territorial Force. Seaham Harbour with 1st Durham Battery, also at Seaham Harbour; 2nd Durham Battery, Durham (detachment at Silksworth); 3rd Durham Battery, The Armoury, West Hartlepool and Ammunition column, Seaham Harbour.

Northumbrian Brigade, Royal Field Artillery (Howitzer) (County of Durham), 4th. Territorial Force. Bolingbroke Street, South Shields with 4th Durham (Howitzer) Battery, also at Bolingbroke Street; 5th Durham (Howitzer) Battery, Hebburn-on-Tyne and Ammunition Column, Bolingbroke Street, South Shields.

Northumbrian Clearing Hospital. Territorial Force. Newcastle-upon-Tyne.

Northumbrian Division. Territorial Force. Frenchgate, Richmond.

Northumberland Infantry Brigade: 6 Eldon Square, Newcastle-upon-Tyne. Battalions – 4th, 5th, 6th, 7th Northumberland Fusiliers.

York and Durham Infantry Brigade: 12 Castlegate, Malton. Battalions – 4th East Yorkshire; 4th, 5th Yorkshire; 5th Durham Light Infantry.

Durham Light Infantry Brigade: Old Elvet, Durham. Battalions – 6th, 7th, 8th, 9th Durham Light Infantry.

Royal Artillery: Frenchgate, Richmond. 1st, 2nd, 3rd, 4th (Howitzer) Northumbrian Brigades, Royal Field Artillery; Northumbrian Royal Garrison Artillery.

Royal Engineers: Barras Bridge, Newcastle-upon-Tyne. 1st, 2nd Northumbrian Field Companies; Northumbrian Divisional Signal Company.

Army Service Corps: St George's Hall, Newcastle-upon-Tyne. Northumbrian Divisional Transport and Supply Column.

Royal Army Medical Corps: 1st, 2nd, 3rd Northumbrian Field Ambulances.

Northumbrian Divisional Engineers. Territorial

Northumbrian Divisional Engineers. *Band, Hornsea, 1912.*

Force. Barras Bridge, Newcastle-upon-Tyne with 1st and 2nd (The Newcastle) Field Companies.

Northumbrian Divisional Signal Company (The Newcastle). Territorial Force. Barras Bridge, Newcastle-upon-Tyne with No.1 Section, No.2 (Northumberland) Section, No.3 (York and Durham) Section, No.4 (Durham Light Infantry) Section.

Northumbrian Divisional Transport and Supply Column. Territorial Force. St George's Hall, Newcastle-upon-Tyne with Headquarters Company, Angus Hall, Gateshead; Northumberland Brigade Company, St George's Hall, Newcastle-upon-Tyne; York and Durham Brigade Company, Walton Street, Hull and Durham Light Infantry Brigade Company, Sunderland.

Northumbrian Field Ambulance, 1st. Territorial Force. Hutton Terrace, Newcastle-upon-Tyne.

Northumbrian Field Ambulance, 2nd. Territorial Force. Larchfield Street, Darlington with "A" and "B" sections, also at Larchfield Street; "C" Section, Shildon.

Northumbrian Field Ambulance, 3rd. Territorial Force. Wenlock Barracks, Walton Street, Hull.

Northumbrian Field Companies (The Newcastle), 1st, 2nd. See Northumbrian Divisional Engineers.

Northumbrian Royal Garrison Artillery (North Riding). Territorial Force. Middlesbrough. There was also a detachment at Thornaby.

Nottingham Cadet Battalion (Church). Park Row Chambers, Nottingham. Nine companies.

Northumbrian Divisional Transport and Supply Column. *Three men of the Northumberland Brigade Company. The uniforms are blue with white facings and the sergeant wears a Wheelwrights' (a wagon wheel) arm badge above his chevrons.*

Northumbrian Divisional Transport and Supply Column.

Nottingham High School Officers Training Corps. One infantry company, Junior Division.

Nottingham University College Officers Training Corps. One infantry company, Senior Division.

Nottinghamshire and Derbyshire Regiment. See Sherwood Foresters (Nottinghamshire and Derbyshire Regiment).

Nottinghamshire Royal Horse Artillery. Territorial Force. Derby Road, Nottingham. Included the Notts & Derby Mounted Brigade Ammunition Column. The Battery also had a detachment at Wiseton.

Nottinghamshire Royal Horse Artillery. *At camp on Salisbury Plain, 1913.*

Nottinghamshire Yeomanry (Sherwood Rangers). Territorial Force. Retford with "A" Squadron, Newark (detachments at Sutton-on-Trent and Collingham); "B" Squadron, Mansfield (detachments at Chesterfield, Alfreton, Pinxton and Kirkby-in-Ashfield); "C" Squadron, Worksop (detachments at Clumber and Normanton); "D" Squadron, Retford (detachments at Ranskill, Trent Port, Melton Ross and Misterton).

Nottinghamshire Yeomanry (South Nottinghamshire Hussars). Territorial Force. Derby Road, Nottingham with "A" Squadron, Bingham (detachments at Carlton, Plumtree and Southwell); "B" Squadron, Watnall (detachments at Arnold and Eastwood); "C" Squadron, Nottingham; "D" Squadron, Wollaton (detachment at Long Eaton).

Notts & Derby Brigade Company, Army Service Corps. See North Midland Divisional Transport and Supply Column.

Notts & Derby Infantry Brigade. See North Midland Division.

Notts & Derby Mounted Brigade. Territorial Force. Derby Road, Nottingham. Included Nottingham, South Nottinghamshire Hussars, Derbyshire Yeomanries; Nottinghamshire Royal Horse Artillery.

Notts & Derby Mounted Brigade Ammunition Column. See Nottinghamshire Royal Horse Artillery.

Notts & Derby Mounted Brigade Field Ambulance. Territorial Force. Derby Road, Nottingham with "A" Section, also at Derby Road; "B" Section, Grimsby.

Notts & Derby Mounted Brigade Signal Troop. Territorial Force. Derby Road, Nottingham.

Notts & Derby Mounted Brigade Transport and Supply Column. Territorial Force. Chesterfield. There was also a detachment at Bolsover.

Notts & Derby Mounted Brigade Transport and Supply Column. *Brass shoulder title.*

Nottinghamshire Yeomanry (South Nottinghamshire Hussars). *The regimental badge, a slip of oak with acorn, can be seen on the caps and collars.*

O

Oakham School Officers Training Corps. One infantry company, Junior Division.

Officers Training Corps. The Officers Training Corps was divided into two divisions, the Senior, consisting of university units, and Junior, which was formed from public schools. Units (known as Contingents) of the OTC were made up in the main of infantry companies, but there were a number of cavalry, artillery, engineer, transport and supply and medical formations. Varying in size of establishment, all came directly under the administration of the War Office and had no affiliations to Regular or other regiments. In addition, and for the purpose of providing officers for the Territorial Force, there was also the Inns of Court OTC.

Senior Division: Made up of contingents from the following universities – Aberdeen, Belfast, Birmingham, Bristol, Cambridge, Dublin, Durham, Edinburgh, Glasgow, Leeds, London, Manchester, Nottingham, Oxford, Reading, Royal Agricultural College, Royal College of Surgeons in Ireland, Royal Veterinary College Edinburgh, Royal Veterinary College of Ireland, St Andrews, Sheffield and Wales.

Junior Division: Made up of contingents from the following schools/colleges – Aldenham, All Hallows, Ampleforth, Ardingly, Beaumont, Bedford Grammar, Bedford Modern, Berkhamsted, Bloxham, Blundell's, Bournemouth, Bradfield, Bridlington Grammar, Brighton, Bristol Grammar, Bromsgrove, Bury Grammar, Cambridge and County, Campbell,

Oxford University Officers Training Corps. *The member of the Cavalry Squadron seen here wears below an Army Scout badge a red four-pointed proficiency star. His cap badge (other components of the Corps wore badges relevant to their arm of service) features a trumpet in the centre of a crossed sabre and scabbard. (Ivor Bush Collection).*

Oxfordshire and Buckinghamshire Light Infantry. *Officer. This photograph shows the officers' distinctive collar ornaments – a regimental button and length of gold Russia braid. Other ranks of the Regiment wore no collar badges. The cap badge (a simple white metal bugle-horn) is also clearly seen.*

Charterhouse, Cheltenham, Chigwell, Christ's Hospital, Churcher's, City of London, Clifton, Cork Grammar, Cranbrook, Cranleigh, Dartford Grammar, Dean Close, Denstone, Derby, Dollar Institution, Dorchester Grammar, Dover, Downside, Dulwich, Eastbourne, Edinburgh Academy, Ellesmere, Elstowe, Emanuel, Epsom, Eton, Exeter, Felstead, Fettes, Forest, Framlingham, George Heriot's, George Watson's, Giggleswick, Glasgow Academy, Glasgow High, Glenalmond, Gresham's, Grimsby Municipal, Haileybury, Handsworth Grammar, Harrow, Hereford Cathedral, Hertford Grammar, Highgate, Hillhead High, Hurstpierpoint, Hymers, Imperial Service, Ipswich, Kelly, Kelvinside Academy, King Alfred's, King Edward VII, King Edward's Grammar, King Edward's (Bath), King Edward's (Birmingham), King William's, King's (Taunton), King's (Wimbledon), King's (Bruton), King's (Canterbury), King's (Grantham), King's (Rochester), King's (Warwick), King's (Worcester), Kirkcaldy High, Lancing, Leeds Grammar, Leys, Liverpool College, Liverpool Institute, Loretto, Louth, Maidstone Grammar, Malvern, Manchester Grammar, Marlborough, Merchant Taylors', Merchiston Castle, Mill Hill, Monkton Combe, Morrison's Academy, Newcastle-under-Lyme High, North Eastern County, Nottingham High, Oakham, Oratory, Oundle, Perse, Plymouth, Portsmouth Grammar, Queen Mary's Grammar, Radley, Reading, Reigate Grammar, Repton, Rossall, Royal Grammar (High Wycombe), Royal Grammar (Lancaster), Royal Grammar (Newcastle-upon-Tyne), Royal Grammar (Worcester), Royal Grammar School of King Edward VI, Roysse's, Rugby, St Albans, St Andrew's, St Bees, St Columba's, St Dunstan's, St Edmund's, St Edward's, St John's, St Lawrence, St Paul's, St Peter's, Sedbergh, Sherborne, Shrewsbury, Sidcup Hall, Sir Roger Manwood's, Skinners', Solihull Grammar, Stonyhurst, Taunton, Tonbridge, Trent, University College, Uppingham, Victoria, Wellingborough Grammar, Wellington College (Berkshire), Wellington College (Shropshire), Wellington School, West Buckland, Westminster, Whitgift Grammar, Wilson's, Winchester, Wolverhampton Grammar, Woodbridge and Worksop.

Ongar Grammar School Cadets. 4th Battalion, See Essex Regiment.

Oratory Cadet Corps. 58 Cromwell Road, London. Four companies.

Oratory School Officers Training Corps. Edgbaston, Birmingham. One infantry company, Junior Division.

Ordnance College. Woolwich.

Orkney Royal Garrison Artillery. Territorial Force. Kirkwall with No.1 Company, also at Kirkwall; No.2 Company, Sanday (detachment at Stronsay); No.3 Company, Shapansey (detachment at South Ronaldshay); No.4 Company, Stromness (detachment at Finstown); No.5 Company, Evie (detachment at Birsay); No.6 Company, Holm (detachments at Tankerness and Deerness); No.7 Company, Kirkwall.

Oxfordshire and Buckinghamshire Light Infantry. *2nd Battalion leaving Aldershot Station in 1911. At the head of the column, two officers and three colour-sergeants escort the cased Colours.*

Oundle School Officers Training Corps. Three infantry companies, Junior Division.

Oxford University Officers Training Corps. One cavalry squadron, a section of field artillery, one signal section, a battalion of infantry and a field ambulance section, Senior Division.

Oxfordshire and Buckinghamshire Light Infantry. Two Regular (1st and 2nd) and one Special Reserve (3rd) battalions. The Regiment was represented in the Territorial Force by two battalions. One numbered as 4th, the other, the Buckinghamshire Battalion, having no numerical titles prior to the First World War. Depot, Oxford.

1st Battalion: Ahmednagar, India.

2nd Battalion: Aldershot.

3rd Battalion: Oxford.

4th Battalion: Oxford with "A" Company, also at Oxford; "B" Company, Oxford (detachment at Thame); "C" Company, Banbury (detachment at Brackley); "D" Company, Henley-on-Thames (detachment at Culham); "E" Company, Chipping Norton (detachments at Kingham, Charlbury, Shipton and Stow-on-the-Wold); "F" Company, Witney (detachments at Woodstock, Burford and Eynsham); "G" Company, Banbury (detachment at Bicester); "H" Company, Oxford (detachment at Woodburn). The Burford Grammar School Cadet Corps and Cowley Cadet Corps, headquarters, 14 Holywell Street, Oxford, were affiliated.

Buckinghamshire Battalion: Aylesbury with "A" Company, Marlow; "B" Company, High Wycombe (detachment at Winslow); "C" Company, Buckingham (detachments at Tingewick and Chesham); "D" Company, Aylesbury; "E" Company, Slough (detachment at Datchet); "F" and "G" Companies, Wolverton; "H" Company, High Wycombe. The Aylesbury Grammar School Cadet Corps was affiliated.

Oxfordshire and Buckinghamshire Light Infantry. *Buckinghamshire Battalion. The sergeant wears a proficiency star above his chevrons and a pouch-belt ornament that still bears the initials of the Buckinghamshire Rifle Volunteers. The dark grey jacket has scarlet collar and piping.*

Oxfordshire and Buckinghamshire Light Infantry. *4th Battalion. The Colours and Colour Party seen here at Windsor shortly after presentation by King Edward VII in June, 1909. Uniforms are scarlet with white facings.*

Oxfordshire Yeomanry (Queen's Own Oxfordshire Hussars). *Machine gun section.*

Oxfordshire and Buckinghamshire Light Infantry. *Buckinghamshire Battalion. Cap badge. In the centre of a Maltese Cross the swan from the county arms of Buckinghamshire.*

Oxfordshire Yeomanry (Queen's Own Oxfordshire Hussars). *Uniform is dark blue with white cord, mantua-purple collars and cuffs. The cap badge features the cypher ("AR") of Queen Adelaide.*

Oxfordshire Yeomanry (Queen's Own Oxfordshire Hussars). Territorial Force. Oxford with "A" Squadron, also at Oxford; "B" Squadron, Woodstock (detachments at Witney and Bicester); "C" Squadron, Henley-on-Thames (detachments at Watlington, Thame and Goring-on-Thames); "D" Squadron, Banbury (detachments at Deddington, Chipping Norton, Shipton, Charlbury and Burford).

P

Paddington Boys' Club and Naval Brigade. Guardians Offices, Harrow Road.

Palmer's School Cadet Corps. See 6th Battalion, Essex Regiment.

Pembroke Royal Garrison Artillery. Territorial Force. Milford Haven with No.1 Company, also at Milford Haven; No.2 Company, Saundersfoot (detachment at Tenby); No.3 Company, Fishguard (detachment at Pembroke Dock).

Pembroke Yeomanry (Castlemartin). Territorial Force. Tenby with "A" Squadron, Tenby (detachments at Pembroke, St Florence, Manorbier, Kilgetty and Templeton); "B" Squadron, Haverfordwest (detachments at Clarbeston Road, Newgale and Fishguard) "C" Squadron, Carmarthen (detachments at Whitland, Llanelly, Llandilo, Llangadock, Pantglas and Llandovery); "D" Squadron, Lampeter (detachments at Aberystwyth, Tregaron, Llandyssil and Llanybyther).

Perse School Officers Training Corps. Cambridge. One infantry company, Junior Division.

Perthshire Battalion. See 6th (Perthshire) Battalion, Black Watch (Royal Highlanders).

Peter Symonds School Cadet Corps. See 4th Battalion, Hampshire Regiment.

Plymouth College Officers Training Corps. One infantry company, Junior Division.

Plymouth Lads' Brigade Cadet Corps. See 5th Battalion, Devonshire Regiment.

Poplar and Stepney Rifles. See 17th Battalion, London Regiment.

Pembroke Yeomanry (Castlemartin). *Cap badge. Exclusive to the Regiment, the battle honour "Fishguard" is the first to be carried by any volunteer unit and the only one for service in the British Isles. It commemorates the landing of a French force in 1797, and its subsequent surrender to the regiment's commander Lord Cawdor.*

Pembroke Yeomanry (Castlemartin). *Sergeants at camp, Builth Wells, Breckonshire, 1914.*

Portsmouth Grammar School Officers Training Corps. One infantry company, Junior Division.

Post Office Rifles. See 8th Battalion, London Regiment.

Poulton Cadet Company, 1st. See 4th Battalion, Cheshire Regiment.

Prestonpans Cadet Corps. See 8th Battalion, Royal Scots (Lothian Regiment).

Prince Albert's Own Hussars. See 11th (Prince Albert's Own) Hussars.

Prince Albert's Own Leicestershire Yeomanry. See Leicestershire Yeomanry.

Prince Albert's (Somerset Light Infantry). Two Regular (1st and 2nd), one Special Reserve (3rd) and two Territorial Force (4th and 5th) battalions. Depot, Taunton.

1st Battalion: Colchester.

2nd Battalion: Quetta, India.

3rd Battalion: Taunton.

4th Battalion: Lower Bristol Road, Bath with "A" and "B" Companies, also at Lower Bristol Road; "C" Company, Keynsham (detachments at Brislington, Whitechurch and Bitton); "D" Company, Frome (detachments at Bruton, Mells and Wanstrow); "E" Company, Weston-super-Mare (detachments at Winscombe and Cheddar); "F" Company, Castle Cary (detachments at Shepton Mallet and Evercreech); "G" Company, Midsomer Norton (detachments at Radstock, Bishop Sutton and Peasedown St John); "H" Company, Glastonbury (detachment at Wells).

5th Battalion: Taunton with "A" Company, also at Taunton; "B" Company, Williton (detachments at Watchet, Minehead and Washford); "C" Company, Bridgwater (detachment at North Petherton); "D" Company, Langport (detachments at Highbridge and Somerton); "E" Company, Yeovil (detachments at Martock and Langport); "F" Company, Crewkerne (detachment at South Petherton); "G" Company, Wellington (detachments at Milverton and Wiveliscombe); "H" Company, Chard (detachment at Ilminster).

Prince Albert's (Somerset Light Infantry). *This officer is in full dress – scarlet tunic with blue facings – and is seen here with foreign service helmet.*

Prince Albert's (Somerset Light Infantry). *2nd Battalion. Machine gun section, Malta, 1911.*

Prince Albert's (Somerset Light Infantry). *4th Battalion forming the Guard of Honour during a royal visit to Wells.*

Prince Albert's (Somerset Light Infantry). *In other regiments both officers and sergeants wear their sashes knotted on the left side. This photograph, however, illustrates how in the Somerset Light Infantry (the origins of the tradition are uncertain) the reverse was the case.*

Prince Albert's (Somerset Light Infantry). *Cap badge. The battle honour "Jellalabad", together with the Mural Crown, was awarded for the regiment's gallant defence of the fort in 1842. The title "Prince Albert's" was conferred at the same time.*

Prince of Wales's Leinster Regiment (Royal Canadians). *Included here, in this central device of the officers' helmet plate, are two recognitions of past service. Maple leaves for service on the Canadian frontier during the American War of 1812–14, and with Sir Hugh Rose's Force during the Indian Mutiny.*

Prince of Wales's Battalion. See 5th (Prince of Wales's) Battalion, Devonshire Regiment.

Prince of Wales's Dragoon Guards. See 3rd (Prince of Wales's) Dragoon Guards.

Prince of Wales's Leinster Regiment (Royal Canadians), Two Regular (1st and 2nd) and three Special Reserve (3rd, 4th and 5th) battalions. Depot, Birr.

1st Battalion: Fyzabad, India.
2nd Battalion: Cork.
3rd Battalion: Birr.
4th Battalion: Maryborough.
5th Battalion: Drogheda.

Prince of Wales's (North Staffordshire Regiment). Two Regular (1st and 2nd), two Special Reserve (3rd and 4th) and two Territorial Force (5th and 6th) battalions. Depot, Lichfield.

1st Battalion: Buttevant, Ireland.
2nd Battalion: Rawal Pindi, India.
3rd Battalion: Lichfield.
4th Battalion: Lichfield.
5th Battalion: Hanley with "A" Company, Longton; "B" Company, Hanley; "C" Company, Burslem; "D" Company, Tunstall; "E" Company, Stoke-on-Trent (detachment at Hanley); "F" Company, Stone; "G" Company, Newcastle-under-Lyme; "H" Company, Stoke-on-Trent.
6th Battalion: Burton-on-Trent with "A" Company, also at Burton-on-Trent; "B" Company, Burton-on-Trent (detachment at Tutbury); "C" Company,

Prince of Wales's (North Staffordshire Regiment). *Cap badge.*

Tamworth; "D" Company, Rugeley; "E" Company, Lichfield; "F" Company, Stafford; "G" Company, Uttoxeter; "H" Company, Burton-on-Trent.

Prince of Wales's Own Civil Service Rifles. See 15th Battalion, London Regiment.

Prince of Wales's Own Royal Hussars. See 10th (Prince of Wales's Own Royal Hussars).

Prince of Wales's Own Royal Regiment. See Royal Wiltshire Yeomanry (Prince of Wales's Own Royal Regiment).

Prince of Wales's Own (West Yorkshire Regiment). Two Regular (1st and 2nd), two Special Reserve (3rd and 4th) and four Territorial Force (5th-8th) battalions. Depot, York.

1st Battalion: Lichfield.

2nd Battalion: Malta.

3rd Battalion: York.

4th Battalion: York.

5th Battalion: York with "A" Company, York (detachment at Tadcaster); "B" and "C" Companies, York; "D" Company, Selby; "E" Company, Harrogate; "F" Company, Harrogate (detachment at Wetherby); "G" Company, Knaresborough (detachments at Borobridge and Starbeck); "H" Company, Ripon (detachment at Pateley Bridge).

6th Battalion: Belle Vue Barracks, Bradford. The Bradford Postal Telegraph Messengers' Cadet Corps, headquarters at Bradford Post Office, was affiliated.

7th Battalion (Leeds Rifles): Carlton Barracks, Leeds.

8th Battalion (Leeds Rifles): Carlton Barracks, Leeds. There was also a detachment at Pudsey.

Prince of Wales's Royal Lancers. See 12th (Prince of Wales's Royal) Lancers.

Prince of Wales's Volunteers (South Lancashire Regiment). Two Regular (1st and 2nd), one Special Reserve (3rd) and two Territorial Force (4th and 5th) battalions. Depot, Warrington.

1st Battalion: Quetta, India.

2nd Battalion: Tidworth.

3rd Battalion: Warrington.

4th Battalion: Warrington with "A" to "D" Companies, also at Warrington; "E" Company, Newton-le-Willows; "F" Company, Warrington; "G" Company, Newton-le-Willows; "H" Company, Warrington.

5th Battalion: St Helens with "A" Company, also at St Helens; "B" Company, Prescot; "C" Company, St Helens; "D" Company, St Helens (detachment at Haydock); "E" Company, St Helens; "F" Company, Prescot; "G" Company, St Helens; "H" Company, Widnes.

Prince of Wales's Own (West Yorkshire Regiment). *2nd Battalion officers. Scarlet tunics with buff facings.*

Prince of Wales's Own (West Yorkshire Regiment). *6th Battalion mobilizing at Bradford, August, 1914.*

Prince of Wales's Own (West Yorkshire Regiment). *Cap badge. The White Horse of Hanover.*

Prince of Wales's Volunteers (South Lancashire Regiment). *Bandmaster.*

Prince of Wales's Volunteers (South Lancashire Regiment). *Cap badge. The Prince of Wales's Volunteers' title dates from 1793 and the formation that year (as 82nd Regiment) of the 2nd Battalion. The 1st Battalion, the old 40th Regiment, served during the 1801 campaign in Egypt.*

Princess Beatrice's Battalion. See 8th (Isle of Wight Rifles "Princess Beatrice's"). Battalion, Hampshire Regiment.

Princess Charlotte of Wales's Dragoon Guards. See 5th (Princess Charlotte of Wales's) Dragoon Guards.

Princess Charlotte of Wales's (Royal Berkshire Regiment). Two Regular (1st and 2nd), one Special Reserve (3rd) and one Territorial Force (4th) battalions. Depot, Reading.

1st Battalion: Mandora Barracks, Aldershot.

2nd Battalion: Jhansi, India.

3rd Battalion: Reading.

4th Battalion: St Mary's Butts, Reading with "A" Company, Reading (detachment at Englefield); "B" Company, Reading; "C" Company, Wantage (detachment at Wallingford); "D" Company, Windsor; "E" Company, Newbury (detachments at Bucklebury, Aldermaston and Hungerford); "F" Company, Abingdon; "G" Company, Maidenhead; "H" Company, Wokingham. The Battalion also had a cadet company, designated 1st Cadet Company at the Maidenhead County Boys School.

Princess Charlotte of Wales's (Royal Berkshire Regiment). *3rd Battalion Band at Pernham Camp, 1913. Scarlet tunics with blue facings.*

Princess Charlotte of Wales's (Royal Berkshire Regiment). *Cap badge. The Dragon of China. Awarded to the 1st Battalion (then 49th Regiment) for service during the China War of 1840–1842.*

Princess Louise's (Argyll and Sutherland Highlanders). Two Regular (1st and 2nd), two Special Reserve (3rd and 4th) and five Territorial Force (5th to 9th) battalions. Depot, Stirling.
1st Battalion: Dinapore, India.
2nd Battalion: Fort George.
3rd Battalion: Stirling.
4th Battalion: Paisley.
5th (Renfrewshire) Battalion: Finnart Street, Greenock with "A" to "D" Companies, also at Finnart Street; "E" Company, Port Glasgow; "F" and "G" Companies, Greenock; "H" Company, Gourock (detachment at Inverkip).
6th (Renfrewshire) Battalion: 66 High Street, Paisley with "A", "B" and "C" Companies, also at 66 High Street, Paisley; "D" Company, Renfrew; "E" Company, Johnstone; "F" Company, Thornliebank; "G" Company, Barrhead; "H" Company, Pollokshaws.
7th Battalion: Stirling with "A" Company, Stirling (detachment at Bridge of Allan); "B" Company, Stenhousemuir (detachment at Denny); "C" Company, Falkirk (detachment at Bonnybridge); "D" Company, Lennoxtown (detachment at Kilsyth); "E" Company, Alloa; "F" Company, Alva (detachments at Dollar, Tillicoultry and Menstrie); "G" Company, Kinross (detachment at Kelty); "H" Company, Alloa (detachments at Sauchie and Clackmannan).
8th (The Argyllshire) Battalion: Dunoon with "A" Company, Inveraray (detachments at Lochgoilhead, Auchnagoul, Dalmally, Furnace, Cairndow, Strachur and Kilchrenan); "B" Company, Campbeltown; "C" Company, Southend (detachments at Campbeltown, Kelkenzie, Glenbarr, Tayinloan, Stewarton and Drumlemble); "D" Company, Dunoon (detachment at Sandbank); "E" Company, Lochgilphead (detachments at Kilmartin, Tighnabruaich, Glendaruel, Ardrishaig and Tayvallich); "F" Company, Ballachulish (detachments at Kinlochleven, Ardgour and Duror); "G" Company, Bowmore (detachments at Jura, Port

Princess Louise's (Argyll and Sutherland Highlanders). *5th Battalion after receiving their Colours from the King at Windsor in 1909. The scarlet doublets have yellow facings and the tartan is Sutherland pattern. Note the badger heads on the sporrans.*

Ellen, Bridgend and Ballygrant); "H" Company, Easdale (detachments at Clachan, Oban, Cullipool, Toberonochy, Benderloch and Ardchattan). The Dunoon Grammar School Cadet Corps was affiliated.

9th (The Dumbartonshire) Battalion: Hartfield, Dumbarton with "A" Company, Helensburgh (detachment at Cardross); "B" Company, Kirkintilloch (detachments at Cumbernauld and Lenzie); "C" Company, Dumbarton; "D" Company, Milngavie; "E" Company, Jamestown (detachment at Bonhill); "F" Company, Alexandria (detachment at Renton); "G" and "H" Companies, Clydebank.

Princess Royal's Dragoon Guards. See 7th (Princess Royal's) Dragoon Guards.

Princess Victoria's (Royal Irish Fusiliers). Two Regular (1st and 2nd) and two Special Reserve (3rd and 4th) battalions. Depot, Armagh.

1st Battalion: Shorncliffe.

2nd Battalion: Quetta, India.

3rd Battalion: Armagh.

4th Battalion: Cavan.

Princess Louise's (Argyll and Sutherland Highlanders). *Collar badge featuring the boar's head of the Argylls and cat belonging to the Sutherlands. The mottos are Ne obliviscaris (Do not forget) and Sans peur (Without fear).*

Princess Louise's (Argyll and Sutherland Highlanders). *Cap badge.*

Princess Victoria's (Royal Irish Fusiliers). *Just visible is the regiment's two-piece cap badge – a coronet above a grenade on the ball of which are the Prince of Wales's plumes and a harp. The same badges, this time placed side-by-side, are worn on the collar. The jacket is scarlet with blue collar and cuffs.*

Q

Queen Alexandra's Imperial Military Nursing Service. Personnel attached to medical establishments. There was also a reserve of staff – the Queen Alexandra's Imperial Military Nursing Service Reserve, and a Territorial Force element know as Territorial Force Nursing Service (*qv*).

Queen Alexandra's Own Royal Hussars. See 19th (Queen Alexandra's Own Royal) Hussars.

Queen Mary's Grammar School Officers Training Corps. Walsall. Two infantry companies, Junior Division.

Queen Alexandra's Imperial Military Nursing Service Reserve. *The Regular, Reserve and Territorial Force (Territorial Force Nursing Service) had the same, grey with scarlet edging to the cape, uniform. The badge, which was worn suspended from a blue ribbon (with two white stripes and two red) attached to the cape, by the Reserve (the Regulars had the Dannebrog, or Danes' Cross of Queen Alexandra) had the letter "R" in the centre. The two scarlet bands worn on the lower sleeves indicate that the wearer is a Sister.*

Queen Mary's Own Hussars. See 18th (Queen Mary's Own) Hussars.

Queen Mary's Regiment. See Surrey Yeomanry (Queen Mary's Regiment).

Queen Victoria School for the Sons of Scottish Sailors and Soldiers. Dunblane.

Queen Victoria's Rifles. See 9th Battalion, London Regiment.

Queen's Bays. See 2nd Dragoon Guards (Queen's Bays).

Queen's Edinburgh Rifles. See 4th and 5th Battalions, Royal Scots (Lothian Regiment).

Queen's Lancers. See 9th (Queen's Royal) Lancers and 16th (The Queen's) Lancers.

Queen's Own Cameron Highlanders. Two Regular (1st and 2nd), one Special Reserve (3rd) and one Territorial Force (4th) battalions. Depot, Inverness.
1st Battalion: Edinburgh.
2nd Battalion: Poona, India.
3rd Battalion: Inverness.
4th Battalion: Inverness with "A" Company, also at Inverness; "B" Company, Nairn (detachments at Cawdor, Ardersier, Auldearn, Croy and Petty); "C" Company, Inverness (detachment at Moy); "D" Company, Broadford (detachments at Torrin, Elgoll and Raasay); "E" Company, Fort William (detachments at Corpach, Fort Augustus and Invergarry); "F" Company, Kingussie (detachments at Dalwhinnie, Newtonmore, Kincraig or Inch, Aviemore and Ardverikie); "G" Company, Beauly (detachments at Struy, Kiltarlity, Balnain, Inchmore and Drumnadrochit); "H" Company, Portree (detachments at Glenmore, Bernisdale, Edinbane, Sconser, Tarbert (Harris), Kilmuir and Lochmaddy).

Queen's Own Cameron Highlanders. *Cap (bottom) and collar (top) badges.*

Queen's Own Cameron Highlanders. *Scarlet doublet with blue collars and cuffs, Cameron of Erracht tartan kilt.*

Queen's Own Dorset Yeomanry. *Note best shot in squadron badge to the left of beer barrel, and above, six efficiency (one for every four years) stars. The blue full-dress uniforms have scarlet facings.*

Queen's Own Royal Glasgow and Lower Ward of Lanarkshire Yeomanry. *Cap badge.*

Queen's Own Dorset Yeomanry. Territorial Force. Sherborne with "A" Squadron, Dorchester (detachments at Bridport, Weymouth, Maiden Newton and Charmouth); "B" Squadron, Sherborne (detachments at Yeovil and Pulham); "C" Squadron, Blandford (detachments at Wimborne, Wareham and Handley); "D" Squadron, Gillingham (detachments at Shaftesbury, Stalbridge and Sturminster Newton).

Queen's Own Hussars. See 4th (Queen's Own) Hussars and 7th (Queen's Own) Hussars.

Queen's Own Oxfordshire Hussars. See Oxfordshire Yeomanry (Queen's Own Oxfordshire Hussars).

Queen's Own Royal Glasgow and Lower Ward of Lanarkshire Yeomanry. Territorial Force. Yorkhill Parade, Yorkhill, Glasgow with "A" and "B" Squadrons, Glasgow; "C" Squadron, Paisley (detachment at Greenock); "D" Squadron, Glasgow.

Queen's Own Royal Regiment. See Staffordshire Yeomanry (Queen's Own Royal Regiment).

Queen's Own (Royal West Kent Regiment). Two Regular (1st and 2nd), one Special Reserve (3rd) and two Territorial Force (4th and 5th) battalions. Depot, Maidstone.

1st Battalion: Dublin.

2nd Battalion: Multan, India.

3rd Battalion: Maidstone.

4th Battalion: Tonbridge with "A" Company, Maidstone; "B" Company, Maidstone (detachment at West Malling); "C" Company, Tonbridge (detachment at Hadlow); "D" and "E" Companies, Tunbridge Wells; "F" Company, Orpington; "G" Company,

Sevenoaks; "H" Company, Westerham (detachment at Edenbridge). The Westerham and Chipstead Cadet Corps, headquarters at Westerham, was affiliated.

5th Battalion: East Street, Bromley with "A" and "B" Companies, also at East Street; "C" Company, Dartford; "D" Company, Beckenham; "E" Company, Sidcup (detachment at Dartford); "F" and "G" Companies, Chatham (detachments at Cliffe-at-Hoo); "H" Company, Swanley. The 1st Cadet (Chatham) Company, Royal Marine Light Infantry at Royal Marine Barracks, Chatham, was affiliated.

1st Cadet Battalion: 241 Stanstead Road, Forest Hill. Affiliated to 5th Battalion.

Queen's Own West Kent Yeomanry. Territorial Force. Union Street, Maidstone with "A" Squadron, Bromley (detachments at Catford and Woolwich); "B" Squadron, Dartford (detachments at Rochester, Gravesend, Sevenoaks and Woolwich); "C" Squadron, Tunbridge Wells (detachments at Tonbridge and Hawkhurst); "D" Squadron, Maidstone (detachments at West Malling, Westminster and Woolwich).

Queen's Own Worcestershire Hussars. See Worcestershire Yeomanry (The Queen's Own Worcestershire Hussars).

Queen's Own Yorkshire Dragoons. See Yorkshire Dragoons Yeomanry (Queen's Own).

Queen's Royal Lancers. See 9th (Queen's Royal) Lancers.

Queen's (Royal West Surrey Regiment). Two Regular (1st and 2nd), one Special Reserve (3rd) and two Territorial Force (4th and 5th) battalions. Depot, Guildford.

1st Battalion: Bordon.

2nd Battalion: Pretoria.

3rd Battalion: Guildford.

4th Battalion: Croydon with "A" and "B" Companies, also in Croydon; "C" Company, Crystal Palace; "D" Company, Croydon; "E" Company, Caterham (detachment at Godstone); "F" Company, Croydon; "G" Company, Lingfield (detachment at Oxted); "H" Company: Croydon. The West Croydon Cadets, headquarters in Drummond Road, West Croydon, were affiliated.

5th Battalion: Guildford with "A" Company, Reigate (detachments at Horley and Brockham); "B" Company, Camberley (detachments at Bagshot and Frimley); "C" Company, Guildford (detachment at Albury); "D" Company, Guildford (detachment at Bramley); "E" Company, Farnham (detachment at Frensham); "F" Company, Godalming (detachments at Haslemere, Chiddingfold, Witley, Elstead and Alford); "G" Company, Dorking (detachments at Holmwood and Shere); "H" Company, Woking (detachments at Knapp Hill, Byfleet and Send). The Frimley and Camberley Cadet Corps, headquarters at "Thornhurst" Camberley, and "G" (Surrey) and "H" (Surrey) Companies, 1st Cadet Battalion, Hampshire Regiment, headquarters, Farnham, were affiliated.

Queen's Westminster Cadet Corps. See 16th London Regiment.

Queen's Westminster Rifles. See 16th Battalion, London Regiment.

Queen's Own (Royal West Kent Regiment). *Cap badge. Both the horse and motto Invicta (Unconquered) are from the arms of Kent.*

Queen's (Royal West Surrey Regiment). *4th Battalion leaving Croydon for war stations shortly after mobilization, August, 1914.*

Queen's (Royal West Surrey Regiment). *5th Battalion. The regimental badge of a Paschal Lamb (the ancient badge of the Regiment, confirmed in 1751) is worn on the cap, collar and black pouch-belt. The uniform is green with scarlet facings.*

R

Radley College Officers Training Corps. Abingdon, Berkshire. Three infantry companies, Junior Division.

Rangers. See 12th Battalion, London Regiment.

Reading School Officers Training Corps. One infantry company, Junior Division.

Reading University Officers Training Corps. One infantry company, Senior Division.

Reigate Grammar School Officers Training Corps. One infantry company, Junior Division.

Remount Service. Units of the Army's Remount Service (Depots) numbered five within the United Kingdom and one in South Africa. No.1 Depot: Lusk Farm, Dublin. No.2 Depot: Woolwich. No.3 Depot: Melton Mowbray. No.4 Depot: Arborfield Cross, near Reading. No.5 Depot: Pinckard's Farm, Chiddingfold, Godalming. South Africa Depot: Roberts' Heights, Pretoria.

Renfrewshire Battalion. See 5th and 6th (Refrewshire) Battalions, Princess Louise's (Argyll and Sutherland Highlanders).

Renfrewshire Batteries, 1st (Howitzer), 2nd (Howitzer). See 3rd Highland Brigade, Royal Field Artillery (Howitzer).

Renfrewshire Fortress Engineers. Territorial Force. Fort Matilda, Greenock with No.1 Works Company at Paisley, No.2 Electric Lights Company, Greenock.

Renfrewshire Small Arm Section Ammunition Column. See 3rd Highland Brigade, Royal Field Artillery (Howitzer)

Repton School Officers Training Corps. Four infantry companies, Junior Division.

Richmond County School Cadet Corps. See 6th Battalion, East Surrey Regiment.

Rifle Brigade (The Prince Consort's Own). Four Regular (1st, 2nd, 3rd and 4th) and two Special Reserve (5th and 6th) battalions. Depot, Winchester.

1st Battalion: Colchester.
2nd Battalion: Kuldana, India.
3rd Battalion: Cork.
4th Battalion: Dagshai, India.
5th Battalion: Winchester.
6th Battalion: Winchester.

Robin Hood Battalion. See 7th (Robin Hood) Battalion, Sherwood Foresters (Nottinghamshire and Derbyshire Regiment).

Ross and Cromarty (Mountain) Battery. See 4th Highland Brigade, Royal Garrison Artillery (Mountain).

Rifle Brigade (The Prince Consort's Own). 1st Battalion shortly after arriving in France, 1914.

Ross Highland Battalion. See 4th (Ross Highland) Battalion, Seaforth Highlanders (Ross-shire Buffs, The Duke of Albany's).

Rossall School Officers Training Corps. Fleetwood, Lancashire. Three infantry companies, Junior Division.

Ross-shire Buffs. See Seaforth Highlanders (Ross-shire Buffs, The Duke of Albany's).

Rough Riders. See City of London Yeomanry (Rough Riders).

Royal Agricultural College Officers Training Corps. Cirencester. One infantry company, Senior Division.

Royal Alderney Militia. Part of the Channel Islands Militia group and comprising two artillery batteries and an engineer section.

Royal Anglesey Royal Engineers Militia. Special Reserve. Beaumaris.

Royal Army Medical College. Grosvenor Road, London.

Royal Army Medical Corps. The Regular element of the RAMC consisted of a series of numbered companies (see details below) and three Depot companies, the latter being designated by letter – "A", "B", "C" – and based in Aldershot. There was one Special Reserve formation designated No.18 Field Ambulance and with headquarters at Upper Chorlton Road, Manchester.

The Territorial Force (details of individual units have been recorded under their designations) mainly comprised a series of Field Ambulances attached either to a Mounted Brigade – Eastern, Highland, London, Lowland, North Midland, Notts & Derby, South Eastern, 1st South Midland, 2nd South Midland, South Wales, 1st South Western, 2nd South Western, Welsh Border, Yorkshire; or TF Division – East Anglian, Highland, Home Counties, East Lancashire, West Lancashire, 1st London, 2nd London, Lowland, North Midland, South Midland, Northumbrian, West Riding, Welsh, Wessex. Within each division, Field Ambulances were numbered 1st, 2nd, 3rd (each comprising three sections lettered "A", "B" and "C") and allotted on to each of the three infantry brigades. In the same way, Clearing Hospitals (all fourteen were in existence prior to the First World War, but, as of August, 1914, a number had not yet received recognition by the Army Council) and Schools of Instruction were attached to TF Divisions. Clearing Hospitals were designated according to division, whereas Schools of Instruction (see details below) were numbered. There were also twenty-three General Hospitals organised within Army Command areas – 1st and 2nd Eastern; 1st, 2nd, 3rd, 4th London; 1st, 2nd, 3rd, 4th, 5th Northern; 1st, 2nd, 3rd, 4th Scottish; 1st, 2nd 3rd, 4th, 5th Southern; 1st, 2nd, 3rd Western – and a Sanitary Service made up of two units based in London.

Companies: No.1, Aldershot; No.2, Aldershot; No.3, Aldershot; No.4, Netley; No.5, Netley; No.6, Cosham; No.7, Devonport; No.8, York; No.9, Colchester; No.10, Chatham; No.11, Shorncliffe; No.12, Woolwich; No.13, Edinburgh; No.14, Dublin; No.15, Belfast; No.16, Cork; No.17, Curragh; No.18, Rochester Row, London; No.19, Chester; No.20, Tidworth; No.21, Netley; No.22, Wynberg; No.23, Roberts' Heights, Pretoria; No.25, Bermuda; No.26, Ceylon; No.27, Hong Kong; No.28, Gibraltar; No.29, Jamaica; No.30, Malta; No.31, Mauritius; No.32, Singapore; No.33, Cairo; No.34, Woolwich; No.35, Grosvenor Road, London.

Royal Army Medical Corps. *Territorial staff-sergeant in full-dress uniform – blue with dull-cherry facings.*

Schools of Instruction: No.1 (Highland Division), Territorial Barracks, Fonthill, Aberdeen; No.2 (Lowland Division), Yorkhill Parade, Yorkhill, Glasgow; No.3 (East Lancashire Division), Upper Chorlton Road, Manchester; No.3 (West Lancashire Division), 14 Harper Street, Liverpool; No.4 (Welsh Division), 15 Newport Road, Cardiff; No.5 (West Riding Division), Harewood Barracks, Woodhouse Lane, Leeds; No.5 (Northumbrian Division), Hutton Terrace, Newcastle-upon-Tyne; No.6 (North Midland Division), Oxford Street, Leicester; No.7 (South Midland Division), The Barracks, Great Brook Street, Birmingham; No.8 (Wessex Division), Leonards Buildings, Goldsmith Street, Exeter; No.9 (East Anglian Division), Woodbridge Road, Ipswich; No.10 (Home Counties Division), The Palace, Maidstone; London (1st and 2nd London Divisions), Duke of York's Headquarters, Chelsea.

Royal Army Medical Corps Training Establishment. Aldershot.

Royal Artillery. See Royal Regiment of Artillery.

Royal Berkshire Regiment. See Princess Charlotte of Wales's (Royal Berkshire Regiment).

Royal Bucks Hussars. See Buckinghamshire Yeomanry (Royal Bucks Hussars).

Royal Canadians. See Prince of Wales's Leinster Regiment (Royal Canadians).

Royal College of Surgeons in Ireland Officers Training Corps. Dublin. One infantry company, Senior Division.

Royal Company of Archers. See King's Body Guard for Scotland.

Royal 1st Devon Yeomanry. Territorial Force. 9 Dix's Field, Exeter with "A" Squadron, Thorverton (detachments at Crediton, Tiverton, Rackenford, Cullompton and Bampton); "B" Squadron, Ottery St Mary (detachments at Exmouth, Exeter, Axminster, Sidmouth and Dawlish); "C" Squadron, Totnes (detachments at Moreton Hampstead, Bovey Tracey, Newton Abbot, Dartmouth, Kingsbridge and Plymouth); "D" Squadron, Bodmin (detachments at Launceston, Camelford, Liskeard, Truro, Helston and Penzance).

Royal (Dick) Veterinary College, Edinburgh Officers Training Corps. Four Army Veterinary Corps sections, Senior Division.

Royal Dragoons. See 1st (Royal) Dragoons.

__Royal 1st Devon Yeomanry.__ Senior NCOs. The party includes a Farrier-Sergeant (third from left, back row) and Signals Instructor (extreme left, front row). Scarlet tunics are worn with blue collars and cuffs.

Royal Dublin Fusiliers. *1st Battalion.*

Royal East Kent (The Duke of Connaught's Own) (Mounted Rifles).

Royal Dublin Fusiliers. *4th Battalion. Major H.R. Beddoes who wears regimental full-dress uniform – scarlet tunic with blue facings. The grenade collar badges have the silver figures of a tiger and elephant and represent long service in India.*

Royal Dublin Fusiliers. Two Regular (1st and 2nd) and three Special Reserve (3rd, 4th and 5th) battalions. Depot, Naas.
1st Battalion: Madras, India.
2nd Battalion: Gravesend.
3rd Battalion: Naas.
4th Battalion: Dublin.
5th Battalion: Dublin.

Royal East Kent (The Duke of Connaught's Own) (Mounted Rifles) Yeomanry. Territorial Force. Canterbury with "A" Squadron, Chatham; "B" Squadron, Faversham (detachments at Sheerness, Sittingbourne, Herne Bay and Canterbury); "C" Squadron, Dover (detachments at Waldershare, Deal, Margate and Ramsgate); "D" Squadron, Ashford (detachments at Folkestone, Tenterden, Bethersden, Headcord, Wye, New Romney and Westminster).

Royal Engineer Cadets (2nd London Division). See 2nd London Divisional Engineers.

Royal Engineers. Regular Army RE units appeared within three main groups: (1) a series of numbered companies (1st to 59th, but several gaps leaving a total of fifty-one) carrying out Fortress, Field, Railway, Survey, Line of Communication and Coast Defence duties; (2) ten lettered companies, nine at the Chatham Depot, one at Army Headquarters, India; (3) Signal Units. These, with the exception of one squadron, were designated as companies. There was also a collection of miscellaneous units and one Coast Battalion made up from personnel from several of the numbered companies. The RE Special Reserve comprised a Motor Cyclist Section and the

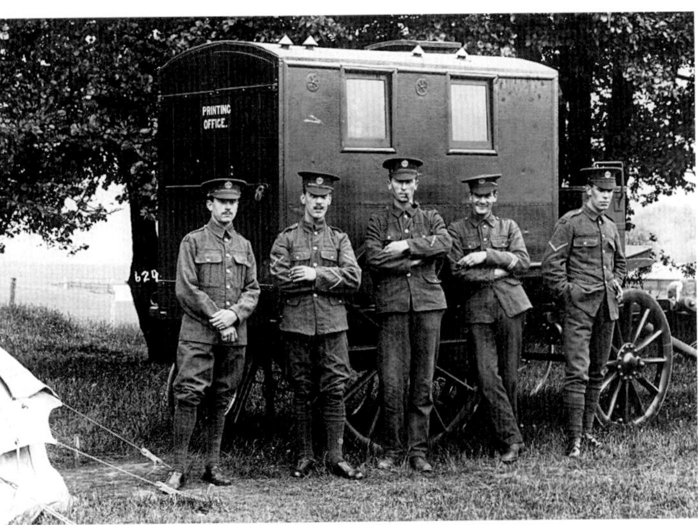

Royal Engineers. *Printing Section.*

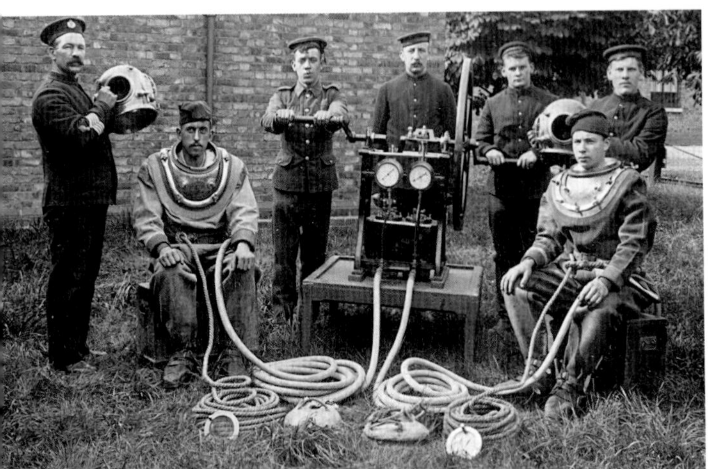

Royal Engineers. *Divers.*

Royal Engineers. *Signal Service Territorial.*

Postal Section based at General Post Office Headquarters in London. There were two other units – the Royal Anglesey and Royal Monmouthshire, and these have been recorded under their own titles. For the Territorial Force (all units recorded under their own titles), there were fourteen groups of Divisional Engineers: East Anglian, Highland, Home Counties, East Lancashire, West Lancashire, 1st London, 2nd London, Lowland, North Midland, South Midland, Northumbrian, West Riding, Welsh and Wessex, each comprising two field companies. The Royal Engineers Territorial Force Signal Service was made up of fourteen units with divisional (East Anglian etc.) designations (HQ and four sections each); five companies allotted as Army Troops: London District, Northern Command, Scottish Command, Southern Command, Western Command (these comprising Wireless, Cable and Airline companies) and three, Lothian, Black Watch and South Wales, Infantry Brigade Signal Sections. Fortress Engineers, designated City of Aberdeen, Cinque Ports, Cornwall, Devonshire, Dorsetshire, City of Dundee, Durham, City of Edinburgh, Essex, Glamorgan, Hampshire, Kent, Lancashire, Renfrewshire, East Riding, Sussex and Wiltshire, comprised varying numbers of Works and Electric Lights companies. Other TF RE units were the London and Tyne Electrical Engineers, and an all officer formation known as the Engineer and Railway Staff Corps.

Companies, 1st to 30th: 1st (Fortress) at Gibraltar; 2nd (Field), Cairo; 3rd (Fortress), Dover; 4th (Fortress), Gosport; 5th (Field), Aldershot; 6th (Fortress), Weymouth; 7th (Field), Shorncliffe; 8th (Railway), Longmoor Camp, East Liss; 9th (Field), Woolwich; 10th (Railway), Longmoor Camp, East Liss; 11th

(Field), Aldershot; 12th (Field), Moore Park, Kilworth; 13th (Survey), York; 14th (Survey), Dublin; 15th (Fortress), Gibraltar; 16th, with Coast Battalion, one section at Paull-on-Humber, one section, Middlesbrough; 17th (Field), Curragh; 18th (Fortress), Falmouth; 19th (Survey), Southampton; 20th (Fortress), Devonport; 21st (Fortress), Harwich; 22nd (Fortress), Yarmouth, Isle of Wight; 23rd (Field), Aldershot; 24th (Fortress), Malta; 25th (Fortress), Hong Kong; 26th (Field), Bordon, 27th (Fortress), Bermuda; 28th (Fortress), Malta; 29th (Works, Line of Communication), Chatham; 30th (Fortress), Plymouth.

Companies, 31st to 59th: 31st (Fortress), Ceylon; 32nd (Fortress), Gibraltar; 33rd (Fortress), Fort Camden, Crosshaven, County Cork, with detachments serving with the Coast Battalion at Berehaven and Lough Swilly; 34th (Fortress), Channel Isles; 35th (Fortress), Pembroke Dock, with detachments serving with the Coast Battalion at Cardiff and Liverpool; 36th (Fortress), Sierra Leone; 38th (Field), Cork; 39th (Fortress), Sheernes, with a detachment serving with the Coast Battalion at Gravesend; 40th (Fortress), Hong Kong; 41st (Fortress), Singapore; 42nd (Fortress), Gosport; 43rd (Fortress), Mauritius; 44th (Fortress), Jamaica; 45th (Fortress), Gibraltar; 47th (Fortress), Simonstown; 49th (Coast Battalion), North Queensferry, with sections at Greenock and Broughty Ferry; 54th (Field), Chatham; 55th (Field), Pretoria; 56th (Field), Bulford, Salisbury Plain; 57th (Field), Bulford, Salisbury Plain, 59th (Field), Curragh.

Lettered Companies: "A", "B", "C", "D", "E", "F", "G", "L" and "M" at Chatham Depot; "H", Army Headquarters, India.

Signal Squadron and Troops: 1st Signal Squadron at Longmoor, East Liss; 1st Signal Troop, Aldershot; 2nd Signal Troop, Tidworth; 3rd Signal Troop, Curragh; 4th Signal Troop, Canterbury; 5th Signal Troop, York.

Signal Companies: "A" at Aldershot; "B", Limerick; "K", Aldborough House, Dublin; 1st, Aldershot; 2nd, Aldershot; 3rd, Bulford, Salisbury Plain; 4th, Woolwich; 5th, Carlow; 6th, Limerick; 7th, South Africa.

Miscellaneous Units: 1st Bridging Train, Aldershot. 2nd Bridging Train, Chatham. 1st Field Squadron, Aldershot. 4th Field Troop, Curragh. Training Depot Field Units), Aldershot. Railway Depot, Longmore. Colonial Survey Section, Federated Malay States, Penang. 1st Printing Company, Chatham.

Coast Battalion: Made up from 6th Company at Weymouth; 16th Company, North Shields, Paull-on-Humber and Middlesbrough; 49th Company, North Queensferry, Greenock and Broughty Ferry, and sections and detachments provided by 18th Company, Falmouth; 33rd Company, Berehaven and Lough Swilly, County Cork; 35th Company, Cardiff and Liverpool, 39th Company, Gravesend.

Royal Field Artillery. *Detraining at Okehampton, 1911. Note the use of hired civilian transport.*

Royal Field Artillery. *137th Battery on exercise, 1914.*

Royal Field Artillery. With Headquarters at Woolwich, the Royal Field Artillery (Regular Army) comprised 147 batteries. These were designated by number and placed into fifty-one (including six reserve) brigades. Brigades were identified by Roman numerals. There were six depots situated around the United Kingdom, and in India, twelve ammunition columns.

1st to 50th Batteries: 1st (XLV Brigade), 2nd (XIII), 3rd (XLV), 4th (VII), 5th (XLV), 6th (XL), 7th (IV), 8th (XIII), 9th (XLI), 10th (XVII), 11th (XV), 12th (XXXV), 13th (I), 14th (IV), 15th (XXXVI), 16th (XLI), 17th (XLI), 18th (III), 19th (IX), 20th (IX), 21st (II), 22nd (XXXIV), 23rd (XL), 24th (XXXVIII), 25th (XXXV), 26th (XVII), 27th (XXXII), 28th (IX), 29th (XLII), 30th (XLIII), 31st (XXXVII), 32nd (XXXIII), 33rd (XXXIII), 34th (XXXVIII), 35th (XXXVII), 36th (XXXIII), 37th (VIII), 38th (VII), 39th (XIV), 40th (XLIII), 41st (XLII), 42nd (II), 43rd (XII), 44th (XIII), 45th (XLII), 46th (XXXIX), 47th (XLIV), 48th (XXXVI), 49th (XL), 50th (XXXIV).

51st to 100th Batteries: 51st (XXXIX Brigade), 52nd (XV), 53rd (II), 54th (XXXIX), 55th (XXXVII), 56th (XLIV), 57th (XLIII), 58th (XXXV), 59th (XVIII), 60th (XLIV), 61st (VIII), 62nd (III), 63rd (V), 64th (V), 65th (VIII), 66th (IV), 67th (I), 68th (XIV), 69th (I), 70th (XXXIV), 71st (XXXVI), 72nd (XXXVIII). 73rd (V), 74th (VI), 75th (III), 76th (X), 77th (VI), 78th (VII), 79th (VI), 80th (XV), 81st (X), 82nd (X), 83rd (XI), 84th (XI), 85th (XI), 86th (XII), 87th (XII), 88th (XIV), 89th (XVI), 90th (XVI), 91st (XVI), 92nd (XVII), 93rd (XVIII), 94th (XVIII), 95th (XIX), 96th (XIX), 97th (XIX), 98th (XX), 99th (XX), 100th (XX).

101st to 147th Batteries: 101st (XXI Brigade), 102nd (XXI), 103rd (XXI), 104th (XXII), 105th (XXII), 106th (XXII), 107th (XXIII), 108th (XXIII), 109th (XXIII), 110th (XXIV), 111th (XXIV), 112th (XXIV), 113th (XXV), 114th (XXV), 115th (XXV), 116th (XXVI), 117th (XXVI), 118th (XXVI), 119th (XXVII), 120th (XXVII), 121st (XXVII), 122nd (XXVIII), 123rd (XXVIII), 124th (XXVIII), 125th (XXIX), 126th (XXIX), 127th (XXIX), 128th (XXX), 129th (XXX), 130th (XXX), 131st (XXXI), 132nd (XXXI), 133rd (XXXI), 134th (XXXII), 135th (XXXII), 136th (I Reserve), 137th (I Reserve), 138th (II Reserve), 139th (II Reserve), 140th (III Reserve), 141st (III Reserve), 142nd (IV Reserve), 143rd (IV Reserve), 144th (V Reserve), 145th (V Reserve), 146th (VI Reserve), 147th (VI Reserve).

I to X Brigades: I, Edinburgh and comprising 13th, 67th and 69th Batteries; II, Cahir, 21st, 42nd and

Royal Field Artillery. *18-pounder gun.*

53rd Batteries; III, Jullundur, India, 18th Battery at Jullundur, 62nd Battery, Multan and 75th Battery, Peshawar; IV, Secunderabad, India, 7th, 14th and 66th Batteries; V, Lucknow, India, 63rd Battery at Cawnpore, 64th Battery, Fyzabad and 73rd Battery, Lucknow; VI (Howitzer), Jhansi, India, 74th (Howitzer) Battery at Jhansi, 77th (Howitzer) Battery, Meerut and 79th (Howitzer) Battery, Jhansi; VII, Rawal Pindi, India, 4th, 38th and 78th Batteries; VIII (Howitzer), Kildare, 37th (Howitzer), 61st (Howitzer) and 65th (Howitzer) Batteries; IX, Meerut, India, 19th Battery at Meerut, 20th Battery, Bareilly and 28th Battery, Meerut; X, Kirkee, India, 76th, 81st and 82nd Batteries.

XI to XX Brigades: XI, Jubbulpore, India and comprising 83rd, 84th and 85th Batteries; XII (Howitzer), Clonmel, 43rd (Howitzer) Battery at Fethard, 86th (Howitzer) Battery, Clonmel and 87th (Howitzer) Battery, Kilkenny; XIII, Bangalore, India, 2nd Battery at Bangalore, 8th Battery, Bellary and 44th Battery, Bangalore; XIV, Colchester, 39th, 68th and 88th Batteries; XV, Kildare, 11th, 52nd and 80th Batteries; XVI, Nowshere, India, 89th, 90th and 91st Batteries; XVII, Allahabad, India, 10th Battery at Barrackpore, 26th Battery, Allahabad and 92nd Battery, Dinapore; XVIII, Lahore Cantonment, India, 59th Battery at Lahore Cantonment, 93rd Battery, Ferozepore and 94th Battery, Lahore Cantonment; XIX, St Thomas' Mount, India, 95th Battery at Kamptee, 96th Battery, Belgaum and 97th Battery, St Thomas' Mount; XX, Neemuch, India, 98th Battery at Nasirabad, 99th and 100th Batteries, Neemuch.

XXI to XXX Brigades: XXI, Hyderabad, India and comprising 101st and 102nd Batteries at Hyderabad and 103rd Battery, Karachi; XXII, Roberts' Heights, Transvaal and comprising 104th Battery at Roberts' Heights, 105th Battery, Potchefstroom and 106th Battery, Roberts' Heights; XXIII, Bulford and comprising 107th, 108th and 109th Batteries; XXIV, Ballincollig and comprising 110th, 111th and 112th Batteries; XXV, Deepcut and comprising 113th, 114th and 115th Batteries; XXVI, Aldershot and comprising 116th, 117th and 118th Batteries; XXVII, Newbridge, Ireland and comprising 119th, 120th and 121st Batteries; XXVIII, Dundalk and comprising 122nd, 123rd and 124th Batteries; XXIX, Shorncliffe and comprising 125th, 126th and 127th Batteries; XXX (Howitzer), Bulford and comprising 128th (Howitzer), 129th (Howitzer) and 130th (Howitzer) Batteries.

XXXI to XL Brigades: XXXI, Sheffield and comprising 131st, 132nd and 133rd Batteries; XXXII, Woolwich, 27th, 134th and 135th Batteries;

XXXIII, Exeter, 32nd, 33rd and 36th Batteries; XXXIV, Aldershot, 22nd, 50th and 70th Batteries; XXXV, Woolwich, 12th, 25th and 58th Batteries; XXXVI, Ewshott, Farnham, 15th, 48th and 71st Batteries; XXXVII (Howitzer), Woolwich, 31st (Howitzer), 35th (Howitzer) and 55th (Howitzer) Batteries; XXXVIII, Fermoy, 24th, 34th and 72nd Batteries; XXXIX, Bordon, 46th, 51st and 54th Batteries; XL, Bulford, 6th, 23rd and 49th Batteries.

XLI to XLV Brigades: XLI, Bordon and comprising 9th, 16th and 17th Batteries; XLII, Bulford, 29th, 41st and 45th Batteries; XLIII (Howitzer), Deepcut, 30th (Howitzer), 40th (Howitzer) and 57th (Howitzer) Batteries; XLIV (Howitzer), Brighton, 47th (Howitzer), 56th (Howitzer) and 60th (Howitzer) Batteries; XLV, Leeds, 1st, 3rd and 5th Batteries.

Reserve Brigades: I, Newcastle-upon-Tyne and comprising 136th and 137th Batteries; II, Preston, 138th and 139th Batteries; III, Hillsea, 140th and 141st Batteries; IV, Woolwich, 142nd and 143rd Batteries; V, Athlone, 144th and 145th Batteries; VI, Glasgow, 146th and 147th Batteries.

Ammunition Columns: No.1, Nowshera; No.2, Rawal Pindi; No.3, Lahore Cantonment; No.4, Hyderabad; No.5, Deesa; No.6, Kirkee; No.7, Meerut; No.8, Fyzabad; No.9, Secunderabad; No.10, Bangalore; No.11, Jubbulpore; No.12 (Howitzer), Jhansi.

Depots: No.1, Newcastle-upon-Tyne; No.2, Preston; No.3, Hilsea; No.4, Woolwich; No.5, Athlone; No.6, Glasgow.

In 1908, field and howitzer artillery units were raised for each of the fourteen newly formed Territorial Force divisions – East Anglian, Highland, Home Counties, East Lancashire, West Lancashire, 1st London, 2nd London, Lowland, North Midland, South Midland, Northumbrian, West Riding, Welsh and Wessex. Four brigades (three field, one howitzer) were allotted to thirteen divisions, the Highland Division having just two field and one howitzer. A brigade designated 4th Highland was made up of mountain artillery, and this was placed within the Royal Garrison Artillery. Each field brigade comprised three batteries (these being designated according to geographical location) and an ammunition column. Howitzer brigades had two batteries and an ammunition column. Records of Territorial Force RFA brigades and batteries can be found under their relevant divisions.

Royal Flying Corps. Until 1918, and the formation in April that year of the Royal Air Force, the Royal Flying Corps formed part of the army and as such appeared in the *Army List*. Divided into Naval and Military Wings, the former being known as the Royal Naval Air Service, the several component units and establishments of the Corps were listed as Flying Schools, Naval Air Stations, a Recruit Depot, Kite Section and Aircraft Park, together with an Aeronautical Inspection Department. Numbered squadrons, just seven shown in the *Monthly Army List* for August, 1914, appear within the Military Wing section only. An 8th was listed, but recorded as "Not yet formed." The Royal Naval Air Service, notes the *Army List*, is "Borne on the Books of HMS Pembroke." The Central Flying School was at Upavon, Salisbury Plain.

Naval Wing (Royal Naval Air Service): Comprised the Naval Flying School at Eastchurch, and eight Naval Air Stations located – Isle of Grain, Calshot,

Royal Flying Corps. *The cloth shoulder titles are white letters on blue.*

Felixstowe, Yarmouth, Fort George, Dundee, Farnborough and Kingsnorth.

Military Wing: Comprised Headquarters at South Farnborough; Recruit Depot, South Farnborough; Kite Section, South Farnborough; 1st Squadron, South Farnborough; 2nd Squadron, Montrose; 3rd Squadron, Salisbury Plain; 4th Squadron, Salisbury Plain; 5th Squadron, Gosport; 6th Squadron, South Farnborough; 7th Squadron, South Farnborough; Aircraft Park, South Farnborough and the Aeronautical Inspection Department, South Farnborough. There was also an Indian Central Flying School at Sitapur.

Royal Fusiliers (City of London Regiment). Four regular (1st, 2nd, 3rd and 4th) and three Special Reserve (5th, 6th and 7th) battalions. Depot, Hounslow. The Royal Fusiliers did not have Territorial Force battalions in the same way as other regiments – i.e. numbered in sequence following the Regular and Special Reserve. Affiliated to the Regiment, however, were the 1st to 4th Battalions of the London Regiment.

1st Battalion: Kinsale, Ireland.
2nd Battalion: Calcutta, India.
3rd Battalion: Lucknow, India.
4th Battalion: Parkhurst, Isle of Wight.
5th Battalion: Hounslow.
6th Battalion: Hounslow.
7th Battalion: Artillery Place, Finsbury, London.
1st Cadet Battalion: With Headquarters at Harben Armoury, Pond Street, Hampstead, the Battalion had companies situated around the London area.

Royal Garrison Artillery. The Royal Garrison Artillery (Regular Army) in August, 1914 comprised Garrison and Siege formations, these styled as companies, and batteries of Heavy Artillery. Companies/batteries were numbered 1 to 108 in a single sequence. Gaps in the line-up, however, left a total of eighty-six companies and twelve batteries. There was also a Mountain Division, which comprised nine batteries (eight in India, one Egypt), and shown in the *Army List* under the heading "Local Battalion of Royal Garrison Artillery" the Hong Kong-Singapore Battalion. Another "Local" formation was the Sierra Leone Company. At home there were two Heavy Brigades, each with three batteries, a Siege Artillery Brigade of two companies, and four Depots.

Two units, the Cork and Antrim, made up the RGA Special Reserve, while the Territorial Force encom-

Royal Fusiliers. *4th Battalion officers at Parkhurst, Isle of Wight. The Battalion left for France on 13 August, 1914 and by the following November had lost (killed or wounded) some fifty officers. Full-dress uniforms are worn – scarlet with blue facings.*

Royal Fusiliers (City of London Regiment). *1st Cadet Battalion at its Pond Street, Hampstead Headquarters.*

Royal Garrison Artillery.

passed one Mountain Brigade, the 4th Highland (for 1st, 2nd and 3rd Highland Brigades, see Royal Field Artillery); fourteen batteries (with ammunition columns) of Heavy Artillery (each attached to a TF division), and units for the defence of ports. The Divisional Heavy Batteries were designated according to the division to which they were attached, those other than London, Lancashire and West Riding including in their title a county location – East Anglian (Essex), Highland (Fifeshire), Home Counties (Kent), 1st Lancashire, 2nd Lancashire, 1st London, 2nd London, Lowland (City of Edinburgh), North Midland (Staffordshire), South Midland (Warwickshire), Northumbrian (North Riding), West Riding, Welsh (Carnarvonshire) and Wessex (Hampshire). Lancashire and London batteries were brigaded as pairs and were administered under the overall titles of Lancashire Brigade and London Brigade. Units for the defence of ports were designated – Clyde, Cornwall, Devonshire, Dorsetshire, Durham, East Riding, Essex and Suffolk, Forth, Glamorgan, Hampshire, Kent, Lancashire and Cheshire, Orkney, Pembroke, North Scottish, Sussex and Tynemouth. These were mixed and comprised both Heavy batteries and Garrison companies. Special Reserve and Territorial Force formations have been recorded under their own titles. Regular formations were:

Mountain Division: Comprised No.1 Battery at Khaira Gali; No.2 Battery, Jutogh; No.3 Battery, Quetta; No.4 Battery, Quetta; No. 5 Battery, Jutogh; No.6 Battery, Rawal Pindi; No.7 Battery, Cairo; No.8 Battery, Quetta and No.9 Battery, Kalabagh.

Heavy Brigades: 1st, Fareham and comprising Nos. 26, 35 and 108 Batteries; 2nd, Woolwich, Nos. 24, 31 and 48 Batteries.

Siege Artillery Brigade: Plymouth and comprising Nos. 39 and 107 Companies.

Hong Kong-Singapore Battalion: Comprising Nos.1, 2, 3 Companies at Hong Kong; No.4 Company, Mauritius and No.5 Company, Singapore.

Sierra Leone Company:

Depots: No.1, Newhaven; No.2, Fort Rowner, Gosport; No.3, Plymouth Citadel; No.4, Great Yarmouth.

Companies and Batteries Nos. 1 to 30: All companies are Garrison unless shown as "(Siege)". Batteries appear as "(Heavy)". No.1, Malta; No.2, Sheerness; No.3, Bermuda; No.4, Gibraltar; No.5, Malta; No.6, Gibraltar; No.7, Gibraltar; No.8, Gibraltar; No.9, Gibraltar; No.10, Queenstown Harbour; No.11, Golden Hill; No.12, Tynemouth; No.13, Landguard Fort, Landguard Point; No.14, Shoeburyness; No.15, Londonderry; No.16, Weymouth; No.17, Alderney; No.18, Sheerness; No.19, Sheerness; No.20, Jersey; No.21, Leith; No.22, Sheerness; No.23 (Siege), Fort Grange, Gosport; No.24 (Heavy), Woolwich; No.26 (Heavy), Fort Wallington; No.28, Weymouth; No.29, Portsmouth; No.30, Weymouth.

Companies and Batteries Nos. 31 to 70: No.31 (Heavy), Woolwich; No.32, Sandown; No.33, Golden Hill; No.34, Sandown; No.35 (Heavy), Fort Fareham; No.36, Plymouth; No.37, Portsmouth; No.38, Plymouth; No.39 (Siege), Plymouth; No.40, Dover; No.41, Plymouth; No.42, Portsmouth; No.43, Queenstown Harbour; No.44, Pembroke Dock; No.45, Plymouth; No.46, Dover; No.47, Tynemouth; No.48 (Heavy), Woolwich; No.49, Queenstown Harbour; No.50, Sierra Leone; No.51, Allahabad; No.52, Bombay; No.54, Gibraltar; No.55, Gibraltar; No.56, Mauritius; No.57, Pembroke Dock; No.59 (Siege), Rurki; No.60, Quetta; No.61, Aden; No.62, Calcutta; No.63, Malta; No.64, Rangoon; No.65, Malta; No.66, Jamaica; No.67, Portsmouth; No.68, Barian; No.69, Manora; No.70, Aden.

Companies and Batteries Nos. 71 to 108: No.71 (Heavy), Nowgong; No.72 (Heavy), Peshawar; No.73, Delhi; No.74, Fort Agra; No.75, Rangoon; No.76, Aden; No.77, Bombay; No.78, Singapore; No.79, Bombay; No.80, Singapore; No.81 (Siege), Rurki; No.82, Ferezepore; No.83, Hong Kong; No.84, Capetown; No.85, Bombay; No.86 (Heavy), Multan; No.87, Hong Kong; No.88, Hong Kong; No.90 (Heavy), Nowgong; No.91 (Heavy), Rurki; No.93, Ceylon; No.94, Rawal Pindi; No.95, Bermuda; No.96, Malta; No.97, Sumonstown; No.99, Malta; No.100, Malta; No.101, Quetta; No.102, Malta; No.104 (Heavy), Campbellpore; No.107 (Siege), Plymouth; No.108 (Heavy), Fort Nelson.

Royal Glasgow Yeomanry. See Queen's Own Royal Glasgow and Lower Ward of Lanarkshire Yeomanry.

Royal Gloucestershire Hussars Yeomanry. Territorial Force. Gloucester with "A" Squadron, Gloucester (detachments at Ledbury, Cheltenham and Winchcombe); "B" Squadron, Stroud (detachments at Westonbirt, Yate, Berkeley, Cirencester and Bourton-on-the-Water); "C" Squadron, Newport (detachments at Cardiff, Chepstow, Ebbw Vale, Monmouth and Abergavenny); "D" Squadron, Bristol (detachments at Broadmead, Tockington and Horfield).

Royal Gloucestershire Hussars Yeomanry. *The regimental-quarter-master-sergeant seen here has on the lower left arm of his blue jacket the crossed swords and crown of "best swordsman in regiment". The crossed rifles below indicate "best shot in squadron".*

Royal Gloucestershire Hussars Yeomanry. *Cap badge. The crest of the Duke of Beaufort.*

Royal Grammar School, High Wycombe Officers Training Corps. One infantry company, Junior Division.

Royal Grammar School, Lancaster Officers Training Corps. One infantry company, Junior Division.

Royal Grammar School, Newcastle-upon-Tyne Officers Training Corps. One infantry company, Junior Division.

Royal Grammar School, Worcester Officers Training Corps. One infantry company, Junior Division.

Royal Grammar School of King Edward VI Officers Training Corps. Guildford. One infantry company, Junior Division.

Royal Guernsey Militia. Part of the Channel Islands Militia group and comprising two light infantry battalions supported by artillery and engineer sections.

Royal Hibernian Military School. Phoenix Park, Dublin.

Royal Highlanders. See Black Watch (Royal Highlanders).

Royal Horse Artillery. With Headquarters and Depot at Woolwich, the Royal Horse Artillery comprised twenty-five Regular batteries. These were placed into thirteen brigades. Batteries were designated by letter ("A" to "Y") while brigades had Roman numerals. There was also a Riding Establishment at Woolwich, and nine lettered ammunition columns stationed in India.

The Territorial Force had fourteen RHA units designated according to geographical location – Ayrshire, Berkshire, 1st City of London, 2nd City of London, Essex, Glamorgan, Hampshire, Inverness-shire, Leicestershire, Nottinghamshire, West Riding, Shropshire, Somerset and Warwickshire. (See under individual titles.) These were made up of one battery and an ammunition column. The latter bore the designation of a TF Mounted Brigade.

Batteries: "A" (I Brigade), "B" (I), "C" (II), "D" (III),

Royal Horse Artillery. *Blue uniform with scarlet facings.*

Royal Horse Guards. *Taken in 1912, this photograph shows the "Blues" at arms inspection.*

Royal Horse Guards. *Dismounted at Horse Guards Parade, London. Blue jacket with scarlet facings, red plume.*

"E" (III), "F" (IV), "G" (V), "H" (VI), "I" (VII), "J" (IV), "K" (VI), "L" (VII), "M" (VIII), "N" (IX), "O" (V), "P" (X), "Q" (VIII), "R" (X), "S" (IX), "T" (XI), "U" (XI), "V" (XII), "W" (XII), "X" (XIII), "Y" (XIII).

Brigades: I, Ambala, India and comprising "A" (The Chestnut Troop) and "B" Batteries; II, "C" Battery at Canterbury; III, Newbridge, "D" and "E" Batteries; IV, "F" Battery at St John's Wood, "J" Battery, Aldershot; V, "G" and "O" Batteries at Ipswich; VI, "H" Battery at Trowbridge, "K" Battery, Christchurch; VII, Aldershot, "I" and "L" Batteries; VIII, India, "M" Battery at Risalpur, "Q" Battery, Sialkot; IX, India, "N" Battery at Secunderabad, "S" Battery, Bangalore; X, Woolwich, "P" and "R" Batteries; XI, India, "T" Battery at Abbassia, "U" Battery, Lucknow; XII, Meerut, India, "V" and "W" Batteries; XIII, Mhow, India, "X" and "Y" Batteries.

Ammunition Columns: "A", Campbellpore; "B", Sialkot; "C", Ambala; "D", Ahmednagar; "E", Mhow; "F", Meerut; "G", Lucknow; "H", Secunderabad; "I", Lahore.

Royal Horse Guards. Windsor.

Royal Hospital, Chelsea. Royal Hospital Road, Chelsea, London.

Royal Hospital, Kilmainham. Kilmainham near Dublin.

Royal Hussars. See 10th (Prince of Wales's Own Royal) Hussars.

Royal Inniskilling Fusiliers. Two Regular (1st and 2nd) and two Special Reserve (3rd and 4th) battalions. Depot, Omagh.
1st Battalion: Trimulgherry, India.
2nd Battalion: Dover.
3rd Battalion: Omagh.
4th Battalion: Enniskillen.

Royal Irish Dragoon Guards. See 4th (Royal Irish) Dragoon Guards.

Royal Irish Fusiliers. See Princess Victoria's (Royal Irish Fusiliers).

Royal Inniskilling Fusiliers. *Cap badge.*

Royal Inniskilling Fusiliers.

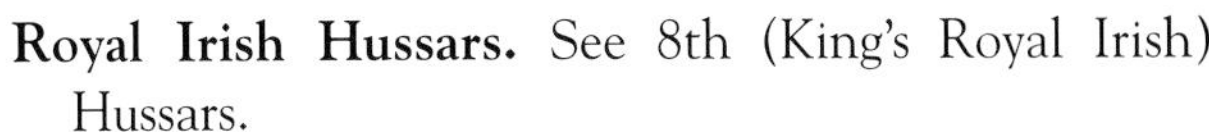

Royal Irish Hussars. See 8th (King's Royal Irish) Hussars.

Royal Irish Lancers. See 5th (Royal Irish) Lancers.

Royal Irish Regiment. Two Regular (1st and 2nd) and two Special Reserve (3rd and 4th) battalions. Depot, Clonmel.
1st Battalion: Nasirabad, India.
2nd Battalion: Devonport.
3rd Battalion: Clonmel.
4th Battalion: Kilkenny.

Royal Irish Rifles. Two Regular (1st and 2nd) and three Special Reserve (3rd, 4th and 5th) battalions. Depot, Belfast.
1st Battalion: Aden.
2nd Battalion: Tidworth.
3rd Battalion: Belfast.
4th Battalion: Newtownards.
5th Battalion: Downpatrick.

Royal Jersey Militia. Part of the Channel Islands Militia group and comprising three light infantry battalions: 1st (or West) Battalion, 2nd (or East) Battalion, 3rd (or South) Battalion supported by artillery, engineer and Medical sections.

Royal Lancaster Regiment. See King's Own (Royal Lancaster Regiment).

Royal Lancers. See 9th (Queen's Royal) Lancers.

Royal Malta Artillery. Malta. Nos.1, 2 and 3 Batteries.

Royal Marine Artillery. See Royal Marines.

Royal Marine Light Infantry.

Royal Marine Cadet Corps. See Depot Royal Marine Cadet Corps, 4th Battalion, Buffs (East Kent Regiment).

Royal Marine Light Infantry. See Royal Marines.

Royal Marine Light Infantry, 1st Cadet (Chatham) Company. See 5th Battalion, Queen's Own (Royal West Kent Regiment).

Royal Marines. Comprised Royal Marine Artillery and Royal Marine Light Infantry formed into three divisions – Chatham, Portsmouth and Plymouth. Depot, Deal.

Royal Military Academy. Woolwich.

Royal Military College. Sandhurst.

Royal Military School of Music. Kneller Hall, Hounslow.

Royal Monmouthshire Royal Engineers Militia. Special Reserve. Monmouth.

Royal Monmouthshire Royal Engineers Militia.

Royal Munster Fusiliers. Two Regular (1st and 2nd) and three Special Reserve (3rd, 4th and 5th) battalions. Depot, Tralee.

1st Battalion: Rangoon, Burma.

2nd Battalion: Malplaquet Barracks, Aldershot.

3rd Battalion: Tralee.

4th Battalion: Kinsale.

5th Battalion: Limerick.

Royal Naval Air Service. See Royal Flying Corps.

Royal North Devon Hussars Yeomanry. Territorial Force. Barnstaple with "A" Squadron, Holsworthy (detachments at Black Torrington, Hatherleigh, Bratton Clovelly, Tavistock, Woodford Bridge and Bradworthy); "B" Squadron, Barnstaple (detachments at Atherington, Bratton Fleming, Blackmore Gate, Fremington, Swimbridge, West Down and Braunton); "C" Squadron, South Molton (detachments at West Buckland, Molland, Chittlehampton, Sandyway, Ashreigny and Chulmleigh); "D" Squadron, Torrington (detachments at Woolsery, Langtree, Parkham, Highbickington, Bideford and Roborough).

Royal Regiment of Artillery. The Royal Regiment of Artillery comprised three sections – Royal Horse Artillery, Royal Field Artillery and Royal Garrison Artillery. See under these listings.

Royal Scots Fusiliers. Two Regular (1st and 2nd), one Special Reserve (3rd) and two Territorial Force (4th and 5th) battalions. An independent company – the Ardeer Company – was attached to the Regiment. Depot, Ayr.

1st Battalion: Gosport.

2nd Battalion: Gibraltar.

3rd Battalion: Ayr.

4th Battalion: Kilmarnock with "A" Company, also at Kilmarnock; "B" Company, Irvine (detachment at Kilwinning); "C" Company, Stewarton (detachment

Royal Scots Fusiliers. *5th Battalion.*

at Kilmaurs); "D" Company, Beith (detachments at Glengarnock and Lochwinnoch); "E" Company, Saltcoats; "F" Company, Dalry (detachment at Kilbirnie); "G" Company, Darvel (detachments at Galston and Newmilns); "H" Company, Kilmarnock.

5th Battalion: Ayr with "A" Company, also at Ayr; "B" Company, Catrine (with a detachment at Darnconnar); "C" Company, Maybole (detachment at Girvan); "D" Company, Stranraer (detachments at Portpatrick and Castle Kennedy); "E" Company, Cumnock (detachment at New Cumnock); "F" Company, Troon; "G" Company, Muirkirk (detachment at Glenbuck); "H" Company, Dalmellington (detachment at Rankinston).

Ardeer Company: Formed from employees of the Nobel's Explosives Company, Ardeer Works, Stevenston.

1st Cadet Battalion: Comprised six companies – "A" Company at The Academy, Ayr and affiliated to 5th Battalion; "B" Company, Kilmarnock Academy and "C" Company, Royal Academy, Irvine, both affiliated to 4th Battalion; "D" Company, Girvan High School, affiliated to 5th Battalion; "E" and "F" Companies, Ardeer Works, Stevenston.

Royal Scots Greys. See 2nd Dragoons (Royal Scots Greys).

Royal Scots (Lothian Regiment). Two Regular (1st and 2nd), one Special Reserve (3rd) and seven Territorial Force battalions (4th to 10th). Depot, Glencorse.

1st Battalion: Allahabad, India.

2nd Battalion: Plymouth.

3rd Battalion: Glencorse.

4th Battalion (Queen's Edinburgh Rifles): Forrest Hill, Edinburgh.

5th Battalion (Queen's Edinburgh Rifles): Forrest Hill, Edinburgh.

6th Battalion: 33 Gilmore Place, Edinburgh.

7th Battalion: Dalmeny Street, Leith with "A" to "G" Companies, also in Dalmeny Street; "H" Company, Musselburgh.

8th Battalion: Haddington with "A" Company, Haddington (detachments at Aberlady, Gifford and Pencaitland); "B" Company, Tranent (detachments at Ormiston, Elphinstone and Macmerry); "C" Company, Prestonpans (detachment at Cockenzie); "D" Company, North Berwick (detachments at East Linton, Dunbar and Gullane); "E" Company, Dalkeith (detachments at Bonnyrigg, Pathhead and Gorebridge); "F" Company, Loanhead (detachment at Penicuik); "G" Company, Peebles; "H" Company, Innerleithen (detachment at Walkerburn). There were four cadet units affiliated – The Haddington Cadet Corps, at the Knox Institute, Haddington; North Berwick Cadet Corps, North Berwick High School; Prestonpans Cadet Corps and Tranent Industrial School Cadet Corps.

9th (Highlanders) Battalion: 89 East Claremont Street, Edinburgh.

10th (Cyclist) Battalion: Linlithgow with "A" Company, Linlithgow (detachment at Philipstoun); "B" Company, Bo'ness (detachment at Carriden); "C" Company, Armadale (detachments at Whitburn, Pumpherston and Blackridge); "D" Company, Bathgate; "E" Company, Uphall (detachments at Broxburn and Livingston); "F" Company, Fauldhouse (detachment at Harthill); "G" Company, West Calder (detachment at Addiewell); "H" Company, Kirkliston (detachments at Dalmeny, Winchburgh and Newbridge).

1st (Highland) Cadet Battalion: Forrest Road, Edinburgh. Four companies.

Royal Scots (Lothian Regiment). *4th Battalion (Queen's Edinburgh Rifles) blackened-brass shoulder title.*

Royal Scots (Lothian Regiment). *6th Battalion, Edinburgh. Full-dress scarlet doublets with blue facings are worn.*

Royal Sussex Regiment. Two Regular (1st and 2nd); one Special Reserve (3rd) and two Territorial Force (4th and 5th) battalions. Depot, Chichester.
1st Battalion: Peshawar, India.
2nd Battalion: Woking.
3rd Battalion: Chichester.
4th Battalion: Horsham with "A" Company, Hayward's Heath (detachment at Cuckfield); "B" Company, Hurstpierpoint (detachments at Burgess Hill and Henfield); "C" Company; East Grinstead (detachments at Crawley and Forest Row); "D" Company, Petworth (detachments at Midhurst and North Chapel); "E" Company, Horsham (detachment at Warnham); "F" Company, Arundel (detachments at Ashington, Littlehampton and Storrington); "G" Company, Chichester (detachments at Bognor and Eastergate); "H" Company, Worthing. The Brighton Preparatory Schools Cadet Corps, headquarters at Cottesmore School, Brighton, was affiliated.

Royal Sussex Regiment. *4th Battalion. The Battalion Pioneers (see crossed axes arm badges) are seen here at camp in Arundel, 1912.*

Royal Sussex Regiment. *Drum-major. The uniform is scarlet with blue facings.*

5th (Cinque Ports) Battalion: Middle Street, Hastings with "A" Company, Hastings (detachments at Eastbourne and Hailsham); "B" Company, Battle (detachments at Dallington, Sedlescombe, Staplecross, Robertsbridge and Bexhill); "C" Company, Wadhurst (detachments at Burwash, Flimwell, Hurst Green, Ticehurst and Frant); "D" Company, Lewes (detachments at Glynde and Stanmer); "E" Company, Rye (detachments at Icklesham, Winchelsea, Peasmarsh and Northiam); "F" Company, Uckfield (detachments at East Hoathly, Hadlow Down, Nutley, Buxted, Newick and Heathfield); "G" Company, Crowborough (detachments at Blackham, Hartfield, Groombridge, Mayfield and Rotherfield); "H" Company, Ore (detachment at Westfield). The 1st (Cinque Ports) Cadets at 17 Silchester Road, St Leonard's-on-Sea of two companies was affiliated.
6th (Cyclist) Battalion: 18 Montpelier Place, Brighton with "A" and "B" Companies, also at 18 Montpelier Place; "C" Company, Brighton (detachment Portslade); "D", Brighton; "E" to "H" Companies, Lewes.

Royal Veterinary College of Ireland Officers Training Corps. Ballsbridge near Dublin. Four Army Veterinary Corps sections, Senior Division.

Royal Warwickshire Regiment. Two Regular (1st and 2nd), two Special Reserve (3rd and 4th) and four Territorial Force (5th-8th) battalions. Depot, Warwick. There were also two Cadet Battalions.
1st Battalion: Shorncliffe.
2nd Battalion: Malta.

Royal Sussex Regiment. *5th (Cinque Ports) Battalion.*

3rd Battalion: Warwick.
4th Battalion: Warwick.
5th Battalion: Thorp Street, Birmingham.
6th Battalion: Thorp Street, Birmingham.
7th Battalion: Coventry with "A", "B", "C" and "D" Companies, also in Coventry; "E" Company, Rugby; "F" Company, Leamington; "G" Company, Warwick (detachment at Kenilworth); "H" Company, Nuneaton. The Bablake School Cadet Company in Coventry was affiliated.
8th Battalion: Aston Manor, Birmingham with "A" Company, also at Aston Manor; "B" Company, Saltley; "C" to "H" Companies, Aston Manor, Birmingham.
1st Cadet Battalion: Aston Manor. Attached to 8th Battalion.
2nd Cadet Battalion: Stevens Memorial Hall, Coventry. Attached to 7th Battalion.

Royal Welsh Fusiliers. Two Regular (1st and 2nd), one Special Reserve (3rd) and four Territorial Force (4th-7th) battalions. Depot, Wrexham.
1st Battalion: Malta.
2nd Battalion: Portland.
3rd Battalion: Wrexham.
4th (Denbighshire) Battalion: Wrexham with "A" Company, also at Wrexham; "B" Company, Gresford (detachment at Wrexham); "C" Company, Ruabon; "D" Company, Denbigh (detachment at Ruthin); "E" Company, Coedpoeth; "F" Company, Gwersyllt; "G" Company, Rhosllanerchrugog; "H" Company, Llangollen (detachment at Chirk).
5th (Flintshire) Battalion: Flint with "A" Company, Mold; "B" Company, Hawarden (detachment at Buckley); "C" Company, Rhyl (detachment at St Asaph); "D" Company, Holywell (detachment at Mostyn); "E" Company, Flint (detachment at Bagillt); "F" Company, Caergwrle; "G" Company, Colwyn Bay; "H" Company, Connah's Quay.
6th (Carnarvonshire & Anglesey) Battalion: Carnarvon with "A" Company, also at Carnarvon; "B" Company, Portmadoc; "C" Company, Penygroes (detachment at Nantlle); "D" Company, Llanberis (detachment at Ebenezer); "E" Company, Conway (detachment at Llandudno); "F" Company, Penmaenmawr; "G" Company, Pwllheli (detachment at Criccieth); "H" Company, Holyhead (detachment at Menai Bridge).
7th (Merioneth & Montgomery) Battalion: Newtown

with "A" Company, Llanidloes (detachments at Montgomery, Caersws and Carno); "B" Company, Newtown; "C" Company, Welshpool (detachments at Llanfair, Llanfyllin, Llanwddyn, Llansantffraid and Llanfechan); "D" Company, Machynlleth (detachments at Llanbrynmair, Cemmaes and Corris); "E" Company, Dolgelly (detachments at Barmouth and Harlech); "F" Company, Towyn (detachments at Aberdovey, Abergwynolwyn and Llwyngwril); "G" Company, Blaenau Festiniog (detachments at Festiniog and Penrhyndeudraeth); "H" Company, Bala (detachments at Corwen and Glyndyfrdwy).

Royal West Kent Regiment. See Queen's Own (Royal West Kent Regiment).

Royal West Surrey Regiment. See Queen's (Royal West Surrey Regiment).

Royal Wiltshire Yeomanry (Prince of Wales's Own Royal Regiment). Territorial Force. The Butts, London Road, Chippenham with "A" Squadron, Warminster (detachments at Longbridge Deverell, Whiteparish, Salisbury, Amesbury and Trowbridge); "B" Squadron, Chirton (detachments at Melksham, Marlborough, Devizes, Lavington and Urchfont); "C" Squadron, Chippenham (detachments at Corsham, Wootton Bassett, Malmesbury, Calne, Purton and Ashton Keynes); "D" Squadron, Swindon.

Roysse's School Officers Training Corps. Abingdon. One infantry company, Junior Division.

Rugby School Officers Training Corps. Three infantry companies, Junior Division.

Ruthin School Cadet Corps. One company.

Rutland Street School (LCC) Cadet Corps. See 10th London Regiment.

Royal Warwickshire Regiment. *Clearly seen is the regiment's antelope badge. The tunic is scarlet with blue facings.*

Royal Wiltshire Yeomanry (Prince of Wales's Own Royal Regiment). *Blue jacket with scarlet facings.*

S

St Albans School Officers Training Corps. One infantry company, Junior Division.

St Andrew's College Officers Training Corps. Dublin. One infantry company, Junior Division.

St Andrew's University Officers Training Corps. Two infantry companies, Senior Division.

St Ann's School Cadet Corps. 57a Dean Street, Soho, London. Two companies.

St Bees School Officers Training Corps. Two infantry companies, Junior Division.

St Columba's College Officers Training Corps. Rathfarnham, Co. Dublin. One infantry company, Junior Division.

St Dunstan's College Officers Training Corps. Catford, London. Two infantry companies, Junior division.

St Edmund's School Officers Training Corps. Canterbury. One infantry company, Junior Division.

St Edward's School Officers Training Corps. Oxford. One infantry company, Junior Division.

St Gabriel's Cadet Corps. See 1st Cadet Battalion, Essex Regiment.

St Helens Divisional Signal Company. See West Lancashire Divisional Signal Company (The St Helens).

St Helens Field Companies, 1st, 2nd. See West Lancashire Divisional Engineers.

St John's School Officers Training Corps. Leatherhead. One infantry company, Junior Division.

St Lawrence College Officers Training Corps. Ramsgate. One infantry company, Junior Division.

St Leonard's Collegiate School Cadet Company. See 2nd Home Counties Brigade, Royal Field Artillery.

St Mark's (Peckham) Cadet Corps. Harders Road, Peckham, London. One company.

St Matthew's Cadet Corps. See 1st Cadet Battalion, Essex Regiment.

St Pancras Battalion. See 19th Battalion, London Regiment.

St Paul's School Officers Training Corps. West Kensington, London. Two infantry companies, Junior division.

St Peter's Cadet Company. See 13th London Regiment.

St Peter's School Officers Training Corps. York. One infantry company, Junior Division.

St Phillip's Cadet Corps. Arundel, Sussex.

St Thomas's (Wandsworth) Cadet Corps. See 23rd Battalion, London Regiment.

St Bees School Officers Training Corps.

Sandroyd School Troop of Scouts. Cobham. One company.
School of Army Sanitation. Aldershot.
School of Gunnery. Shoeburyness.
School of Military Engineering. Chatham.
School of Musketery. Hythe.

School of Musketry. *Sergeant instructor with Lewis gun.*

School of Musketry. *Sergeant instructor (centre) seen here with Territorials of (back row left to right) Huntingdonshire Cyclists, Suffolk Regiment, Cambridgeshire Regiment, Northamptonshire Regiment, Cambridgeshire Regiment; (seated) Norfolk Regiment, Essex Regiment, Welsh Regiment; (front row) Northern Cyclist Battalion, Yorkshire Dragoons.*

Schools of Electric Lighting. Plymouth and Portsmouth.
Scots Fusiliers. See Royal Scots Fusiliers.
Scots Greys. See 2nd Dragoons (Royal Scots Greys).
Scots Guards. Two Regular battalions.
1st Battalion: Aldershot.
2nd Battalion: Tower of London.

Scots Guards. *Pipers. Service dress jackets are worn with Dress Stewart kilts.*

Scots Guards. *Marching order. Buttons arranged in groups of three.*

Scots Guards. *Seen here at the Sidney Street siege, East London, of 3 January, 1911.*

Scottish Airline Signal Company. See Scottish Command Signal Companies (Army Troops).

Scottish Borderers. See King's Own Scottish Borderers.

Scottish Cabel Signal Company. See Scottish Command Signal Companies (Army Troops).

Scottish Command Signal Companies (Army Troops). Territorial Force. 21 Jardine Street, Glasgow with Scottish Wireless Signal Company, Scottish Cable Signal Company and Scottish Airline Signal Company

Scottish General Hospital, 1st. Territorial Force. Aberdeen.

Scottish General Hospital, 2nd. Territorial Force. 4 Lindsay Place, Edinburgh.

Scottish General Hospitals, 3rd, 4th. Territorial Force. Yorkhill, Glasgow.

Scottish Horse, 1st. Territorial Force. Dunkeld with "A" Squadron, Blair Atholl (detachments at Ballinluig, Pitlochry, Kirkmichael and Kinloch Rannoch); "B" Squadron, Dunkeld (detachments at Murthly, Bankfoot, Dupplin, Perth, Cluny and Aberfeldy); "C" Squadron, Coupar-Angus (detachments at Blairgowrie, Alyth and Invergowrie); "D" Squadron, Dunblane (detachments at Crieff, Comrie, Lochearnhead, Auchterarder, Muthill, Dunning and Methven).

Scottish Horse, 2nd. Territorial Force. Aberdeen with "E" Squadron, Elgin (detachments at Pluscarden, Craigellachie, Cullen, Dallas, Dufftown, Forres, Keith and Archiestown); "F" Squadron, Kintore (detachments at Peterhead, Fraserburgh, Ellon, Huntly, Insch, Inverurie, Monymusk, Cluny, Alford, Turriff, Fyvie, Rothie-Norman, Maud, Mintlaw, Newmachar and Bucksburn); "G" Squadron, Aberdeen (detachments at Torphins, Aboyne, Tarland, Ballater and Braemar); "H" Squadron, Connell (detachments at Kilchrenan, Appin, Easdale, Ardrishaig, Taynuilt, Calgary, Tiree, Craignure, Campbeltown, Bunessan, Torloisk, Port Ellen, Port Charlotte, Bowmore and Bridgend).

Scottish Rifle Brigade. See Lowland Division.

Scottish Rifle Brigade Company, Army Service Corps. See Lowland Divisional Transport and Supply Column.

Scottish Rifles. See Cameronians (Scottish Rifles).

Scottish Wireless Signal Company. See Scottish Command Signal Companies (Army Troops).

Scottish Horse. *The two yeomen standing left and right wear the regimental Atholl-grey full-dress uniforms. The facings are yellow. Note the man seated right who is wearing his Imperial Service badge on the wrong side.*

Scottish Horse. *Cap badge. The date 1900 refers to the year of formation.*

Seaford College Cadet Company. Seaford, Sussex.

Seaforth and Cameron Infantry Brigade. See Highland Division.

Seaforth Highlanders (Ross-Shire Buffs, The Duke of Albany's). Two Regular (1st and 2nd), one Special Reserve (3rd) and three Territorial Force (4th, 5th and 6th) battalions. Depot, Fort George.

1st Battalion: Agra, India.

2nd Battalion: Shorncliffe.

3rd Battalion: Fort George.

4th (Ross Highland) Battalion: Dingwall with "A" Company, Tain (detachments at Nigg, Fearn, Edderton and Portmahomack); "B" Company, Dingwall; "C" Company, Munlochy (detachments at Avoch, Rosemarkie, Culbokie, Muir of Ord and Fortrose); "D" Company; Gairloch (detachments at Opinan, Poolewe, Kinlochewe and Torridon); "E" Company, Ullapool (detachments at Coigach and Braemore); "F" Company, Invergordon (detachment at Kildary); "G" Company, Alness (detachment at Evanton); "H" Company, Maryburgh (detachments at Strathpeffer, Garve, Strathconon and Fairburn).

5th (The Sutherland and Caithness Highland) Battalion: Golspie with "A" Company, Golspie (detachments at Melvich and Bettyhill); "B" Company, Dornoch (detachment at Rogart); "C" Company, Bonar Bridge (detachments at Lairg, Lochinver and Elphin); "D" Company, Brora (detachments at Helmsdale, Kildonan and Kinbrace); "E" Company, Thurso (detachment at Reay); "F" Company, Wick (detachment at Lybster); "G" Company, Halkirk (detachments at Watten and Westfield); "H" Company, Castletown (detachments at Dunnet, Mey and Bower Madden).

6th (Morayshire) Battalion: Elgin with "A" Company, Forres (detachment at Altyre); "B" Company, Elgin (detachments at Lossiemouth and Pluscarden); "C" Company, Elgin (detachment at Lossiemouth); "D" Company, Rothes (detachment at Archiestown); "E" Company, Fochabers (detachment at Bogmuir); "F" Company, Grantown (detachments at Nethy Bridge and Carrbridge); "G" Company, Garmouth (detachment at Lhanbryde); "H" Company, Lossiemouth (detachments at Hopeman and Burghead).

***Seaforth Highlanders (Ross-Shire Buffs, The Duke of Albany's).** 5th (The Sutherland and Caithness Highland) Battalion. A special badge was worn by the Battalion comprising a cat-a-mountain within a strap bearing the motto Sans Peur (Without fear). Officers had in addition feathers donating rank – Lieutenant-Colonel (four feathers), Major (three feathers), Captain (two feathers), Lieutenant (one feather).*

***Seaforth Highlanders (Ross-Shire Buffs, The Duke of Albany's).** "D" Company, 2nd Battalion at Shorncliffe, 1912. The men are in full dress – scarlet doublets with buff facings. Kilts are MacKenzie pattern tartan.*

Seaforth Highlanders (Ross-Shire Buffs, The Duke of Albany's). *From left to right, Bugler Campbell, Bugler Sutcliffe and Drummer Walter Ritchie. Drummer Ritchie would win the Victoria Cross on the Somme in 1916 while serving with 2nd Seaforth.*

Seaforth Highlanders (Ross-Shire Buffs, The Duke of Albany's). *Cyclist Section.*

Seaforth Highlanders (Ross-Shire Buffs, The Duke of Albany's). *Cap badge. The motto means "help the king". This, with the stag's head, is that of the MacKenzies and is said to have been given in recognition of the founder of the clan having saved King Alexander II of Scotland from an attack by a stag.*

Seaforth Highlanders (Ross-Shire Buffs, The Duke of Albany's). *Two collar badges were worn (two either side). Closest to the opening of the collar, the cypher "F" of Frederick, Duke of York with the motto Caber Feidh (Antlers of the Deer). Either side of these, an elephant. This commemorates the service in India of the old 78th Regiment (later 2nd Battalion).*

Sedbergh School Officers Training Corps. Two infantry companies, Junior Division.

Settle Cadet Battalion. See 6th Battalion, Duke of Wellington's (West Riding Regiment).

Sharpshooters. See 3nd County of London Yeomanry (Sharpshooters)

Sherborne School Officers Training Corps. Three infantry companies, Junior Division.

Sherwood Foresters (Nottinghamshire and Derbyshire Regiment). Two Regular (1st and 2nd), two Special Reserve (3rd and 4th) and four Territorial Force (5th to 8th) battalions. Depot, Derby.

1st Battalion: Bombay, India.

2nd Battalion: Sheffield.

3rd Battalion: Derby.

4th Battalion: Derby.

5th Battalion: Derby with "A", "B" and "C" Companies, also at Derby; "D" Company, Long Eaton (detachment at Melbourne); "E" Company, Ripley (detachments at Codnor Park, Alfreton and Butterley); "F" Company, Belper (detachments at Horsley, Crich and Kilburn); "G" Company, Ilkeston (detachments at Long Eaton, Heanor and Langley Mill); "H" Company, Swadlincote (detachment at Repton).

6th Battalion: 10 Corporation Street, Chesterfield with "A" Company, also at 10 Corporation Street; "B" Company, Chapel-en-le-Frith (detachments at Edale, Hathersage, Peak Dale and Chinley); "C" Company, Buxton (detachment at Ashbourne); "D" Company, Bakewell (detachment at Stoney Middleton); "E" Company, Wirksworth (detachments at Cromford and Matlock); "F" Company, Staveley (detachments at Clowne, Eckington and Brimington); "G" Company, Claycross (detachments at New Tupton and South Wingfield); "H" Company, Whaley Bridge (detachments at New Mills, Disley and Hayfield).

7th (Robin Hood) Battalion: Derby Road, Nottingham.

8th Battalion: Newark with "A" Company, Retford (detachment at Ollerton); "B" Company, Newark; "C" Company, Sutton-in-Ashfield; "D" Company, Mansfield; "E" Company, Carlton (detachments at Burton Joyce and Bingham); "F" Company, Arnold (detachments at Basford, Eastwood, Daybrook and Hucknall); "G" Company, Worksop (detachment at Shireoaks); "H" Company, Southwell (detachments at Calverton and Farnsfield). The Welbeck Cadet Battalion, seven companies at the Cadet Drill Hill, Mansfield, was affiliated.

Sherwood Rangers. See Nottinghamshire Yeomanry (Sherwood Rangers).

Shetland Companies. See Gordon Highlanders.

Shrewsbury School Officers Training Corps. Three infantry companies, Junior Division.

Shropshire Light Infantry. See King's (Shropshire Light Infantry).

Shropshire Royal Horse Artillery. Territorial Force. Shrewsbury. Included the Welsh Border Mounted Brigade Ammunition Column at Church Stretton. The Battery also had a detachment at Wellington.

Shropshire Yeomanry. Territorial Force. Shrewsbury with "A" Squadron, Shrewsbury (detachments at Baschurch, Pontesbury, Pulverbach and Wem); "B" Squadron, Oswestry (detachments at Whitchurch and Ellesmere), "C" Squadron, Ludlow (detachments at Craven Arms, Ross-on-Wye, Hereford, Leominster, Tenbury and Kington); "D" Squadron, Wellington (detachments at Much Wenlock, Shifnal, Market Drayton, Newport and Bridgnorth).

Sherwood Foresters (Nottinghamshire and Derbyshire Regiment). *6th Battalion brass shoulder title.*

Shropshire Royal Horse Artillery. *Staff-sergeants and sergeants, Salisbury Plain, 1912.*

Sidcup Hall School Officers Training Corps. Sidcup, Kent. One infantry company, Junior Division.

Sierra Leone Battalion. Daru.

Sir Roger Manwood's School Officers Training Corps. Sandwich. One infantry company, Junior Division.

Sir Walter St James School Cadet Corps. High Street, Battersea, London. One company.

Skinners' School Officers Training Corps. Tunbridge Wells. One infantry company, Junior Division.

Solihull Grammar School Officers Training Corps. One infantry company, Junior Division.

Somaliland India Contingent. Berera.

Somerset Light Infantry. See Prince Albert's (Somerset Light Infantry).

Somerset Naval Cadet Corps. Recognised in December, 1912. Location unknown.

Somerset Royal Horse Artillery. Territorial Force. County Territorial Hall, Taunton. Included the 2nd South Western Mounted Brigade Ammunition Column. The Battery also had a detachment at Glastonbury, and the Ammunition Column detachments at Shepton Mallet, Portishead and Wells.

Somerset Yeomanry, North. See North Somerset Yeomanry.

Somerset Yeomanry, West. See West Somerset Yeomanry.

South Eastern Mounted Brigade. Territorial Force. 43 Russell Square, London. Included East Kent, West Kent and Sussex Yeomanries; "B" Battery, Honourable Artillery Company. The Surrey Yeomanry was attached for training.

South Eastern Mounted Brigade Ammunition Column. See Honourable Artillery Company.

South Eastern Mounted Brigade Field Ambulance. Territorial Force. Victoria Road, Margate. There was also a detachment in Ramsgate.

South Eastern Mounted Brigade Signal Troop. Territorial Force. 43 Russell Square, London.

South Eastern Mounted Brigade Transport and Supply Column. Territorial Force. One company at Croydon.

South Irish Horse. Special Reserve. Beggars Bush Barracks, Dublin. Shown in the *Army List*, together with the North Irish Horse, under the collective heading of Irish Horse.

South Lancashire Brigade Company, Army Service Corps. See West Lancashire Divisional Transport and Supply Column.

South Lancashire Infantry Brigade. See West Lancashire Division.

South Lancashire Regiment. See Prince of Wales's Volunteers (South Lancashire Regiment).

South London Cadets. See 21st Battalion, London Regiment.

South Midland Brigade Company, Army Service Corps. See South Midland Divisional Transport and Supply Column.

South Midland Brigade, Royal Field Artillery (Gloucestershire), 1st. Territorial Force. Clifton, Bristol with 1st and 2nd Gloucestershire Batteries, also at Clifton; 3rd Gloucestershire Battery, Gloucester and Ammunition Column, Clifton.

South Midland Brigade, Royal Field Artillery, 2nd. Territorial Force. 24 Southfield Street, Worcester with 1st Worcestershire Battery, also at Southfield Street; 2nd Worcestershire Battery, George Street, Kidderminster (detachment at Malvern); 3rd Worcestershire Battery, Easemore Road, Redditch and Ammunition Column, Clarence Road, Malvern.

South Irish Horse. *The shamrock cap badge has (one on each leaf) the letters S, I and H.*

1st South Midland Brigade, Royal Field Artillery. *The bombardier on the right is seen with other Gloucestershire Territorials, including to his right a corporal of the Royal Gloucestershire Hussars.*

South Midland Brigade, Royal Field Artillery, 3rd. Territorial Force. Stoney Lane, Birmingham with 1st, 2nd and 3rd Warwickshire Batteries and Ammunition Column.

South Midland Brigade, Royal Field Artillery (Howitzer), 4th. Territorial Force. Quinton Road, Coventry with 4th Warwickshire (Howitzer) Battery, also at Quinton Road (detachment at Rugby); 5th Warwickshire (Howitzer) Battery, Rugby and Ammunition Column, Coventry.

South Midland Clearing Hospital. Territorial Force. Birmingham.

South Midland Division. Territorial Force. The Old Barracks, Warwick.

Warwickshire Infantry Brigade: The Old Barracks, Warwick. Battalions – 5th, 6th, 7th, 8th Royal Warwickshire.

Gloucester and Worcester Infantry Brigade: Charlecote, Battledown, Cheltenham. Battalions – 4th, 6th Gloucestershire; 7th, 8th Worcestershire.

South Midland Infantry Brigade: 20 Magdalen Street, Oxford. Battalions – 5th Gloucestershire; 4th Oxfordshire and Buckinghamshire; Buckinghamshire Battalion; 4th Royal Berkshire.

Royal Artillery: Draycott Lodge, Kempsey, Worcester. 1st, 2nd, 3rd, 4th (Howitzer) South Midland Brigades, Royal Field Artillery; South Midland Royal Garrison Artillery.

Royal Engineers: 32 Park Row, Bristol. 1st, 2nd South Midland Field Companies; South Midland Divisional Signal Company.

Army Service Corps: Aston, Birmingham. South Midland Divisional Transport and Supply Column.

Royal Army Medical Corps: 1st, 2nd, 3rd South Midland Field Ambulances.

Attached: Southern, Wireless, Cable, Airline Signal Companies.

South Midland Divisional Engineers. Territorial Force. 32 Park Row, Bristol with 1st and 2nd South Midland Field Companies.

South Midland Divisional Signal Company. Territorial Force. 32 Park Row, Bristol with No.1 Section, No.2 (Warwickshire) Section, No.3 (Gloucester and Worcester) Section, No.4 (South Midland) Section.

South Midland Divisional Transport and Supply Column. Territorial Force. Aston, Birmingham with Headquarters Company, also at Aston; Warwickshire Brigade Company, Court Oak House, Harborne; Gloucester and Worcester Brigade Company, Wallbridge, Stroud and South Midland Brigade Company, Taplow.

South Midland Field Ambulances, 1st, 2nd. Territorial Force. The Barracks, Great Brook Street, Birmingham. There was also a detachment at Sutton Coldfield that formed part of 2nd South Midland Field Ambulance.

South Midland Field Ambulance, 3rd. Territorial Force. Colston Fort, Montague Place, Kingsdown, Bristol.

South Midland Field Companies, 1st, 2nd. See South Midland Divisional Engineers.

South Midland Infantry Brigade. See South Midland Division.

South Midland Mounted Brigade, 1st. Territorial Force. St John's, Warwick. Included Warwickshire, Gloucestershire, Worcestershire Yeomanries; Warwickshire Royal Horse Artillery.

South Midland Mounted Brigade, 2nd. Territorial Force. 12 Lonsdale Road, Oxford. Included Buckinghamshire, Berkshire, Oxfordshire Yeomanries; Berkshire Royal Horse Artillery.

South Midland Mounted Brigade Ammunition Column, 1st. See Warwickshire Royal Horse Artillery.

South Midland Mounted Brigade Ammunition Column, 2nd. See Berkshire Royal Horse Artillery.

South Midland Mounted Brigade Field Ambulance, 1st. Territorial Force. Great Brook Street, Birmingham.

South Midland Mounted Brigade Field Ambulance, 2nd. Territorial Force. Stony Stratford.

South Midland Mounted Brigade Signal Troop, 1st. Territorial Force. St John's, Warwick.

South Midland Mounted Brigade Signal Troop, 2nd. Territorial Force. 12 Lonsdale Road, Oxford.

South Midland Mounted Brigade Transport and Supply Column, 1st. Territorial Force. Taunton Road, Sparkbrook, Birmingham.

South Midland Mounted Brigade Transport and Supply Column, 2nd. Territorial Force. Yeomanry House, Castle Hill, Reading.

South Midland Royal Garrison Artillery (Warwickshire). Territorial Force. The Metropolitan Works, Saltley, Birmingham. There were also detachments in Wednesbury.

South Nottinghamshire Hussars. See Nottinghamshire Yeomanry (South Nottinghamshire Hussars).

South Scottish Infantry Brigade. See Lowland Division.

South Staffordshire Regiment. Two Regular (1st and 2nd), two Special Reserve (3rd and 4th) and two Territorial Force (5th and 6th) battalions. Depot, Lichfield.

1st Battalion: Pietermaritzburg, South Africa.

2nd Battalion: Aldershot.

3rd Battalion: Lichfield.

4th Battalion: Lichfield.

5th Battalion: Walsall with "A", "B" and "C" Companies, also at Walsall; "D" Company, Bloxwich; "E" Company, Brierley Hill; "F" Company, Hednesford; "G" Company, Handsworth; "H" Company, Wednesbury.

6th Battalion: Headquarters, "A" and "B" Companies at Wolverhampton; "C" Company, Wednesfield; "D" Company, Willenhall; "E" Company, Tipton; "F" Company, Darlaston; "G" Company, Bilston; "H" Company, Tettenhall. The Brierley Hill Cadet Corps, headquarters at the Temperance Hall, Brierley Hill was affiliated.

South Wales Borderers. Two Regular (1st and 2nd) and one Special Reserve (3rd) battalions. The Regiment's only Territorial Force element, the Brecknockshire Battalion, bore no numerical designation prior to the war. Depot, Brecon. Although associated with the South Wales Borderers, the Monmouthshire Regiment constituted an independent Territorial Force regiment.

1st Battalion: Bordon.

2nd Battalion: Tientsin, China.

3rd Battalion: Brecon.

Brecknockshire Battalion: Brecon with "A" Company, also at Brecon; "B" Company, Brynmawr; "C" Company, Crickhowell; "D" Company, Hay-on-Wye; "E" Company, Builth Wells (detachment at Llanwrtyd Wells); "F" Company, Talgarth; "G" Company, Cefn-Coed; "H" Company, Ystradgynlais (detachments at Brynamman and Seven Sisters).

South Wales Infantry Brigade. See Welsh Division.

South Wales Mounted Brigade. Territorial Force. Carmarthen. Included Pembrokeshire, Montgomeryshire, Glamorgan Yeomanries; Glamorgan Royal Horse Artillery.

South Wales Mounted Brigade Ammunition Column. See Glamorgan Royal Horse Artillery.

South Wales Mounted Brigade Field Ambulance. Territorial Force. Hereford. There was also a detachment at Burghill.

South Wales Mounted Brigade Signal Troop. Territorial Force. Carmarthen.

South Wales Mounted Brigade Transport and Supply Column. Territorial Force. 7 Rutland Street, Swansea.

South Wales Borderers. *2nd Battalion, Tientsin, China, 1914.*

South Wales Borderers. Brecknockshire Battalion

South Western Brigade Company, Army Service Corps. See Wessex Divisional Transport and Supply Column.

South Western Infantry Brigade. See Wessex Division.

South Western Mounted Brigade, 1st. Territorial Force. 28a Butcher Row, Salisbury. Included Royal Wiltshire, North Somerset, Hampshire Yeomanries; Hampshire Royal Horse Artillery. The Dorset Yeomanry was attached for training.

South Western Mounted Brigade, 2nd. Territorial Force. Lennards Buildings, Goldsmith Street, Exeter. Included 1st Devon, Royal North Devon, West Somerset Yeomanries; Somerset Royal Horse Artillery.

South Western Mounted Brigade Ammunition Column, 1st. See Hampshire Royal Horse Artillery.

South Western Mounted Brigade Ammunition Column, 2nd. See Somerset Royal Horse Artillery.

South Western Mounted Brigade Field Ambulance, 1st. Territorial Force. Church Place, Swindon. There were also detachments at Marlborough, Calne, Pewsey and Devizes.

Southern Command Signal Companies (Army Troops). Southern Airline Signal Company.

South Western Mounted Brigade Field Ambulance, 2nd. Territorial Force. Frome with "A" Section in Bath, "B" Section, Weston-super-Mare.

South Western Mounted Brigade Signal Troop, 1st. Territorial Force. 28a Butcher Row, Salisbury.

South Western Mounted Brigade Signal Troop, 2nd. Territorial Force. Goldsmith Street, Exeter.

South Western Mounted Brigade Transport and Supply Column, 1st. Territorial Force. The Armoury, Tisbury. There were also detachments at Hindon, East Knoyle, Semley, Donhead, Ludwell, Berwick St John, Fovant, Dinton, Salisbury, Longford Park and Amesbury.

South Western Mounted Brigade Transport and Supply Column, 2nd. Territorial Force. High Street, Weston-super-Mare. There was also a detachment at Wedmore.

Southend High School Cadet Corps. See 6th Battalion, Essex Regiment.

Southern Airline Signal Company. See Southern Command Signal Companies (Army Troops).

Southern Cable Signal Company. See Southern Command Signal Companies (Army Troops).

Southern Command Signal Companies (Army Troops). Territorial Force. Great Brook Street, Birmingham with Southern Wireless Signal Company, Southern Cable Signal Company and Southern Airline Signal Company.

Southern General Hospital, 1st. Territorial Force. Great Brook Street, Birmingham.

Southern General Hospital, 2nd. Territorial Force. Colston Fort, Montague Place, Kingsdown, Bristol.

Southern General Hospital, 3rd. Territorial Force. Oxford.

Southern General Hospital, 4th. Territorial Force. Territorial Buildings, Millbay, Plymouth.

Southern General Hospital, 5th. Territorial Force. Connaught Drill Hall, Gosport.

Southern Wireless Signal Company. See Southern Command Signal Companies (Army Troops).

Southport Cadet Corps. See 7th Battalion, King's (Liverpool Regiment).

Special Reserve. Special Reserve battalions formed part of each infantry regiment. These were numbered on from the regulars (3rd and 4th usually) and followed by the Territorials. There were three Yeomanry regiments – North Irish Horse, South Irish Horse and King Edward's Horse (The King's Oversea Dominions Regiment) – the Antrim and

Cork Royal Garrison Artillery, and with the Royal Engineers, the Royal Anglesey Militia and Royal Monmouthshire Militia. There was also a unit known as No. 18 Field Ambulance and another titled Eastern Telegraph Reserve. Special Reserve elements, but with no particular designation, were included in most other arms of the Army.

Staff College. Camberley.

Staff for Royal Engineer Services. Superintending Inspectors of Works and Inspectors of Works at various locations throughout the British Isles and other Colonial stations.

Staffordshire Batteries, 1st, 2nd, 3rd. See 2nd North Midland Brigade, Royal Field Artillery.

Staffordshire Batteries, 4th, 5th, 6th. See 3rd North Midland Brigade, Royal Field Artillery.

Staffordshire Brigade Company, Army Service Corps. See North Midland Divisional Transport and Supply Column.

Staffordshire Infantry Brigade. See North Midland Division.

Staffordshire Royal Garrison Artillery. See North Midland Royal Garrison Artillery (Staffordshire).

Staffordshire Yeomanry (Queen's Own Royal Regiment). Territorial Force. Bailey Street, Stafford with "A" Squadron, Walsall (detachments at West Bromwich, Tamworth, Lichfield and Sutton Coldfield); "B" Squadron, Stoke-on-Trent (detachments at Stafford, Leek, Cannock and Newcastle-under-Lyme); "C" Squadron, Burton-on-Trent (detachment at Uttoxeter); "D" Squadron, Wolverhampton (detachment at Himley).

Steyne School Cadet Corps. See 1st Home Counties Brigade, Royal Field Artillery.

Stonyhurst College Officers Training Corps. Blackburn. Three infantry companies, Junior Division.

Suffolk Batteries, 1st (Howitzer), 2nd (Howitzer). See 3rd East Anglian Brigade, Royal Field Artillery (Howitzer).

Staffordshire Yeomanry (Queen's Own Royal Regiment). *The uniforms are blue with scarlet facings, and the cap badge a crown over the Staffordshire Knot.*

Suffolk Regiment. Two Regular (1st and 2nd), one Special Reserve (3rd) and three Territorial Force (4th, 5th and 6th) battalions. Depot, Bury St Edmunds.

1st Battalion: Khartoum, Sudan.

2nd Battalion: Curragh.

3rd Battalion: Bury St Edmunds.

4th Battalion: Portman Road, Ipswich with "A", "B", "C" and "D" Companies, also at Portman Road; "E" Company, Lowestoft; "F" Company, Halesworth (detachment at Saxmundham); "G" Company, Framlingham (detachment at Woodbridge); "H" Company, Leiston (detachment at East Bridge).

5th Battalion: Bury St Edmunds with "A" Company, Stowmarket (detachment at Eye); "B" Company, Beccles (detachment at Bungay); "C" Company, Hadleigh (detachment at Bildeston); "D" Company, Sudbury (detachments at Long Melford and Bures); "E" Company, Bury St Edmunds (detachment at Barrow); "F" Company, Bury St Edmunds (detachment at Lavenham); "G" Company, Haverhill (detachment at Clare); "H" Company, Newmarket (detachment at Mildenhall).

6th (Cyclist) Battalion: Ipswich with "A" and "B" Companies, also in Ipswich; "C" Company, Ipswich (detachment at Brantham); "D" Company, Southwold (detachment at Aldeburgh); "E" Company, Lowestoft; "F" Company, Bungay (detachment at Beccles); "G" Company, Stowmarket; "H" Company, Bury St Edmunds.

Suffolk Regiment. *Drummer. The scarlet jacket has yellow facings.*

Suffolk Yeomanry (The Duke of York's Own Loyal Suffolk Hussars). Territorial Force. Bury St Edmunds with "A" Squadron, Cambridge (detachment at Ely); "B" Squadron, Bury St Edmunds (detachments at Eye, Thetford, Sudbury and Stowmarket); "C" Squadron, Ipswich (detachments at Felixstowe, Framlingham and Woodbridge); "D" Squadron, Beccles (detachments at Bungay, Halesworth, Lowestoft and Leiston).

Sunbury House School Cadet Company. See 9th Battalion, Duke of Cambridge's Own (Middlesex Regiment).

Surrey Brigade Company, Army Service Corps. See Home Counties Divisional Transport and Supply Column.

Surrey Infantry Brigade. See Home Counties Division.

Surrey Yeomanry (Queen Mary's Regiment). Territorial Force. Melbourne House, King's Avenue, Clapham Park with "A" Squadron, Clapham Park (detachment at Aldershot); "B" Squadron, Guildford (detachments at Woking and Camberley); "C" Squadron, West Croydon (detachment at Clapham); "D" Squadron, Wimbledon (detachment at Clapham). The Regiment also had a squadron of cadets, designated "E" Cadet Squadron.

Sussex Batteries, 1st, 2nd, 3rd. See 1st Home Counties Brigade, Royal Field Artillery.

Sussex Batteries, 4th, 5th, 6th. See 2nd Home Counties Brigade, Royal Field Artillery.

Sussex Fortress Engineers. Territorial Force. Seaford with No.1 Works Company. There was also a detachment at Newhaven.

Sussex Regiment. See Royal Sussex Regiment.

Sussex Royal Garrison Artillery. Territorial Force. 117 Gloucester Road, Brighton with No.1 Company, also at Gloucester Road; No.2 Company, Lewes.

Sussex Yeomanry. Territorial Force. Church Street, Brighton with "A" Squadron, Brighton (detachments at Horsham, Worthing, Hayward's Heath and Crawley); "B" Squadron, Lewes (detachments at Burgess Hill, Eridge, Brighton, Uckfield, Tunbridge

Above:* *Suffolk Yeomanry (The Duke of York's Own Loyal Suffolk Hussars).

Wells and Hayward's Heath); "C" Squadron, Chichester (detachment at Bognor); "D" Squadron, Eastbourne (detachments at St Leonards-on-Sea, Bexhill and Rye).

Sutherland and Caithness Highland Battalion. See 5th (The Sutherland and Caithness Highland) Battalion, Seaforth Highlanders (Ross-shire Buffs, The Duke of Albany's)

Suffolk Yeomanry (The Duke of York's Own Loyal Suffolk Hussars). *Cap badge. The castle is said to be that of Bury St Edmunds and the date 1793 was the year in which the Regiment was formed.*

Right: *Sussex Yeomanry (Queen Mary's Regiment).* *Father and son. On the right, D.J. Geall of "E" Cadet Squadron, Sussex Yeomanry, and on the left his father, J.H. Geall in the uniform of the Sussex Volunteer Training Corps (formed 1914).*

T

Taunton School Officers Training Corps. One infantry company, Junior Division.

Territorial Force. Intended for home defence only and made up of part-time soldiers, the TF comprised cavalry (the Yeomanry), infantry battalions (affiliated to and numbered within most regiments), a number of independent named infantry regiments – Honourable Artillery Company, Monmouthshire, Cambridgeshire, London, Inns of Court, Hertfordshire and Herefordshire, four Cyclist battalions – Highland, Huntingdonshire, Kent and Northern, and elements of the Royal Horse Artillery, Royal Field Artillery, Royal Garrison Artillery, Royal Engineers, Army Service Corps and Royal Army Medical Corps (see under RHA, RFA, RGA, RE, ASC and RAMC for details of each). There was also a TF Nursing Service and several Chaplains. Administered by the TF Associations, cadet units were formed with establishments ranging from company to battalion strength, and these in the main were affiliated to TF units.

The Higher Formation of the Territorial Force (Divisions, Brigades) comprised fourteen Mounted Brigades, fourteen Divisions and forty-five Infantry Brigades.

Mounted Brigades: Eastern, South Eastern, London, Yorkshire, 1st South Western, 2nd South Western, Welsh Border, South Wales, Notts & Derby, North Midland, Highland, Lowland, 1st South Midland and 2nd South Midland.

Divisions: East Anglian, Highland, Home Counties, East Lancashire, West Lancashire, 1st London, 2nd London, Lowland, North Midland, South Midland, Northumbrian, West Riding, Welsh and Wessex.

Infantry Brigades: Argyll and Sutherland, Black Watch, Cheshire, Devon and Cornwall, Durham Light Infantry, East Lancashire, East Midland, Essex, Gloucester and Worcester, Gordon, Hampshire, Highland Light Infantry, Kent, Lancashire Fusiliers, Lincoln and Leicester, Liverpool, 1st to 6th London, Lothian, Manchester, Middlesex, Norfolk and Suffolk, North Lancashire, Northumberland, North Wales, Notts & Derby, Scottish Rifle, Seaforth and Cameron, South Lancashire, South Midland, South Scottish, South Wales, South Western, Staffordshire, Surrey, Warwickshire, Welsh Border, 1st, 2nd, 3rd West Riding, York and Durham.

Territorial Force Nursing Service. Part of Queen Alexandra's Imperial Military Nursing Service (*qv*).

The Blues. See Royal Horse Guards.

The Border Battalion. See 4th (The Border) Battalion, King's Own Scottish Borderers.

The Haytor (Newton Abbot) Cadet Corps. See 5th Battalion, Devonshire Regiment.

Tollington School Cadet Company. See 7th Battalion, Duke of Cambridge's Own (Middlesex Regiment).

Tonbridge School Officers Training Corps. Three infantry companies, Junior Division.

Tranent Industrial School Cadet Corps. See 8th Battalion, Royal Scots (Lothian Regiment)

Trent College Officers Training Corps. Long Eaton, Derbyshire. One infantry company, Junior Division.

Tyne Electrical Engineers. Territorial Force. Four companies, North Shields.

Tynemouth Royal Garrison Artillery. Territorial Force. Military Road, North Shields with Nos.1 and 2 Companies, also at Military Road; No.3 Company, Seaton Delaval; No.4 Company, Blyth.

Territorial Force Nursing Service. *Grey uniform, the cape having scarlet edging. Note the small letter "T" at the points of the cape and the badge worn suspended from a red ribbon (with central white stripe) attached to the cape. In the centre, the intertwined cypher of Queen Alexandra. The nurse on the right is a Sister (two scarlet bands on the lower sleeves).*

U

University College School Officers Training Corps. Frognal, Hampstead, London. Three infantry companies, Junior Division.

University of London Officers Training Corps. One field artillery section, a company of engineers, one infantry battalion, a transport and supply section and four sections of field ambulance, Senior Division.

University of Sheffield Officers Training Corps. One infantry company, Senior Division.

University of Wales Officers Training Corps. One infantry company at Aberystwyth University College and one section heavy artillery at Bangor University College, Senior Division.

University School Cadet Company. See Home Counties Divisional Engineers.

Upper Tooting High School Cadet Corps. 3 St James Road, Upper Tooting, London. One company,

Uppingham School Officers Training Corps. Three infantry companies, Junior Division.

***University of Wales Officers Training Corps.** The cap badge comprised a Welsh Dragon within a wreath of daffodils.*

V

Ventnor Cadet Company. See 8th Battalion, Hampshire Regiment.

Victoria College Officers Training Corps. Jersey. One infantry company, Junior Division.

W

Wandsworth Boys' Naval Brigade. 37 East Hill, Wandsworth, London. Two companies.

Waring Cadet Corps. 164 Oxford Street, London. One company.

Warley Garrison Cadets. See 4th Battalion, Essex Regiment.

Warwickshire Batteries, 1st, 2nd, 3rd. See 3rd South Midland Brigade, Royal Field Artillery.

Warwickshire Batteries, 4th (Howitzer), 5th (Howitzer). See 4th South Midland Brigade, Royal Field Artillery (Howitzer).

Warwickshire Brigade Company, Army Service Corps. See South Midland Divisional Transport and Supply Column.

Warwickshire Infantry Brigade. See South Midland Division.

Warwickshire Regiment. See Royal Warwickshire Regiment.

Warwickshire Royal Garrison Artillery. See South Midland Royal Garrison Artillery (Warwickshire).

Warwickshire Royal Horse Artillery. Territorial Force. 9 Clarendon Place, Leamington. Included the 1st South Midland Mounted Brigade Ammunition Column. The Battery also had a detachment at Coventry, and the Ammunition Column one at Henley-in-Arden.

Warwickshire Royal Horse Artillery.

***Warwickshire Yeomanry.** Blue uniform with white facings and busby bag.*

Welsh Border Mounted Brigade Transport and Supply Column.

Warwickshire Yeomanry. Territorial Force. St John's, Warwick with "A" Squadron, Birmingham; "B" Squadron, Warwick (detachments at Kineton, Brailes and Southam); "C" Squadron, Coventry (detachments at Rugby and Nuneaton); "D" Squadron, Stratford-on-Avon (detachments at Henley-in-Arden, Salford Priors and Weston Subedge).

Weald of Kent Battalion. See Buffs (East Kent Regiment).

Welbeck Cadet Battalion. See 8th Battalion, Sherwood Foresters (Nottinghamshire and Derbyshire Regiment)

Wellingborough Grammar School Officers Training Corps. One infantry company, Junior Division.

Wellington College, Berkshire Officers Training Corps. Four infantry companies, Junior Division.

Wellington College, Shropshire Officers Training Corps. One infantry company, Junior Division.

Wellington School Officers Training Corps. Wellington, Somerset. One infantry company, Junior Division.

Welsh Border Brigade Company, Army Service Corps. See Welsh Divisional Transport and Supply Column.

Welsh Border Infantry Brigade. See Welsh Division.

Welsh Border Mounted Brigade. Territorial Force. 15 High Street, Shrewsbury. Included Shropshire, Cheshire, Denbighshire Yeomanries; Shropshire Royal Horse Artillery. The Duke of Lancaster's Own, Westmorland and Cumberland and Lancashire Hussars Yeomanries were attached for training.

Welsh Border Mounted Brigade Ammunition Column. See Shropshire Royal Horse Artillery.

Welsh Border Mounted Brigade Signal Troop. Territorial Force. High Street, Shrewsbury.

Welsh Border Mounted Brigade Transport and Supply Column. Territorial Force. 79a Harrowby Road, Birkenhead.

Welsh Brigade, Royal Field Artillery (Howitzer), 1st. Territorial Force. Swansea with 1st Glamorgan (Howitzer) Battery, also at Swansea; 2nd Glamorgan (Howitzer) Battery, Briton Ferry (detachment at Neath), and Ammunition Column, Morriston.

Welsh Brigade, Royal Field Artillery, 2nd. Territorial Force. Cardiff with 3rd and 4th Glamorgan Batteries, also at Cardiff; Cardiganshire Battery, Aberystwyth and Ammunition Column, Cardiff.

Welsh Brigade, Royal Field Artillery, 3rd. See Cheshire Brigade, Royal Field Artillery.

Welsh Brigade, Royal Field Artillery, 4th. Territorial Force. Lime Street, Newport with 1st Monmouthshire Battery, also at Lime Street; 2nd Monmouthshire Battery, Risca; 3rd Monmouthshire Battery, Griffithstown and Ammunition Column, Lime Street, Newport. The Newport Cadet Corps, with Headquarters at Newport Post Office, was affiliated.

Welsh Clearing Hospital. Territorial Force. Cardiff.

Welsh Division. Territorial Force. 3 Belmont, Shrewsbury.

Cheshire Infantry Brigade: Chester. Battalions – 4th, 5th, 6th, 7th Cheshire.

North Wales Infantry Brigade: Wrexham. Battalions – 4th, 5th, 6th, 7th Royal Welsh Fusiliers.

Welsh Border Infantry Brigade: 15 High Street, Shrewsbury. Battalions – 1st, 2nd, 3rd Monmouthshire; 1st Herefordshire.

Royal Artillery: 15 High Street, Shrewsbury. 1st (Howitzer), 2nd, 3rd, 4th Welsh Brigades, Royal Field Artillery; Welsh Royal Garrison Artillery.

Royal Engineers: 59 Charles Street, Cardiff. Cheshire, Welsh Field Companies; Welsh Divisional Signal Company.

Army Service Corps: Hereford. Welsh Divisional Transport and Supply Column.

Royal Army Medical Corps: 1st, 2nd, 3rd Welsh Field Ambulances.

Attached: South Wales Infantry Brigade, 29 Windsor Place, Cardiff, (comprising the Brecknockshire Battalion, 4th, 5th, 6th Welsh Regiment); 4th Kings Shropshire Light Infantry

Welsh Divisional Engineers. Territorial Force. 59 Charles Street, Cardiff with Cheshire Field Company at 79a Harrowby Road, Birkenhead, Welsh Field Company, Llanelly (detachment at Carmarthen).

Welsh Divisional Signal Company. Territorial Force. Park Street, Cardiff with No.1 Section, No.2 (Cheshire) Section, No.3 (North Wales) Section, No.4 (Welsh Border) Section.

Welsh Divisional Transport and Supply Column. Territorial Force. The Barracks, Hereford with Headquarters Company, Weobley (detachments at Kingsland, Hereford and Staunton-on-Wye); Cheshire Brigade Company, 79a Harrowby Road, Birkenhead; North Wales Brigade Company, Ruthin (detachments at Cerrig-y-Druidion, Caerwys and St Asaph), and Welsh Border Brigade Company, Ystrad (Glamorgan).

Welsh Divisional Engineers. *Cheshire Field Company.*

Welsh Divisional Engineers. *Cheshire Field Company. On the left, Sergeant-Major Jackson, a long-serving Volunteer/Territorial (note his collection of efficiency stars).*

Welsh Horse. *Regimental Sergeant-Major Knowles holding bomb dropped by German aeroplane shortly after the regiment's arrival at camp in Melton, Suffolk, 1915.*

Welsh Field Ambulance, 1st. Territorial Force. Ebbw Vale. There were also detachments at Newport and Cwm.

Welsh Field Ambulance, 2nd. Territorial Force. 15 Newport Road, Cardiff.

Welsh Field Ambulance, 3rd. Territorial Force. Swansea.

Welsh Field Company. See Welsh Divisional Engineers.

Welsh Fusiliers. See Royal Welsh Fusiliers.

Welsh Horse. Territorial Force. Although not strictly "in existence" when war was declared in 1914, formation of the Welsh Horse was well under way by 4th August. Its services being official recognised by the War Office on 15th August. The responsibility of the Glamorgan Territorial Force Association, the Regiment had its Headquarters at 3–4 Park Place, Cardiff.

Welsh Mounted Brigade Field Ambulance. Territorial Force. Thomas Street, Chester. There was also a detachment at Ellesmere Port.

Welsh Regiment. Two Regular (1st and 2nd), one Special Reserve (3rd) and four Territorial Force (4th to 7th) battalions. Depot, Cardiff.

1st Battalion: Chakrata, India.

2nd Battalion: Bordon.

3rd Battalion: Cardiff.

4th Battalion: Carmarthen with "A" Company, Haverfordwest (detachment at Milford Haven); "B" Company, Pembroke (detachment at Narberth); "C" Company, Cardigan; "D" Company, Llandilo (detachment at Llandovery); "E" Company, Carmarthen; "F" Company, Llanelly (detachment at Tumble); "G" Company, Llanelly; "H" Company, Ammanford.

5th Battalion: Pontypridd with "A" and "B" Companies, also at Pontypridd; "C" and "D" Companies, Mountain Ash; "E" Company, Aberdare; "F" Company, Treharris; "G" Company, Merthyr Tydfil (detachment at Dowlais); "H" Company, Merthyr Tydfil.

6th (Glamorgan) Battalion: Swansea with "A" Company, Maesteg; "B", "C" and "D" Companies, Swansea; "E" Company, Hafod, Swansea (detachment at Morriston); "F" Company, Neath; "G" Company, Clydach; "H" Company, Gorseinon.

7th (Cyclist) Battalion: 11 Newport Road, Cardiff with "A" and "B" Companies, also at 11 Newport Road; "C" Company, Barry; "D" Company, Bridgend; "E" and "F" Companies, Swansea; "G" Company, Neath; "H" Company, Aberavon, Port Talbot.

Welsh Regiment. *7th (Cyclist) Battalion. Green with scarlet facings uniform, rifle-style black fur cap.*

Welsh Royal Garrison Artillery (Carnarvonshire). Territorial Force. Bangor. The Battery was also in Bangor, with a section at Carnarvon, and the Ammunition Column, Llandudno.

Wessex Brigade, Royal Field Artillery, 1st. Territorial Force. St Paul's Road, Portsmouth with 1st and 2nd Hampshire Batteries, also at St Paul's Road; 3rd Hampshire Battery, Walpole Road, Gosport and Ammunition Column, St Paul's Road, Portsmouth.

Wessex Brigade, Royal Field Artillery (Howitzer), 2nd. Territorial Force. Ryde, Isle of Wight with 4th Hampshire (Howitzer) Battery, Ventnor (detachment at Ryde); 5th Hampshire (Howitzer) Battery, Freshwater (detachment at Newport), and Ammunition Column, Ryde (detachments at Binstead and Ventnor).

Wessex Brigade, Royal Field Artillery, 3rd. Territorial Force. The Armoury, Prospect Place, Swindon with 6th Hampshire Battery, Victoria Drill Hall, Bournemouth; Dorsetshire Battery, Bridport (detachment at Dorchester); Wiltshire Battery, Prospect Place, Swindon and Ammunition Column, Malmesbury.

Wessex Brigade, Royal Field Artillery, 4th. Territorial Force. Exeter with 1st Devonshire Battery, also at Exeter (detachment at Exmouth); 2nd Devonshire Battery, Paignton (detachments at Torre and Dartmouth); 3rd Devonshire Battery, Tavistock (detachments at Lydford and Milton Abbot), and Ammunition Column, Crediton (detachment at Teignmouth).

Wessex Clearing Hospital. Territorial Force. Exeter.

4th Welsh Brigade, Royal Field Artillery. *Musicians arriving at camp in Merionethshire, 1911.*

4th Wessex Brigade, Royal Field Artillery. *1st Devonshire Battery.*

Wessex Royal Garrison Artillery (Hampshire).

Wessex Division. Territorial Force. 19 Cathedral Close, Exeter.

Devon and Cornwall Infantry Brigade: Lennards Buildings, Goldsmith Street, Exeter. Battalions – 4th, 5th Devonshire; 4th, 5th Duke of Cornwall's Light Infantry.

South Western Infantry Brigade: County Territorial Hall, Taunton. Battalions – 4th, 5th Somerset Light Infantry; 4th Dorsetshire; 4th Wiltshire.

Hampshire Infantry Brigade: 30 Carlton Place, Southampton. Battalions – 4th, 5th, 6th, 7th Hampshire.

Royal Artillery: Lennards Buildings, Goldsmith Street, Exeter. 1st, 2nd (Howitzer), 3rd, 4th Wessex Brigades, Royal Field Artillery; Wessex Royal Garrison Artillery.

Royal Engineers: Upper Bristol Road, Bath. 1st, 2nd Wessex Field Companies; Wessex Divisional Signal Company.

Army Service Corps: 14 Oxford Road, Exeter. Wessex Divisional Transport and Supply Column.

Royal Army Medical Corps: 1st, 2nd, 3rd Wessex Field Ambulances.

Attached: 6th Devonshire Regiment.

Wessex Divisional Engineers. Territorial Force. Upper Road, Bath with 1st Wessex Field Company, also at Upper Road (detachment at Long Ashton), 2nd Wessex Field Company, Churchill Road, Weston-super-Mare (detachment at Clevedon).

Wessex Divisional Signal Company. Territorial Force. The Priory, Colleston Crescent, Exeter with No.1 Section, No.2 (Devon and Cornwall) Section, No.3 (South Western) Section, No.4 (Hampshire) Section.

Wessex Divisional Transport and Supply Column. Territorial Force. 14 Oxford Road, Exeter with Headquarters Company, Andover (detachments at Barton Stacey, St Mary Bourne and Winchester); Devon and Cornwall Brigade Company, Mutley Barracks, Plymouth; South Western Brigade Company, Bridgwater and Hampshire Brigade Company, Redan Hill, Aldershot (detachments at Church Crookham and Farnborough). The Aldershot Church Cadet Corps was affiliated to the Hampshire Company.

West Somerset Yeomanry. *Uniforms, blue with scarlet facings.*

Wessex Field Ambulance, 1st. Territorial Force. 71 Holloway Street, Exeter with "A" and "B" Sections, also at 71 Holloway Street; "C" Section, Teignmouth.

Wessex Field Ambulance, 2nd. Territorial Force. Millbay, Plymouth.

Wessex Field Ambulance, 3rd. Territorial Force. Portsmouth with "A" Section, also in Portsmouth; "B" Section, Whitchurch (detachments at Overton, Andover, Sutton Scotney, Basingstoke and Winchester); "C" Section, Southampton.

Wessex Field Companies, 1st, 2nd. See Wessex Divisional Engineers.

Wessex Royal Garrison Artillery (Hampshire). Territorial Force. Cosham. There was also a detachment at Fareham.

West African Regiment. Sierra Leone.

West Buckland School Officers Training Corps. South Molton, Devon. One infantry company, Junior Division.

West Croydon Cadets. See 4th Battalion, Queen's (Royal West Surrey Regiment).

West Somerset Yeomanry. *Cap badge.*

West Ham Cadet Corps. See 1st Cadet Battalion, Essex Regiment.

West India Regiment. Two battalions.
1st Battalion: Sierra Leone.
2nd Battalion: Jamaica.

West Kent Regiment. See Queen's Own (Royal West Kent Regiment).

West Kent Yeomanry. See Queen's Own West Kent Yeomanry.

West Lancashire Brigade, Royal Field Artillery, 1st. Territorial Force. Windsor Barracks, Spekeland Street, Liverpool with 1st, 2nd, 3rd Lancashire Batteries and Ammunition Column.

West Lancashire Brigade, Royal Field Artillery, 2nd. Territorial Force. Stanley Street, Preston with 9th Lancashire Battery, also at Stanley Street; 10th Lancashire Battery, Dallas Road, Lancaster; 11th Lancashire Battery, Yorkshire Street, Blackpool (detachment at Bamber Bridge), and Ammunition Column, Stanley Street, Preston.

West Lancashire Brigade, Royal Field Artillery, 3rd. Territorial Force. 65 Admiral Street, Liverpool with 12th Lancashire Battery, also at Admiral Street, 13th Lancashire Battery, 1 Earp Street, Garston; 14th Lancashire Battery, Widnes and Ammunition Column, 65 Admiral Street, Liverpool.

West Lancashire Brigade, Royal Field Artillery (Howitzer), 4th. Territorial Force. Edge Lane, Liverpool with 7th Lancashire (Howitzer), 8th Lancashire (Howitzer) and Ammunition Column.

West Lancashire Clearing Hospital. Territorial Force. Kendal.

West Lancashire Division. Territorial Force. 21 Islington, Liverpool.

North Lancashire Infantry Brigade: 16 Castle Park, Lancaster. Battalions – 4th, 5th King's Own; 4th, 5th Loyal North Lancashire.

Liverpool Infantry Brigade: 73 Shaw Street, Liverpool. Battalions – 5th, 6th, 7th, 8th King's Liverpool.

South Lancashire Infantry Brigade: 21 Victoria Street, Liverpool. Battalions – 9th, 10th King's Liverpool; 4th, 5th South Lancashire.

Royal Artillery: Derby Buildings, 24 Fenwick Street, Liverpool. 1st, 2nd, 3rd, 4th (Howitzer) West Lancashire Brigades, Royal Field Artillery; 1st Lancashire Royal Garrison Artillery.

Royal Engineers: Engineer Drill Hall, Cropper's Hill, St Helens. 1st, 2nd West Lancashire Field Companies; West Lancashire Divisional Signal Company.

Army Service Corps: Southport. West Lancashire Divisional Transport and Supply Column.

Royal Army Medical Corps: 1st, 2nd, 3rd West Lancashire Field Ambulances.

Attached: Western Wireless, Cable and Airline Signal Companies; 7th Volunteer Battalion, King's Liverpool Regiment.

West Lancashire Divisional Engineers. Territorial Force. Engineer Drill Hall, Cropper's Hill, St Helens with 1st and 2nd (The St Helens) West Lancashire Field Companies. The 2nd Field Company also had a detachment at Widnes.

West Lancashire Divisional Signal Company (The St Helens). Territorial Force. Engineer Drill Hall, Cropper's Hill, St Helens with No.1 Section, No.2 (South Lancashire) Section, No.3 (Liverpool) Section, No.4 (North Lancashire) Section.

West Lancashire Divisional Transport and Supply Column. Territorial Force. Manchester Road, Southport with Headquarters Company, also at Manchester Road; North Lancashire Brigade Company, Tramway Road, Aigburth, Liverpool; Liverpool Brigade Company, Tramway Road, Liverpool and South Lancashire Brigade Company, 46 Legh Street, Warrington.

West Lancashire Field Ambulance, 1st. Territorial Force. Tramway Road, Liverpool.

West Lancashire Field Ambulance, 2nd. Territorial Force. 14 Harper Street, Liverpool.

West Lancashire Field Ambulance, 3rd. Territorial Force. Cropper's Hill, St Helens with "A" Section, also at Cropper's Hill; "B" Section, Kendal (detachment at Barrow-in-Furness); "C" Section, Cropper's Hill.

West Lancashire Field Companies (The St Helens), 1st, 2nd. See West Lancashire Divisional Engineers.

West Riding Batteries, 1st, 2nd, 3rd. See 1st West Riding Brigade, Royal Field Artillery.

West Riding Batteries, 4th, 5th, 6th. See 2nd West Riding Brigade, Royal Field Artillery.

West Riding Batteries, 7th, 8th, 9th. See 3rd West Riding Brigade, Royal Field Artillery.

West Riding Batteries, 10th (Howitzer), 11th (Howitzer). See 4th West Riding Brigade, Royal Field Artillery (Howitzer).

West Riding Brigade Companies, Army Service Corps, 1st, 2nd, 3rd. See West Riding Divisional Transport and Supply Column.

West Riding Brigade, Royal Field Artillery, 1st. Territorial Force. Fenton Street, Leeds with 1st West Riding Battery, also at Fenton Street; 2nd West Riding Battery, Bramley; 3rd West Riding Battery and Ammunition Column, Fenton Street.

West Riding Brigade, Royal Field Artillery, 2nd. Territorial Force. Valley Parade, Bradford with 4th West Riding Battery, also at Valley Parade; 5th West Riding Battery, Halifax; 6th West Riding Battery, Heckmondwike and Ammunition Column, Valley Parade.

West Riding Brigade, Royal Field Artillery, 3rd. Territorial Force. Norfolk Barracks, Sheffield with

7th, 8th, 9th West Riding Batteries and Ammunition Column.

West Riding Brigade, Royal Field Artillery (Howitzer), 4th. Territorial Force. Otley with 10th West Riding (Howitzer) Battery, also at Otley; 11th West Riding (Howitzer) Battery, Ilkley and Ammunition Column, Burley.

West Riding Clearing Hospital. Territorial Force. Leeds.

West Riding Division. Territorial Force. 9 St Leonards, York.

1st West Riding Infantry Brigade: 5 Tower Street, York. Battalions – 5th, 6th, 7th, 8th West Yorkshire.

2nd West Riding Infantry Brigade: Skipton-in-Craven. Battalions – 4th, 5th, 6th, 7th Duke of Wellington's.

3rd West Riding Infantry Brigade: 7 Bank Court Chambers, Sheffield. Battalions – 4th, 5th King's Own Yorkshire Light Infantry; 4th, 5th York and Lancaster.

Royal Artillery: Red House, Marygate, York. 1st, 2nd, 3rd, 4th (Howitzer) West Riding Brigades, Royal Field Artillery; West Riding Royal Garrison Artillery.

Royal Engineers: Glossop Road, Sheffield. 1st, 2nd West Riding Field Companies; West Riding Divisional Signal Company.

Army Service Corps: Harewood Barracks, Woodhouse Lane, Leeds. West Riding Divisional Transport and Supply Column.

Royal Army Medical Corps: 1st, 2nd, 3rd West Riding Field Ambulances.

Attached: Northern Wireless, Cable and Airline Signal Companies.

West Riding Divisional Engineers. Territorial Force. Glossop Road, Sheffield with 1st and 2nd West Riding Field Companies.

West Riding Divisional Signal Company. Territorial Force. Glossop Road, Sheffield with No.1 Section, No.2 (1st West Riding) Section, No.3 (2nd West Riding) Section, No.4 (3rd West Riding) Section.

West Riding Divisional Transport and Supply Column. Territorial Force. Harewood Barracks, Woodhouse Lane, Leeds with Headquarters Company, Lumley Barracks, Burton Stone Lane, York; 1st, 2nd and 3rd West Riding Brigade Companies, Harewood Barracks, Leeds.

West Riding Field Ambulances, 1st, 2nd. Territorial Force. Harewood Barracks, Woodhouse Lane, Leeds. The 2nd West Riding Field Ambulance also had a detachment at Shipley.

West Riding Field Ambulance, 3rd. Territorial Force. Brook House, 2 Gell Street, Sheffield.

West Riding Field Companies, 1st, 2nd. See West Riding Divisional Engineers.

West Riding Infantry Brigade, 1st, 2nd, 3rd. See West Riding Division.

West Riding Regiment. See Duke of Wellington's (West Riding Regiment).

West Riding Royal Garrison Artillery. Territorial Force. York.

West Riding Royal Horse Artillery. Territorial Force. Wentworth Woodhouse, Rotherham. Included the Yorkshire Mounted Brigade Ammunition Column.

West Somerset Yeomanry. Territorial Force. Taunton with "A" Squadron, Wellington (detachments at Minehead, Wiveliscombe, Washford, Dulverton and Williton); "B" Squadron, Taunton (detachments at Churchinford, Buckland St Mary, Bishop's Lydeard, Churchstanton and Hatch Beauchamp); "C" Squadron, Bridgwater (detachments at Highbridge,

Westmorland and Cumberland Yeomanry. *Wireless Section with Marconi equipment provided (at his own expense) by Major C. Beddington. Penrith camp, 1914.*

Glastonbury, Langport, Nether Stowey and North Petherton); "D" Squadron, Yeovil (detachments at Crewkerne, Chard, Ilminster, South Petherton and Martock).

West Surrey Regiment. See Queen's (Royal West Surrey Regiment).

West Yorkshire Regiment. See Prince of Wales's Own (West Yorkshire Regiment).

Westerham and Chipstead Cadet Corps. See 4th Battalion, Queen's Own (Royal West Kent Regiment).

Western Airline Signal Company. See Western Command Signal Companies (Army Troops).

Western Cable Signal Company. See Western Command Signal Companies (Army Troops).

Western Command Signal Companies (Army Troops). Territorial Force. 38 Mason Street, Edge Hill, Liverpool with Western Wireless Signal Company, Western Cable Signal Company and Western Airline Signal Company.

Western General Hospital, 1st. Territorial Force. 73 Shaw Street, Liverpool.

Western General Hospital, 2nd. Territorial Force. Manchester.

Western General Hospital, 3rd. Territorial Force. 15 Newport Road, Cardiff.

Western Wireless Signal Company. See Western Command Signal Companies (Army Troops).

Westminster Cadet Company. Guildhall, London.

Westminster Dragoons. See 2nd County of London Yeomanry (Westminster Dragoons)

Westminster Rifles. See 16th Battalion, London Regiment.

Westminster School Officers Training Corps. Dean's Yard, Westminster. Two infantry companies, Junior Division.

Wolverhampton Grammar School Officers Training Corps. *The plain shield cap badge is from the arms of its founder Sir Stephen Jenyns.*

Westmorland and Cumberland Yeomanry. Territorial Force. Penrith with "A" Squadron, Kendal (detachments at Carnforth, Kirkby Lonsdale, Ulverston and Windermere); "B" Squadron, Penrith (detachments at Keswick, Temple Sowerby and Cockermouth); "C" Squadron, Whitehaven (detachments at Workington, Maryport and Barrow-in-Furness); "D" Squadron, Carlisle (detachments at Wigton and Alston).

Weymouth Secondary School Cadets. One company.

Whitgift Grammar School Officers Training Corps. Croydon. Two infantry companies, Junior Division.

Wilson's School Officers Training Corps. Camberwell, London. One infantry company, Junior Division.

Wiltshire Battery. See 3rd Wessex Brigade, Royal Field Artillery.

Wiltshire Fortress Engineers. Territorial Force. Church Road, Swindon with No.1 Works Company.

Wiltshire Regiment. See Duke of Edinburgh's (Wiltshire Regiment).

Wiltshire Yeomanry. See Royal Wiltshire Yeomanry (Prince of Wales's Own Royal Regiment).

Wimbledon Boys' Naval Brigade. The Institute, Bridges Road, South Wimbledon. One company.

Worcestershire Yeomanry (The Queen's Own Worcestershire Hussars). *Uniforms are blue with scarlet facings.*

Winchester College Officers Training Corps. Four infantry companies, Junior Division.

Wolverhampton Grammar School Officers Training Corps. One infantry company, Junior Division.

Woodbridge School Officers Training Corps. One infantry company, Junior Division.

Woolwich Cadet Corps, 1st. See 2nd London Brigade, Royal Field Artillery.

Woolwich Scout Cadet Company. Oakleigh, Hill Street, Woolwich, London.

Worcestershire Batteries, 1st, 2nd, 3rd. See 2nd South Midland Brigade, Royal Field Artillery.

Worcestershire Regiment. Four Regular (1st, 2nd, 3rd and 4th), two Special Reserve (5th and 6th) and two Territorial Force (7th and 8th) battalions. Depot, Worcester.

1st Battalion: Cairo.

2nd Battalion: Aldershot.

3rd Battalion: Tidworth.

4th Battalion: Meiktila, Burma.

5th Battalion: Worcester.

6th Battalion: Worcester.

7th Battalion: Kidderminster with "A" Company, also at Kidderminster; "B" Company, Tenbury (detachments at Kidderminster and Bockleton); "C" Company, Stourport (detachment at Bewdley); "D" Company, Stourbridge (detachment at Kinver); "E" Company, Oldbury; "F" Company, Halesowen; "G" and "H" Companies, Dudley.

8th Battalion: Silver Street, Worcester with "A" and "B" Companies, also at Silver Street; "C" Company, Pershore (detachments at Malvern, Upton-on-Severn, Elmley Castle and Fladbury); "D" Company, Evesham (detachment at Badsey); "E" Company, Droitwich (detachment at Stoke Works); "F" Company, King's Norton (detachment at Rubery); "G" Company, Bromsgrove; "H" Company, Redditch.

Worcestershire Yeomanry (The Queen's Own Worcestershire Hussars). Territorial Force. Worcester with "A" Squadron, Kidderminster (detachments at Bewdley, Dudley and Witley); "B" Squadron, Camp Hill (detachments at Birmingham, Bromsgrove, Redditch and King's Heath); "C" Squadron, Malvern (detachments at Upton-on-Severn, Leigh Sinton and Ledbury); "D" Squadron, Worcester (detachments at Droitwich and Pershore).

Worksop College Officers Training Corps. Two infantry companies, Junior Division.

Worcestershire Regiment. *Cap badge. Both the lion and motto "Firm" are from the old 29th Regiment (later 1st Battalion).*

Worcestershire Yeomanry (The Queen's Own Worcestershire Hussars). *Cap badge.*

Y

Yeoman of the Guard. See King's Body Guard of the Yeoman of the Guard.

Yeoman Warders of the Tower. See King's Body Guard of the Yeoman of the Guard.

Yeomanry. The Yeomanry, the mounted element (cavalry) of the Territorial Force, in 1914 comprised fifty-five regiments, each organised on a four squadron basis. Squadrons were lettered "A" to "D", or in the case of 2nd Lovat's Scouts and 2nd Scottish Horse, "E" to "H". Unlike Territorial Force infantry battalions, which were affiliated to regiments of the line, the Yeomanry had no direct association with the Regular cavalry. Each was, however, modelled (titles and dress) along the lines of the several Dragoon, Hussar and Lancer regiments of the Line Cavalry. Yeomanry regiments were as follows: Ayrshire; Bedfordshire; Berkshire; Buckinghamshire; Cheshire; Denbighshire; Derbyshire; Devonshire (1st Royal); Devonshire (Royal North); Dorset; Essex; Fife and Forfar; Glamorgan; Gloucestershire; Hampshire; Hertfordshire; Kent (Royal East); Kent (West); Lanarkshire; Lanarkshire (Glasgow); Lancashire (Hussars); Lancaster's (Duke of); Leicestershire; Lincolnshire; London (City of); London (1st County of); London (2nd County of); London (3rd County of); Lothians and Border Horse; Lovat's Scouts (1st); Lovat's Scouts (2nd); Montgomeryshire; Norfolk; Northamptonshire; Northumberland; Nottinghamshire (Sherwood Rangers); Nottinghamshire (South Notts Hussars); Oxfordshire; Pembroke; Scottish Horse (1st); Scottish Horse (2nd); Shropshire; Somerset (North); Somerset (West); Staffordshire; Suffolk; Surrey; Sussex; Warwickshire; Westmorland and Cumberland; Wiltshire; Worcestershire; Yorkshire (Dragoons); Yorkshire (East Riding); Yorkshire (Hussars). Although not strictly "in existence" at the declaration of war in 1914, the Welsh Horse is included, its formation being well under way by 4 August. Also classified as Yeomanry, but part of the Special Reserve, were three regiments – North Irish Horse, South Irish Horse and King Edward's Horse (The King's Oversea Dominions Regiment).

York and Durham Brigade Company, Army Service Corps. See Northumbrian Divisional Transport and Supply Column.

York and Lancaster Regiment. *Men of the 4th and 5th Battalions (3rd West Riding Brigade, West Riding Division) unloading stores from a railway waggon onto an allotted Army Service Corps vehicle.*

York and Lancaster Regiment. *5th Battalion at King Edward VII's funeral procession, 20 May, 1910.*

York and Durham Infantry Brigade. See Northumbrian Division.

York and Lancaster Regiment. Two Regular (1st and 2nd), one Special Reserve (3rd) and two Territorial Force (4th and 5th) battalions. Depot, Pontefract.
1st Battalion: Jubbulpore, India.
2nd Battalion: Limerick.
3rd Battalion: Pontefract.
4th (Hallamshire) Battalion: Sheffield.
5th Battalion: Rotherham with "A" and "B" Companies, also at Rotherham; "C" Company, Barnsley; "D" Company, Wath (detachments at Wombwell and Mexborough); "E" Company, Barnsley; "F" Company, Rotherham; "G" Company, Treeton; "H" Company, Birdwell.

Yorkshire Dragoons Yeomanry (Queen's Own). Territorial Force. Doncaster with "A" Squadron, Sheffield (detachment at Rotherham); "B" Squadron, Wakefield (detachments at Dewsbury and Pontefract); "C" Squadron, Doncaster (detachments at Barnsley and Goole); "D" Squadron, Huddersfield (detachment at Halifax).

York and Lancaster Regiment. *Cap badge. Here we see the Royal Tiger, commemorating the services of the 65th Regiment (later 1st Battalion) in India between 1796 and 1819, the Union Rose, authorised in 1820, and a coronet. The latter is an old badge of the 84th Regiment (later 2nd Battalion).*

Yorkshire Hussars Yeomanry (Alexandra, Princess of Wales's Own). Territorial Force. York with "A" Squadron, Leeds (detachment at Ilkley); "B" Squadron, York (detachments at Bedale, Thirsk, Helmsley and Malton); "C" Squadron, Knaresborough (detachments at Harrogate, Bradford, Easingwold and Ripon); "D" Squadron,

Yorkshire Hussars Yeomanry (Alexandra, Princess of Wales's Own). *Seen here at camp in 1914, the two signal-instructor-sergeants (see crossed flags above chevrons) are wearing full dress – blue with silver cord and lace.*

Yorkshire Dragoons Yeomanry (Queen's Own). *This officer wears mess-dress. On his lapels, the regimental badge of a Yorkshire Rose surmounted by crown.*

Middlesbrough (detachment at Scarborough). The Regiment also had attached, at 103 North Street, Leeds, the Yorkshire Squadron, Imperial Cadet Yeomanry

Yorkshire Light Infantry. See King's Own (Yorkshire Light Infantry).

Yorkshire Mounted Brigade. Territorial Force. 9 St Leonards, York. Included Yorkshire Hussars, Yorkshire Dragoons, East Riding Yeomanries; West Riding Royal Horse Artillery. The Northumberland Hussars Yeomanry was attached for training.

Yorkshire Mounted Brigade Ammunition Column. See West Riding Royal Horse Artillery.

Yorkshire Mounted Brigade Field Ambulance. Territorial Force. Vicarage Street, Wakefield with "A" Section, also at Vicarage Street, and "B" Section, Halifax.

Yorkshire Mounted Brigade Signal Troop. Territorial Force. 9 St Leonards, York.

Yorkshire Mounted Brigade Transport and Supply

Yorkshire Hussars Yeomanry (Alexandra, Princess of Wales's Own). *Yorkshire Squadron, Imperial Cadet Yeomanry.*

Yorkshire Hussars Yeomanry (Alexandra, Princess of Wales's Own). *Bandmaster Cramer-Suckley.*

Column. Territorial Force. Lumley Barracks, York. There were also detachments at Malton and Scarborough.

Yorkshire Regiment. See Alexandra, Princess of Wales's Own (Yorkshire Regiment).

Yorkshire Squadron, Imperial Cadet Yeomanry. See Yorkshire Hussars Yeomanry (Alexandra, Princess of Wales's Own).

Yorkshire Yeomanry, Dragoons. See Yorkshire Dragoons Yeomanry (Queen's Own).

Yorkshire Yeomanry, East Riding. See East Riding of Yorkshire Yeomanry.

Yorkshire Yeomanry, Hussars. See Yorkshire Hussars Yeomanry (Alexandra, Princess of Wales's Own).

LOCATION INDEX

SOURCES OF INFORMATION AND BIBLIOGRAPHY

Monthly Army Lists
Cadet List
Army Orders
Army Council Instructions
Territorial Force Returns
Ray Westlake Unit Archives
Regimental histories, various.

Adams, Frank, *The Clans, Septs and Regiments of the Scottish Highlands*. W.& A.K. Johnston Ltd., Edinburgh, 1908.

Edwards, Major T.J.: *Military Customs*. Gale & Polden, Aldershot, 1961.

Edwards, D. and Langley, D., *British Army Proficiency Badges*. Wadley, Pestatyn, 1984.

Gaylor, John, *Military Badge Collecting*. Seeley Service, London, 1971.

Parkyn, Major H.G. OBE, *(Military) Shoulder-Belt Plates and Buttons*. London, 1956.

Westlake, Ray, *A Register of Territorial Force Cadet Units 1910–1922*. Wembley, 1984.

Westlake, Ray, *The Territorial Battalions*. Spellmount, Tunbridge Wells, 1986.

Westlake, Ray, *The Territorial Force 1914*. Malpas, 1988.

Westlake, Ray, *British Territorial Units 1914–18*. Osprey, Oxford, 1991.

RECOMMENDED FURTHER READING

Readers wishing to delve further into the records of those units listed in this volume – be it in either direction – will need to seek out the appropriate regimental history. Of these there are thousands and most can be found recorded in *A Bibliography of Regimental Histories of the British Army* by Arthur S. White. Information provided – title, author, date of publication, etc. – will enable any library or (if still in print) bookshop to locate them. Not all units however have published histories. Whether this be the case or not, a visit to the National Archive at Kew (formerly PRO) – where unit War Diaries can be inspected – is highly recommended.

An understanding of the higher organisation of the British Army (divisions, brigades) during the war years will be necessary if research into war service is to be undertaken. What division or brigade a particular unit served in during 1914–18 is important to know and two works will prove invaluable for this purpose. *British Regiments 1914–1918* by Brigadier E.A. James will provide a quick reference – at least as far as the Cavalry, Yeomanry and Infantry are concerned (Royal Artillery, Royal Engineers and other supporting arms of service are not listed unfortunately) – and in addition give dates of going overseas, theatres of war served in, and where located at 11 November, 1918.

Having then established what division a regiment served in, the next step is to consult *Order of Battle of Divisions*. Compiled by Major A.F. Becke, and part of the "Official History of the Great War" series, these volumes (there are five) are arranged by division. Each chapter gives a brief record of service, together with a more comprehensive listing of the battles and engagements fought. Of course, and as the title of the series suggests, the main purpose of Beck's work is to provide details of the make-up of each division. The term "Order of Battle" means in this case a highly detailed and accurate record of who (all arms of service are covered on this occasion) was with what, when, and where.

Although this section is intended to direct the reader towards reference works of a regimental nature, I would, however, put high on the list of further reading that fine series produced in the 1920s/30s under the overall title of *Official History of the Great War Based on Official Documents*. Comprising more than twenty-five volumes of "Military Operations" alone (the naval and air wars are dealt with in separate volumes) the work provides detailed and readable records of battles and engagements – often at a regimental or battalion level.

General histories of the First World War are these days plentiful. But they generally do not go into the detail required by the regimental researcher. Books specialising in particular battles are usually more rewarding.

Leaving aside the regimental aspect of the First World War, there are two sources available for research concerning individual men and women killed. *Soldiers Died in the Great War* (available either in book or CD-ROM format) and on the Internet – are the records of the Commonwealth War Graves Commission.

Regimental museums provide an important source of information. Most regiments have these and details of location, times of opening, telephone numbers etc. are included in *A Guide to Regimental Museums* by T. and S. Wise.